CHAKRA AWAKENING.

2 BOOKS IN 1:

REIKI & CHAKRAS FOR BEGINNERS +

THIRD EYE AWAKENING.

ANXIETY RELIEF, SPIRITUAL ENLIGHTENMENT & ENERGY HEALING USING GUIDED MEDITATIONS AND MINDFULNESS

By Ellen Cure

Table of Contents

Book 1

REIKI & CHAKRAS FOR BEGINNERS:

GUIDED MEDITATIONS TO AWAKEN AND BALANCE CHAKRAS, RADIATE POSITIVE ENERGY AND EXPAND YOUR MIND POWER. LEARN REIKI HEALING SECRETS FOR IMPROVING YOUR BODY ENERGY LEVELS

PART 1

Chakras healing

Introduction

By reading this book you will learn how to do self-healing, balance chakras, radiate positive energy and many more. You will love to do all the meditation until you will realize that you are doing it daily. That is fun, right?

While it would be nice if you could simply pop in an instructional video and learn how to do yoga this is not the way that you want to learn how to do things. Yes, it is an option and many people do this rather than ever visiting a yoga studio. Not only are you causing yourself potential injury and damage by trying to take things into your own hands, but you might also face the trouble of learning improper techniques, the last thing that you want to happen as you are trying to advance yourself and the life that you are living. This is just the start of the many dangers that can come along with trying to learn yoga on your own.

Now, if you want to purchase of one of those DVDs that teach you yoga from the comfort of your home, this is an option that is available to you. But why would you want to cause potential damage to your life when you are trying to make great changes? Someone, somewhere, is looking to make money off of you through these DVDs. But this is probably not the option that you want to choose, especially if you are new to the world of yoga. Not only do you need a certified yoga instructor to teach you how to do things so that you are not injuring yourself or hurting your body, but it is also important that you can mentally connect with the chakra so that you can benefit, as you should be from doing yoga.

Tips for Success

Once you have made the decision to perform yoga and have chosen the studio that will help teach you, a few other things are in store for you to learn to fully benefit from your newfound teachings.

First, as we have mentioned countless times throughout this life, you need to be in tune with your body, as well as your mind. Some of the moves and positions of yoga are not for the light-hearted, as they stretch your body in ways that you might not have even realized possible for the body to move.

Have you purchased an outfit that is designed especially for participation in yoga? You must be wearing clothing that is comfortable and easy on the body, and while it may not necessarily be the yoga outfit that you want to wear, they are a lot of fun to purchase.

While you are out shopping, choose a mat. The yoga mat is a very important piece of the puzzle of success. You want to be as comfortable as you possibly can as you are performing the various techniques of yoga, and it's with the mat and the comfortable yoga-type clothing that you are wearing that will make a world of difference in things. Many different types of mats are available for yoga. They are made of various materials and constructed of various sizes. One of the mats can be purchased at an affordable price, and you want to make sure that you are choosing a good mat. Again, your entire experience with yoga is dependent upon a nice, comfortable mat and the clothing that you are wearing.

There is no way for you to know just what to do during the first few classes. So, it is okay to look and to listen, but make sure that you are trying. Take special note of the alignment of the instructor. This is one of the first things that must be done to conquer yoga. As you are looking at other people and observing what they are doing you will begin to pick up on things and better learn how to do yoga.

Finally, make sure that you take things slowly and never try to rush. Anything worth having taken time to achieve, and you should not expect those great changes to be made in a night or even in a week. The more that you are participating the easier that things will become, and before you know it, you will be a yoga pro! As long as you have patience and the eagerness and desire to succeed you can certainly do just that! No matter who you are, what type of background you come from or the ideal results that you want, they can be found!

Opening the Chakras

Just as you start participating in yoga, opening the chakras is a process that must be taken slowly. It is not something that you will fully grasp in a single night, nor is it something that should be expected. Understanding that there are chakras, and that you want to change your overall being, is the first step in identifying and connecting with the chakras that are within you.

To open the chakras that you have, you must discard all of the distrust that you may have, and that you can form a connection mentally. The first chakra is the red chakra, or the root chakra. This is the root chakra because it is the one that is responsible for helping you become aware of yourself and your mental state.

You will need to determine the ways that you will open the chakra as well. This guide has presented you with the many different ways that this can be done. You must focus on each of them and ensure that you are prepared. You must be willing to do them all to attain the best amount of success possible. As we have mentioned time and time again, yoga is one of the very best ways that you can become in tune with the seven chakras that are found within your body.

It is usually with the help of your instructor that you learn the best ways of becoming in tune with your chakras. For most people it takes years and years of practice to be able to gain a full sense of wellbeing with the chakras. Once you have gained the proper instruction and have begun to feel energized through the different chakras it is then that you may be able to start doing things on your own.

Learning your chakras, as well as how to become in tune with them, is certainly a life-changing experience. It can change your entire persona, the whole person that you are. It isn't for those who aren't truly focused upon becoming a success, however; so, make sure that you are committed from the start.

As you learn the different chakras and yoga techniques to perform them you will be able to become a new you, the person that you always wanted to be, the person that you knew was there but did not know how to break out. It is something that can now be done if you can connect to yourself: body, mind and soul.

Understanding Your Chakras

Chakra requires that each of the elements is opened and stable. Yoga as a method of healing uses different centers of energy from within the body. When yoga is practiced, the individual can gain a better awareness of them; body, mind and soul, increasing the energy flow into the energy centers. As we have already discussed, there are a total of 7 of these chakras within the body. The chakras are responsible for awareness and are needed to keep our bodies balanced and our energy levels high. The key to being successful at chakra is to bring awareness to the mind by releasing various blockages that stand in the way. There are several different ways to increase the awareness of the chakra. For anyone who is looking to benefit from the form of the chakra, it is necessary that a deep understanding is met. You must be in touch with your inner being to target the various chakras in the body. When you can mentally connect yourself to this capacity, only great things can result.

Although all forms of yoga work to enhance an individual's overall well-being, using yoga to excite the chakra senses provides a far better understanding of yourself and the things that keep you energized. You are more in tune with your inner self and can develop many attributes when all of the chakras are well balanced and energized as they should be. And, yoga is a wonderful way to help yourself become more toned, mentally energized and feeling your best all the way around.

There are many different ways that you can use to enhance your chakras and feel your best. This includes exercise, mediation, and of course yoga. This guide is designed to help you learn more about the benefits that can come with you when practicing yoga to enhance the chakras.

Origin of the Chakra

Chakras go back to the start of our being, the start of time. Tanzania, Africa, is the root of the human race. There, Mount Meru exists, a large mountain that represents the journey of life. The top of the mountain is the Crown Chakra, the bottom is the root. It is here where the energy of the chakras was first developed. The mountain has been shown in Egyptian mythology, but it is from the Indian Tantra that the world today has developed much of their ways of doing things and the knowledge of the chakras and yoga to benefit them.

Chakras are something that we all have. However, it is not something that every person is in tune with. If you want to be a better person it is a must that you take all of the steps necessary to learn more about yoga and energizing the chakras within you. It is something that anyone who wants to change can do with only a bit of determination needed.

Chapter 1: History and Origins of Chakras

While the chakras are part of an ancient tradition, they are starting to make a reappearance again. There are many new interpretations of their meaning and their functions, and sometimes it is easy to get confused since there are so many ways to think about these chakras. While the popularity is starting to make the chakras more of a word that people recognize, there are a lot of times when this information is going to be erroneous, conflicting, and even confusing. Before you work on making the chakras a part of your life, it is important to understand some of the history that comes with these chakras and can better explain how they should be used.

The Vedas are some of the oldest written traditions from the area of India and it was recorded from the oral tradition of the upper caste Brahmins. The original meaning of this word of chakra is "wheel" which refers to the chariot wheels that were used by the rulers of that time. The word has also been used in these texts as a metaphor for the sun, which can traverse the world just like a triumphant chariot and will denote the eternal wheel of time, which also represents balance and order, just like the idea of the wheel and what the chakras are going to focus on.

The birth of the chakras was said to herald in a brand-new age, and they were often described as being preceded by a disk of light, such as the halo of Christ, but there was a spinning disk that was in front of them. It is also said that Vishnu, the god, descended to Earth, carrying the charka, a club, a conch shell, and a lotus flower.

In these texts, there are also some mentions of the chakras being like a psychic center of consciousness in several different versions of this text including the Yoga Sutras of Patanjali and the Yoga Upanishads. The implied goal of Yoga was to rise above nature and the world that you are living in, to find the realization of a pure consciousness, one that was free from any fluctuations that came in with the emotions and the mind. Yet the word of yoga stands for yoke or union, so the realization that happens in between consciousness and realizations must ultimately reintegrate with nature to get a higher synthesis.

So, since the idea of yoga and the chakras arose inside of the same tradition, the Tantric tradition, it is no wonder that they are often associated together. As we will discuss later on, you will be able to find that yoga is one of the ways that you will be able to bring the chakras into line because they were both developed in the same traditions and both can be used at the same time.

In the traditional ideas of chakras, there are seven of the basic ones and they are all going to exist inside of your body. Through modern physiology, it is easy to see that the seven chakras are going to correspond exactly to the main nerve ganglia inside of the body, which all come from the spinal column. While many people assume that these chakras have nothing to do with them any longer, the chakras were well placed, put into specific parts of the body where nerves are located and where different parts can influence how the rest of the body is going to react. Interestingly, chakras were able to develop based on these thoughts, even before all of the nerves and pressure points would have been realized.

In addition to the main seven chakras that most people concentrate on, there are a few minor chakras that are mentioned inside of the ancient tasks. For example, there is the soma chakra which you will be able to find right above the third eye chakra and then there is the Ananda Kanda lotus, which is going to be near the heart chakra, plus some more options based on how deep into the ancient texts that you choose to go.

Many people assume that the chakras are an ancient idea that you shouldn't pay any attention to. They figure that the chakras have nothing to do with how they live their modern life and they may assume it was all a bunch of spirituality that is just made up. But in reality, you will find that in modern times, the chakras are more important compared to any other time. We need to understand how easy we can get out of balance. We are always running around, always stressed out and worried, and often we have trouble with some of our relationships. Chakras can get these back in line better than anything else.

People who practice balancing their chakras are often going to be so much healthier and happier, and better able to get through the day, compared to others who don't even believe in the chakras and just keep going through all of the bad things that are in their lives. It is worth your time to ensure that you can get the great life that you would like without all the issues.

Chakras and Science

For a long time, science was unable, or unwilling, to explore the chakras and chakra healing. While there is still limited Western science "backing up" the chakra energy centers, it is clear that your body functions thanks to the systems or energetic impulses inside it. Everything you do and think is controlled by this system of energy, which Western science has proven time and time again. Simply looking at the brain's electrical pulses shows how energy rules this vital organ. Before modern science, the chakras were a good method for describing how the body functioned or was even able to function. Now, science may have labeled these properties something different or still cannot explain why certain things in your body work the way they do, but there are some things that this ancient science and today's modern understanding do agree on.

The first thing that science and the charkas agree on is that your body is made up of energy, and so is everything else around you. Nothing around you is a solid piece of reality; it is simply a collection of energy particles deciding to hold together for a short time. Think about a chair. It may appear solid and sturdy to you; however, at its most basic level, it is just a combination of atoms. Atoms are not solid or static items. Inside these atoms are even smaller particles that are constantly moving and adjusting. Those particles are not solid, either. These particles inside the atom are called subatomic particles and are the electrons, neutrons, and protons. The neutrons and protons huddle together at the center of the atom, while the electrons race around on the outside. These move so quickly that scientists cannot determine where an electron is exactly at from one instance to the next.

In addition to being made up of energy and racing electrons and huddling subatomic particles, an atom is mostly made up of space. It is estimated that each atom is 99.99% space. This space is what allows for all this movement. And this information is true, not just about your chair, but about everything around you! Your body and mind are always moving and changing, much more subtle than you may ever feel or know. Nothing in this world exists without energy.

Science now can understand and prove this, but religions have understood for thousands of years the powerful role energy plays in your life. Chakras, tai chi, yoga, QiGong, and reiki are all examples of spiritual practices that deal with moving your energy. And the purpose of this movement is to help your body and your existence find a state of well-being and harmony. These ancient religions understand that we are influenced by and can similarly influence back, this transference and movement of energy through your actions, including your thoughts. This is because your brain is also moving and thoughts are your reality.

Science has begun to explain some of this movement and transference. For example, even when you are sleeping, your body is moving energy around. According to science, this happens mainly through your neurons and nerve pathways. In the ancient sciences and spirituality, it was explained through the chakras and the nadis. No matter what you are consciously or unconsciously doing, your body is a course of flowing energy. This includes digesting your food, thinking, moving your limbs, breathing, and even healing yourself.

The signals the nervous system transmits go from the brain to the body and from the body back to the brain. There are receptors all along the length of your body and throughout, so you can coordinate your actions with your needs and wants. Again, this includes both the conscious and unconscious actions your body takes. When you lift your arm, you are making use of your nervous system and sending energy to your arm to lift it up. When you eat something, your body begins a series of energetic processes to digest, absorb, and remove the waste of that food. These are examples of voluntary and involuntary actions that require energy and communication between receptors and your brain.

In ancient religions, there are many ways to move this energy so it can continue to support the proper functioning of your body. Things like yoga poses, meditation, and breathing practices are all ways to move energy and restore harmonious balance in your life. Chakra healing and balancing is another method, and this often includes a combination of various techniques to move your energy. Both quantum mechanics and "traditional" science suggest that focusing on your thoughts can make a large difference in your overall well-being. For example, visualization techniques have been successfully used to help improve mental functioning and prevent deterioration of the brain in patients that suffered negative side effects from a stroke. Focusing on the chakras and the movement of energy through the nadis is a great method, used for thousands of years and supported through modern science, for bringing peace and well-being to your life. It may be called something different, but it is similar to one another.

Your energetic body, made up of these subtle energetic impulses, is best revealed in your heart and brain. Your brain is probably one of the best places to "look" to see how powerful energy is at work in your body. In your brain alone, there are more than one hundred billion "wires" that conduct energetic impulses. These impulses are charged up ions coursing through your body, making sure your heart is pumping and your muscles are moving. They are biological pathways that are critical to your proper functioning. Observing the electricity of the brain is a great way to understand how your body is made up of energy.

In addition to the energy living inside of you, there is an energy surrounding your body, too. It is often hard to comprehend when you see and feel the boundary of skin and know the solidity of bones, but there is an electromagnetic field surrounding your body. This has a certain frequency. This can seem like New Age and ancient "nonsense" until you realize that scientist uses this understanding when they measure these frequencies with machines like an MRI or ECG machine. A change in energy in a certain location tells them something is out of balance, and they can see it through the image these machines produce.

Psychology is another modern scientific field that examines the mind and why we think and behave in certain ways. According to Psychology Today, every person is a physical embodiment of an energetic field. The chakras go further to explain that there are centers in the body for this energy to flow through. These movements control your emotions, organs, and immune system, among other things. When all things are flowing as they should, you are balanced spiritually, physically, emotionally, and mentally. That is why your chakras are so important to your overall well-being.

On the contrary, if there is a blockage in your energy, you become ill. This is seen in scientific tests such as a CT scan or an MRI. A tumor appears like a black spot in an otherwise energetic and moving system. It is blocking your energy in that place and you are not well. Other times, it manifests in your mental ability. An energy block can cause mental illness such as anxiety, depression, or more. Practicing ways to clear and move your energy is a powerful tool. A recent study showed that participants that suffered from a stroke saw marked improvements in the health of their brain when they spent time visualizing lifting a limb that was paralyzed during the stroke. The stroke damaged a part of their brain that sends the energetic information to that limb to move but visualizing it moving helped strengthen the brain tissue around that damaged area so the deterioration did not spread. This is just one modern scientific example of how an ancient tradition of moving energy with your thoughts can cause significant improvement to your physical well-being.

Your mental state is known to impact your physical body. We see this most in the correlation between stress and your health. Stress is an emotional and mental state, but when it is too prevalent, it causes a cascade of physical ailments along with it. According to the National Institute of Health, stress is an imbalance in your life. This imbalance, real or perceived, triggers the body to try to find and restore balance. These situations cause stress release hormones that are incredibly powerful and that lead to the feeling of anxiety and stimulation. Contemporary science lists stress as a major factor in numerous illnesses, such as cancer and mental illness. Stress costs millions of dollars a year in medical expenses. This is a constant discussion in modern science and most doctors and scientists agree that reducing stress is vital in supporting your overall health.

Also, contemporary science and medicine are beginning to understand and promote healthy mental health alongside physical health. It has become more and more obvious that a person's mental state is as important, if not more so, than their physical body in restoring balance in their overall health. Good treatment not only includes treating the physical body but the mental and spiritual as well. According to the National Institute of Health, most books dealing with the spiritual or mental treatment of an individual is more spiritual, keeping the topic foreign to most physicians, but Western medicine must begin to create a more comprehensive model to treat the gross and subtle bodies of a person. This means Western science needs to continue their understanding of how the energy in the mind and spirit connect to the physical body as they treat patients.

Almost a century ago, in the West, Sir William Osler documented a case where a patient suffered from an asthma attack after smelling an artificial rose. This posed a curious question that science, at the time, could not explain. There was no physical reason that this should have happened. Dr. Robert Adler, in 1975, explained this question; a person's thoughts can control their immune system. Sir William Osler was curious about why mammals were able to have controlled immune responses, and Dr. Adler was finally able to explain it. In his experiments, Dr. Adler was able to prove that a person's emotions and thoughts could create significant changes in their physical body and immune system.

Before these findings, Western science thought each body system worked independently of one another. The foundation of our modern science considered your immune system to not be impacted by your emotional or mental state. Dr. Adler proved this is not the case. His findings showed that, indeed, your entire body works together impacting each part to find balance or homeostasis. It was also his findings that first explained that stress negatively impacts your physical well-being.

You can finally begin to see more traditional, Western doctors embracing the understanding that your mental state is a major impact on your physical body, but it is something that Eastern traditions have known for thousands of years. Ancient science knew that energy is life and an imbalance in this energy, in any form, disrupts your physical existence. Energy needs to flow freely, and one of the best ways you can do this is by taking certain actions to find this balance. You can use meditation, visualization, eating certain foods, performing certain physical actions, etc. to move this life force, or vital energy, through your body and find balance. When you can keep these hubs or channels of energy clear, like keeping plaque out of your arteries for proper blood flow, you can live a more healthy and harmonious life. Unfortunately, many Western cultures do not focus on this integrated approach. This results in dormant, inactive, or blocked energy centers. This leads to a disruption in the flow of energy, and ultimately, to disease and imbalance.

Chapter 2: What are Chakras?

As energy moves through the body, it is in a perpetual state of motion and is regulated, and processed by seven main wheel-like structures, or chakras, which keep this dynamic flow of life-force energy moving and circulating through the energy system to avoid an accumulation of toxic energy.

They absorb this energy, cleanse it and send it out into the energy bodies to feed them with appropriate quality of energy that will be uplifting, health-giving and life-enhancing.

The word chakra is derived from the Sanskrit word, cakra, which simply means 'wheel' or 'disc'. The chakras resonate at different vibrational frequencies, depending on their function and the area of life-experience to which they are related. For example, the lower chakras are more connected to our day-to-day existence and vibrate at a much lower and more tangible frequency.

They allow us to fulfill our earthly needs and everything we need to manifest fulfilling lives on the material plane, for example, food, shelter, security and financial stability (root chakra), creativity, sexuality/reproduction (sacral chakra) and personal power (solar plexus chakra), whereas, the upper chakras are more connected to our emotions and spiritual development.

Each chakra absorbs from the spectrum, the color that is most resonant with its level of vibration and function and feeds this color/vibration back into the energy system through a complex circuitry of energy channels, known as nadis, to facilitate the optimal health and wellbeing of each individual. If one or more of the chakras is blocked or out of balance, our mental, emotional and physical health will suffer.

The Root or the First Chakra

For example, the first chakra - the root chakra (sometimes called the base chakra) is situated at the base of the spine and is the chakra that is most connected to our physical lives on Earth. This chakra vibrates at the same vibrational frequency as the color red, and, therefore, absorbs this color to give us the courage, strength and grounding to take care of our earthly survival needs and feel balanced and connected to our Earthly lives.

The root chakra governs and sends vitality to the hips, legs, bowels, intestines and adrenal glands – the body parts and organs related to movement, survival, fight or flight mechanisms and, in general, our ability to survive on Earth.

When the root chakra is healthy, balanced and spinning effectively, we feel at peace with our physical existence and able to meet our basic survival needs with ease. There are no major issues with money or with finding a nice home and if problems do arise in these areas, we can handle them with grace and without panic or fear. When the root chakra is in balance, we feel at home in our bodies and perfectly able to find enjoyment in the things of this world.

When the root chakra is blocked or not functioning correctly, we struggle to feel safe in the world and to meet our survival needs with ease. We may feel anxious, spaced out and somewhat detached from our physical and material lives. We might also experience lower back pain, stiffness in the hips and legs, or even problems in the reproductive areas of the body.

This chakra is thought to be related to the planets Earth, Saturn and Pluto (Experience, karmic lessons and cycles of birth, death and rebirth).

The Sacral or the Second Chakra

The second chakra, the sacral chakra, vibrates at the same frequency as the color orange and relates to our ability to be creative and to enjoy expressing our sexuality and sensuality. While the root chakra supports us in creating a fulfilling material life, the sacral chakra supports our ability to enjoy the life we create. This chakra is located below the navel and governs the bladder, ovaries, testes and all reproductive functions.

This chakra is thought to be related to The Moon and Pluto (emotions, feeling, birth, death, rebirth and transformation – karmic cycles).

When the sacral chakra is healthy and functioning correctly, we feel creative and happy to be alive. We feel connected to the more passionate side of our nature and able to express our sexuality in appropriate ways. We feel connected to our bodies and enjoy feeding, clothing them and derive pleasure from the fruits of physical existence.

When this chakra is blocked or out of balance, there may be a reluctance to be creative and an inability to enjoy life. We may feel overwhelmed by work routines and cut off from our creativity and passion. In some cases, there may be a tendency to compensate for a lack of vitality and vibrancy with the use of stimulants such as coffee and other intoxicants. In extreme cases, dysfunctions of the sacral chakra can lead to addictive behaviors.

The Solar Plexus or the Third Chakra

The third chakra, the solar plexus chakra, vibrates at the same frequency as the color yellow and is related to our power, intuitive knowing (gut feelings) and our ability to develop healthy levels of self-esteem, wisdom and confidence in our abilities. It is at this level that we begin to reflect on life and observe it, rather than simply surviving or enjoying it. We ascend in awareness and evolve into *psychic* beings who can discern the qualities of the energies around us.

The solar plexus chakra has been referred to as the psychic brain, and it is one of the most important centers for developing intuition. When we can connect with this center and follow our gut feelings, we develop wisdom and greater self-awareness. This chakra is located above the navel but below the rib cage and governs the stomach, digestive organs and nervous system.

If the solar plexus is blocked or is not functioning correctly, we feel a lack of self-esteem and an inability to respond authentically to the energies we experience in the world. When this chakra (our center of personal power) is compromised, we might feel controlled or manipulated by others. We might feel disempowered and out of touch with our truest will and desires. On the physical level we might experience stomach issues, digestive complaints or nervous conditions that stem from not trusting our gut instincts and following our true path in life. Within the stomach, we register our first responses to energy, our gut feelings, butterflies or clenching, and of course our nervous system becomes tense when we're exposed to too much unsettling energy for too long.

This chakra also governs the liver and the spleen, which are also related to the many ways our bodies react to the people and situations around us. The spleen reminds us to look for the natural sweetness in life, and when we feel drained by others, our first impulse is to replace lost vital energies through the unhealthy use of sugar and comfort foods. The liver is where we hold most of our anger at an energetic level.

This chakra is thought to be related to the planets the Sun, Mars and Mercury (selfhood, force of will and communication).

The Heart or the Fourth Chakra

The fourth chakra is the heart chakra, which vibrates at the same frequency as deep, forest green. This is the center that allows us to feel love and compassion for others and to process our emotions in healthy ways. Through a healthy heart chakra, we become able to express our feelings and sustain healthy, loving connections and intimate relationships with others. This chakra is located at the center of the chest and governs the healthy functioning of the physical heart, chest, lungs and thymus gland. This chakra is thought to be related to the planets Venus and Earth (manifesting love on the physical plane).

If the heart chakra is not functioning correctly, we feel cut off emotionally and may seek to isolate ourselves from others. Love feels unsafe and it seems easier to become cynical about relationships and avoid them altogether. It's interesting to note that the Sanskrit name for the heart chakra is Anahata which means unwounded, intact, unhurt, unbeaten. (Please see the Chakra Colours and Functions Chart below for the Sanskrit names of all seven chakras). This implies that a healthy heart chakra is one that is 'like new', full of innocence and wonder; it is like a heart that has never been hurt before and which, therefore, feels safe, open and receptive.

If the heart chakra is overactive, we tend to give too much of ourselves and make unwise choices in love – giving our time and devotion to those who don't truly value us or the love we bring. When we bring the heart chakra back into balance, we make wiser, more loving (and self-loving) choices, and all our relationships flourish and feel good.

The Throat or the Fifth Chakra

The fifth chakra is the throat chakra, which vibrates at the same frequency as the color blue and relates to our ability to find a voice in the world and to express ourselves truthfully and with pure intention. A healthy throat chakra supports us in expressing our true inner essence in the world and is, therefore, also connected to finding our true purpose in life.

The throat chakra is also related to our ability (or inability) to speak up for ourselves. Essentially, the throat chakra supports us in our ability to be ourselves more fully and to communicate our truth with purity, love, compassion and clarity.

Physically, this chakra rules the thyroid, tonsils, throat, neck and shoulders. It is located between the collar bones, over the physical throat area.

This chakra is thought to be related to the moon and Venus (expressions of emotion, love and beauty).

If the throat chakra is blocked or functioning incorrectly, we find it hard to share our true feelings or to truly be ourselves in the world. We may have problems with expressing our thoughts and feelings publicly, and in taking the necessary steps to break out of unhealthy work situations to follow our true calling in life. We may experience persistent problems with throat complaints, stiffness in the neck and shoulders and even digestive issues (the result of constantly swallowing our true feelings). If the throat chakra is overactive, we may find ourselves speaking inappropriately or speaking over others, desperate to get our point across because we feel generally unheard.

When the throat chakra is healthy, we can speak and listen with compassion and find the kindest and wisest words in every situation – words that will inspire others to become their greatest selves.

The Third Eye or the Sixth Chakra

The sixth chakra is the third eye chakra, which is related to our sixth sense and our ability to use our extrasensory perception and psychic faculties to receive psychic information and guidance. This chakra vibrates on the same frequency as the color indigo and is located between and slightly above the physical eyes.

When this chakra is healthy, we can receive psychic information to guide our lives more wisely and with more insight. In a more practical sense, when the third eye is balanced, we can see the truth with our inner vision, and with the support of this chakra, we can see into a range of possible futures and make informed choices, based on our ability to predict the events that might follow a particular action. This, in turn, allows us to make wiser choices, as we make plans and dream dreams for the future.

This chakra governs the physical eyes, sinuses, head, pituitary and pineal gland. The effective functioning of these glands is essential for the effective functioning of our inner and outer vision.

This chakra is thought to be related to the planets Neptune and Jupiter (psychic ability and expansion).

If the third eye chakra is blocked or functioning incorrectly, we may lose our sense of purpose and direction, and feel unable to connect with our inner wisdom. Psychic faculties will be limited or impaired and we may feel a sense of spiritual disconnection. In extreme cases, there may also be problems with headaches, blocked sinuses and fogginess or dizziness.

The Crown or Seventh Chakra

It is located at the top of the head or slightly above the head. Often described as the thousand petal lotus, this chakra is the seat of our ability to connect with the God of our understanding and to transcend the human condition. This chakra is the one which is the most mysterious and perhaps misunderstood. It is the chakra through which we go beyond ourselves, into the unknown and the indescribable.

The time-honoured way to achieve balance in the crown chakra is to develop a daily practice of meditation, yoga, chanting or any other spiritual practice that allows us to switch off the mind and journey into the silent stillness. The crown chakra is a gateway to heaven, or what the Buddhist call Nirvana. It is the chakra through which we experience the unknown and embrace the unknowable.

This chakra governs the brain, skull, skin and hypothalamus. When this chakra is healthy and balanced, we feel a connection with all other beings and can extend compassion towards everyone, because we see the bigger picture and the higher plan in everything. If you wish to connect with guides, angels and ascended masters, or receive inspired and channelled guidance, developing this chakra will connect you with higher sources of guidance and wisdom.

This chakra is thought to be related to the planets Uranus and Mercury (innovation, change and communication).

If the crown chakra is blocked, we may feel cut off spiritually and unable to believe in anything beyond the physical realm. We may feel forgotten or abandoned by God and have no sense of connection with those who love and guide us from the spirit realms. In extreme cases, there may be headaches, migraines, insomnia, faithlessness and irritability.

The Whole Balance

The seven main chakras are individuals. They are distinctly different and have their personalities and attributes. When you look at them as individuals, you might be able to see how one might be stronger or more open than others, in your system, and here is where it gets fun. Now, you can start asking why you feel so strongly in one part of your energy system, but diminished or deficient in another.

As you begin to explore your chakras, you get to be your energy detective and solve the mystery of what is out of balance, remembering all of the qualities each one expresses and how that is involved in your daily life experiences.

When you get better acquainted with your chakra system, it will become more obvious and you will be better able to intuit the direction your healing journey wants to go. As you gain trust in yourself and your energy work, you will know more about the dynamics each one plays in the greater whole.

The idea is to create a balance between all of the chakras so that they can exist in harmony and flow well. Think of a river flowing. The water pushes forward in a direction and moves on its journey that way. What if a dam starts to form? Driftwood starts to build up over time until the water won't flow freely any more in several spots in the river, causing algae to build up and stagnation in the water.

It is your journey to find where the dams are blocking your flowing river so that you can remove the obstacles and refresh your energy flow. Here are the places you can go forward on this journey with a whole and balanced chakra system:

- Abundance and joy regularly

- Lack of fear about your life choices

- Direction, focus and ambition about your life goals and dreams

- Attitude of gratitude every day

- Physical/ emotional/ mental/ spiritual well-being

- Drama-free lifestyle and relationships

- Heartfelt appreciation of the self and others

- Strong sense of self-worth and confidence

- Past pains, traumas and wounds resolved, healed and forgiven

- Expressive and communicative nature and quality of life

- Powerful creative energy, passion and desire for joy and happiness

These are just some of the ways a balanced chakra system can affect your life. Your wholeness doesn't just depend on your physical health and your mental state. Both of those things are connected to your energy centers and your whole energy system. They are all always working together and the key to a healthy and abundant life is the balance chakras.

Chapter 3: The Chakra System

Our chakra system is not open to view with the naked eye. Some are capable of seeing the auric field with their vision, which will usually be represented by a color. This color that is present as "aura" is a reflection of the chakra energy of the body. If you have ever had a photograph taken of your auras, or seen someone else's aura photo, you can see an ethereal wisp of color coming off of the person's body.

This is a lot like what the chakra areas of the body look like as they radiate frequency inside of you. It has been proven that each frequency of energy on a certain spectrum is associated with a specific color. The reason for this pertains to the light spectrum.

Have you ever seen a prism? When you hold it up to the light and rotate it in your hand, some colors shift inside of it and they are all the colors of the rainbow. Sometimes, when the sunlight catches the prism at the right angle, it will cast a rainbow-colored reflection onto the wall or ceiling. The point of knowing this is to understand that color is light and frequency, and so when dealing with the energies of your chakra system, you can connect it to the reality of having your light frequency within.

This is why each chakra is known to have a different color and also how the science behind energy can support this reality. We are made of light, just like the prism casting the rainbow on the wall.

When you ask yourself what all of this means, what is the first thing that pops into your head? How likely are you to see your light and feel your vibration? Is that something you are prepared to do, knowing what you know now about how your internal vibrational frequencies are? Can you picture them in your mind right now?

Try this exercise: close your eyes and see your body in your mind's eye. Project the image of yourself in your internal eye so that you can see the detail of yourself. Now, at the base of your spine, at the tail end of your coccyx, see an orb of reddish colored light. Ask it what it does and why it is there. It is okay if you don't get a response.

Now, move up to your pelvis, just below your navel and picture an orb of orange-colored light. How big is it? Is it moving at all? Spinning? Can you feel any energy here while you picture this orangey orb?

Moving up your spinal column some more, see just above your belly button and below your sternum, a yellow orb of light. How does it feel here? What kind of energy can you notice if any?

Continue up into your chest to your heart space. Here you will picture a green-glowing orb of light. Are you noticing any energy when you focus here? How are you feeling when you settle in this area?

Following the spine up to the neck, right at the base of the throat, see a bluish colored orb of light. What kind of energy is here? Are you able to see the orb well in this area? Can you picture its color?

Continuing further up, focus on the area just above and between your eyebrows. Your third eye is here and it is how you have been picturing this entire meditation in your head. Picture an indigo-colored orb of light here and notice any energy that you may have when you focus on this space. How does it feel?

Lastly, continue your view up to the top of your head and see a violet orb of light sitting just barely outside the top of your skull. What does it feel like in this place? Are you able to access an energy or vibration when you concentrate on this orb of energetic light?

Now, zoom out a little and see your whole body and every orb of colorful light that exists inside of you. You have just taken a tour through your chakra system and can now see how it looks from within. You may not be able to see it clearly with your eyes open, but you can certainly picture these bodies of energy with your eyes closed and your third eye focused on what is under your surface.

Take a moment to reflect on this energy. Question the energies that you may have felt as you rose up your spine picturing each, colorful orb of light. What sensations were there, if any? Did you have any thoughts or feelings creep in with certain placements? Were you able to clearly see them, or did they look faint and hardly noticeable? Do you like asking these questions?

12 Chakra System

But wait, there's more! There are not just seven chakras to contend with; there are more subtle chakras all over your body. Meridians are the channels in the body where Chinese medicine believes your Qi, or life-force energy flows. All of the needle placement points are tiny chakra centers that when stimulated with the point of the needle can rebalance and refresh a healthier flow of energy throughout the body.

By this estimation and theory, there are hundreds of these energy centers in the body. In general, however, when working with your chakras, you will mostly deal with the seven main chakras. Outside of that, there are a few more, larger chakra points in the body that have a huge impact on your overall energy.

The five additional chakras in your body that make a twelve-point chakra system are as follows:

- 2 chakras in the hands- one in each palm

- 2 chakras on the feet- one in each sole

- 1 chakra reaching out of the top of the head above the crown.

These additional five chakras are important to know about as much as any other energy center in the body, however, they are supportive to the rest of the system and will not hold onto energy in the same way that the seven main chakras will.

They are more like receivers. These chakras are gateways to the rest of your energy and are transmitters of energy as well. Have you ever heard of the healing art known as Reiki? Reiki is a traditional Japanese healing technique that supports the rebalancing and energetic healing of the chakra system. A Reiki practitioner becomes attuned to healing these energies and will perform an energetic transformation of the chakra energies through the palm chakras, by moving and removing unwanted, stagnate, or stuck energies within the chakras.

A Reiki practitioner learns how to take away, but not absorb someone's energy that they are working with through their hand chakras. The chakra centers in the soles of the feet are also receiving information while you are standing on the ground, lying on your back, or doing various other activities, but are not typically used in Reiki sessions, or for healing purposes.

Other ways that you are using your hand chakras are infinite: shaking someone's hand and getting a "feeling" about them; picking up an object at an antique store and "sensing" where it came from; feeling your child's forehead when they have a fever; picking out produce at the grocery store. Our hand chakras are aligning with everything that we touch.

Your feet are where you ground and how you walk through this world. Your ability to sense the world around you through your feet is very impactful and can connect you with things that you might not mentally be conscious of. The soles of your feet tell the story of where you have been and where you are going and should be considered when you are putting up your feet and kicking off your shoes at the end of a long day.

The energy center that extends out of the top of your head from your crown chakra is like an extended antenna. It is how you are pursuing the world around you. This is how you sense that it is about to rain, even when there isn't a storm cloud in sight yet, or how you get a feeling about the energy of a crowd when you walk into an office party. This chakra is your ability to receive input from the world around you from your eye level and up. It is less about the path you walk (foot chakras) and more about what other things are happening outside of you, for you to take in and respond to.

These 5 additional chakras comprise a more sensory impact on your whole chakra system. You are experiencing and pulling the world around you and giving it to your main chakra system. All of this links to your perception, brain function, physical consciousness and more.

Your entire chakra system is the subtle, ethereal body of experience that strongly correlates with the physical, mental and emotional path you take every day. Knowing this energetic cycle will help you unfold and unravel more of what lies under your surface and how it can cause a lot of distortion, imbalance and challenge when not properly dealt with and nurtured.

Chapter 4: Earth Star Chakra

While there are seven major chakras, there are believed to be additional major energetic centers in your body; one being the Earth Star Chakra. This chakra is also called a "subpersonal" chakra and is about one foot below the souls of your feet. It is connected to your feet and the minor energy foci in your feet. This chakra is typically a dark brown or even black color and can be called your "super root." Occasionally, you will see this chakra associated with the color aqua because of the amount of water found on the planet, but this is rarer to find. This "root" ties your physical and energetic body to the earth's core. This is not the same as the first chakra, the "root," but it functions similarly. What makes this energy center different is that it does not just ground your one location to the Earth, but rather grounds your entire chakra system to the Universe.

The Earth Star Chakra is what holds the origins of your DNA. It knows your karmic patterns linked to your soul and the past lives you have lived. To feel the deep connection and oneness with the Universe, you need to clear and align your Earth Star Chakra. Your day-to-day living can shuffle you around, causing you to become detached from your energy and the Universe.

Activities like racing from one place to another, working on your computer, or completing errands can all disrupt your grounded energies. The Earth Star Chakra can help you remain fully centered and grounded in this hectic society.

Many healers tap into the Earth Star Chakra to provide therapeutic energy balancing. If you notice you have picked up too much energy from another source and it is not serving you, you can release it using the wisdom of this chakra. Also, if you are lacking a certain energy, you can draw it to you from the Earth using this chakra. The beauty of this chakra is that it provides the security for your soul to fully display itself.

You may have a balanced Earth Star Chakra if you:

Feel deeply rooted in our inner power.

Feel connected to the earth and the Universe.

Can see the big picture.

Work in some capacity for something greater. Experience peace of mind.

Feel secure.

You may have an unbalanced Earth Star Chakra if you:

Lose your balance easily. Experience vertigo.

Have an eating disorder.

Your lower body experiences issues (any problems in your ankles, knees, pelvis, feet hips, or legs).

Struggle with circulation issues.

If you are currently unbalanced or experience imbalance at some point, there are several things you can do to bring it back into alignment. Some of these healing methods include meditation, crystals, and yoga poses.

Guided Meditations for Balancing Your Earth Star Chakra

The purpose of this meditation is to make you feel the connection you have to all things in this Universe and the universal wisdom. It connects your spiritual body to this world, but in a way that empowers and supports your physical and energetic odyssey. Follow one of the meditations below to help you connect, activate, and balance your Earth Star Chakra:

1.   Begin standing upright with your feet firmly flat on the ground. If it is more comfortable, you can remain seated, but try to keep the soles of your feet flat on the ground to help connect you more firmly to the Earth. Begin to relax your body and bring awareness to breathing.

2.   Close your eyes or find a soft gazing point and begin to visualize your feet touching the Earth.

3.   As your feet connect to the Earth, they begin to grow roots, extending far down and out, securely rooting you to your place. The roots you spread into the Earth reach to the center core and wrap around it, binding you tighter to the Earth. You have formed an unbreakable connection to the planet.

4.   With your roots wrapped around the magnetic and solid core of the planet, you feel the energy draw up into your roots. The energy is a pure white light pulsing up towards your feet.

5.   The energy reaches the soles of your feet and begins to fill them with the white, pure light.

6.   Keeping your body relaxed, allow the energy and light to travel up your legs, filling your ankles, shins, knees, upper legs, and hips. Guide this energy into your Root Chakra and the base of your spine. From here, allow the earth's energy to continue up your body, filling your sacrum, solar plexus, heart, lungs, throat, and then course down your arms to your fingertips. Bring your thoughts back to your neck and allow the energy to move up towards the top of your head.

7.   When your entire body is full of this core energy, imagine how it is coursing through your body and flowing like a river out of each one of your fingertips.

8.   When you are ready, allow your thoughts to shift to your present body. Begin to bring your awareness back to the room and the place you are standing or sitting. Take a deep inhale and full, clearing exhale. Open your eyes or blink a few times to bring yourself more fully back to your place.

The next guided meditation uses a similar visualization, but this time the energy enters you from the Universe and then travels down into the earth. Try out each meditation and determine which vibrates best with your energetic needs.

1.   Find a comfortable and quiet place to sit or lay down. Ideally, try to be directly connected to nature by sitting on the grass or the ground. Allow your eyes to close and your breath soften. Let your body relax.

2.   Imagine your body is a pillar of pure light. Bring your thoughts to the sun shining. If it is dark, imagine what the sun looks like when you can see it. Notice a single shaft

or pure light piercing through the sun and coming down to you. The shaft of light enters through the top of your head.

3.   The light travels down the length of your body, illuminating, and healing your body as it moves towards your feet.

4.   When the light shoots out through your feet, watch it extend below your feet, about 12 inches or more, and bathe the place in pure and healing light.

5.   The light that has cleansed your body is now cleansing your Earth Star Chakra, and it begins to grow and spin more smoothly and quickly as it heals. It is now perfectly balanced.

6.   The shaft of light that entered your body begins to leave through your Earth Star Chakra and descend into the Earth. Watch as it continues down, finally reaching the core.

7.   As you observe this movement, express your gratitude for the Earth, for your part in life, and being connected to your purpose. Take time to think about how you want the Earth to heal and thrive.

8.   When you are done communicating with the Universe, allow the energy from the core of the Earth to return to you. It enters through your Earth Star Chakra and travels up to the crown of your head. The light and energy it brings, balances and connects all your energy before it emanates from the crown of your head and travels back to the sun. Watch this light as it drives back up to where it came from.

9.   When you are ready, allow your thoughts to shift to your present body. Begin to bring your awareness back to the room and the place you are standing or sitting. Take a deep inhale and full, clearing exhale. Open your eyes or blink a few times to bring yourself more fully back to your place.

Balancing with Crystals

Another method for balancing your Earth Star Chakra is with crystals. This is a great tool to add to your meditation above or carry them on their own to help remind and keep you grounded and connected. Additionally, you can ask Sandalphon, the archangel of our earthly existence, to keep you firmly connected to the Earth and balanced in your Earth Star Chakra, so you can fulfill your higher purpose. Call on this archangel while in a relaxed position, holding one of the following crystals in your hand:

Red Jasper, Fire Agate, Dalmatian Jasper, Hematite Rainbow Quartz, Chiastolite Smoky Quartz, Black Tourmaline, Black Kyanite, Aqua Aura Quartz

Remember, this chakra is linked to deep browns, black, or Earth-associated colors. Most crystals with these colors will help you activate your Earth Star Chakra, but a popular recommendation is a Black Obsidian or Black Kyanite crystal. Hold it in your hands while meditating or around your neck during your day-to-day life so you continuously are brought back to your central point with the Universe. If you want to integrate the crystal more into your meditation, place one of the crystals mentioned above under your feet before starting one of the guided meditations outlined above. When you extend your roots down from the bottoms of your feet, imagine that they wrap around and connect to the crystal and drive that crystal down to the core of the earth.

When it reaches the center, your roots place the crystal on the core and wrap themselves around both. Now, bring the energy back up and continue your meditation. If you are meditating on the light passing from the sun to the core and back again, allow the light to travel through the crystal after leaving your Earth Star Chakra and returning. It can also travel with the light to the core and then up to the sun if you feel it should make the journey.

Chapter 5: Soul Star Chakra

Like your Earth Star Chakra, the Soul Star Chakra is another major energy center that is outside the traditional seven chakras most people talk about. While your Earth Star is also called a "subpersonal", your Soul Star is called a "transpersonal" chakra. This energy center is located about ½ a foot to a foot above the Crown and is considered the "seat of your soul," or "super soul." This focus is usually depicted in a white or golden color. The ties between your physical self and specifically your Crown with a higher power and the Universe are secured through this chakra. For your Crown to be able to receive the light and energy from the Universe, you need to have an open and flowing Soul Star. If you find that you are still struggling with your ego, consider focusing on your Soul Star so you can move beyond this human state. From an active Soul Star state, you can find a joy-filled healthy and enlightened existence.

Your Soul Star is the holder of your spirituality. Without it, you would not be able to channel the energy of the Universe through your body in a balanced manner. Without this chakra, you would also suffer because it would be impossible to use the Universal knowledge and connection to the whole.

When you are in a situation that stifles your connection to a higher power or spirituality, you can experience an imbalanced Soul Star Chakra. When you find balance in your Soul Star, you can enjoy the connection and ascension from your physical being.

When reading over this introduction to your Soul Star, it may sound very similar to your Crown. Many people become very confused about the similarities and differences between the two. It is important to understand that your Crown Chakra is still located inside your physical self, keeping it connected to your body and mind. Your connection to your higher power and the Universe is still ego-based. It is only your relationship to these powers, while your Soul Star is not connected to yourself. Your Crown still shows yourself as an individual entity connected to the whole, but your Soul Star fuses your identity with the whole. There is no separation from the Universe; therefore, you do not need to ask for guidance from it, you already have it!

A great way to consider your Soul Star is that it is the seed of your existence. From this point your identity is formed, creating your physical self. You transform from this point, for better or for worse. This is why it is very important to have a balanced Soul Star Chakra.

You may have a balanced Soul Star Chakra if you:

Feel connected to your true purpose.

Recognize that you have chosen to be living this human existence. Feel confident that everything is one.

Have a clear direction you are heading.

You may have an unbalanced Soul Star Chakra if you:

Feel spacey or out of touch.

Are ungrounded and unconnected.

Feel separate from the Earth and others. Are confused often.

Do not know what your purpose is in this life. Do not have a direction or path.

Feel disturbed in this life or in your body.

If you are currently unbalanced or experience imbalance at some point, there are several things you can do to bring it back into alignment. Some of these healing methods include meditation, crystals and yoga poses.

Guided Meditations for Balancing Your Soul Star Chakra The following meditation is provided to strengthen your fusion with all things. It is designed to take you from your body and allow you to see how you are not a separate entity but rather mixed into the whole.

Follow the meditation below to help you connect, activate, and balance your Soul Star Chakra:

1.   Begin standing upright with your feet firmly flat on the ground. If it is more comfortable, you can remain seated, but try to keep the soles of your feet flat on the ground to help connect you more firmly to the Earth. Begin to relax your body and bring awareness to breathing.

2.   Close your eyes or find a soft gazing point. Allow your body to settle into a relaxed state.

3.   When you are relaxed, call on the support of the angels guarding your Soul Star Chakra, Zadkiel and Mariel. Also call upon the archangel Butyalil, the controller of all cosmic energies. Entreat them to intercede on your behalf and to strengthen and heal your Soul Star Chakra.

4. Picture each of the angles standing before you; all three are in front of you, holding a pure-white orb. Inside you see alternating violet and magenta light. The light leaves the orbs from the archangels and enters your Soul Star Chakra.

5. When the light hits your Soul Star, you feel the blocks dissipate, your karmic deposit lifts and become one with the Universe and the angels.

6. When you begin to fuse with the Whole, allow your Spirit to leave the human experience and physical body. Feel the warmth and love as you dissipate into the collective.

7. As you join the Universe, recognize the joy, purpose, and wisdom you all have together. Sit in the knowing and the connection. Feel the pure Divine light pulsing through the Universe.

8. After a few minutes of enjoying your fusion with the One, allow the angels to guide you back to your body, coming back into your physical self. When your Spirit returns to your physical identity, recognize the continued connection you feel filtering into your other energy centers from your Soul Star.

9. Sit in the feeling of peace, purpose, and direction. Slowly allow your mind to come back into the room where you are sitting. If your eyes are closed, allow them to slowly open. Softly blink a few times.

10. When you are ready, take a deep inhale and full, clearing exhale. Before moving your body, thank the angels for helping you clear your Soul Star, and connect again with the feeling of a clear and healthy Soul Star. Slowly move your body when you are ready to return to your day.

Balancing Your Soul Star with Crystals

Crystals can also be used to help you balance your Soul Star Chakra. You can easily add crystals to your daily life or while you are meditating. Carrying them on your body, either in your pocket or incorporated into jewelry, can help you remember to seek situations that support your Soul Star rather than suppress it. Because you are more readily connected to your authentic self when in a state of sleep, placing one of the following crystals under your pillow at night can also help you speed up balancing your Soul Star:

Blue Kyanite Spirit Amethyst Celestite

Snowflake Obsidian Selenite

Amethyst Clear Quartz

If you do not have the time or do not want to use the meditation above, consider holding on to one of the above-mentioned crystals while repeating the following affirmations:

1. "I am one."

2. "I am the Universe."

3. "I am pure love."

4. "I am purpose."

5. "I am direction."

Balancing Your Soul Star with Reiki

The following directions are for a Reiki practitioner. If you have not trained or utilized Reiki before, please consult a professional before trying this on yourself. You want to make sure you move and clear your energy appropriately.

1. Ask the archangels Mariel and Zadkiel to assist in activating and expanding your Soul Star. Remember, these angels look after your Soul Star and can help speed up clearing your chakra.

2. Connect your Soul Star to your drawing of HSZSN.

3. At the location where your Soul Star is situated, about six to 12 inches above the Crown Chakra, draw DKM.

4. On the palm of your hand, draw every symbol so you can activate energy healing and the flow.

5. In a comfortable, seated position, lay your hands on your lap with your palms facing the sky.

6. With Reiki flowing, channels the energy to your Soul Star with the attached intention of clearing away any lodged Karma deposits. When the block lifts, continue to let the Reiki energy flow so your Soul Star can fill with light after it is fully activated.

7.   While your Soul Star is activating, repeat the above affirmations to aid in your concentration and balancing efforts.

8.   Repeat this process as often as necessary to continue to clear and activate your Soul Star Chakra.

Chapter 6: Chakra Symbols and Meaning, Location, Colors and Associated Glands

Primary Chakras

Of the 114 chakras in the human body, seven are considered primary—the most important chakras. Let us see the location and colors of these important chakras:

Root Chakra / Muladhara

The Root Chakra is symbolized as a four-petalled lotus with a square at the center, within which is a triangle. The square is a representation of the element earth and the triangle represents the female energy that gives life. Here lies the kundalini energy, which when awakened moves upward, passing all chakras to the Crown Chakra and connecting with universal life force.

- Location of Root Chakra: Base of the spine
- Color: Red

- Corresponds with: Adrenal glands

Sacral Chakra / Svadhisthana

The Sacral Chakra is symbolized as a six-petalled lotus with a crescent moon shape within it which represents the element water.

- Location of Sacral Chakra: Above the genitals
- Color: Orange

- Corresponds with: Sexual glands

Solar Plexus Chakra / Manipura

The Solar Plexus Chakra is symbolized as a ten-petalled lotus with a downward-pointing triangle in the center. This triangle represents the element of fire.

- Location of Solar Plexus Chakra: Below the navel

- Color: Yellow

- Corresponds with: Pancreas

Heart Chakra / Anahata

The Heart Chakra is symbolized as a twelve-petalled lotus with a six-pointed star within it. The six-pointed star is formed by two triangles that overlap each other. This star symbolizes the unity of female and male energies.

- Location of Heart Chakra: In the heart

- Color: Green

- Associated with: Thymus gland

Throat Chakra / Vishuddha

The Throat Chakra is symbolized as a sixteen-petalled lotus with a triangle inside that is pointed downwards. This triangle in turn contains a circle, which represents the element ether.

- Location of Throat Chakra: In the throat

- Color: Blue

- Associated with: Thyroid gland

Third Eye Chakra / Ajna

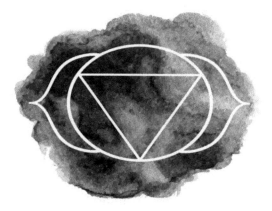

The Third Eye Chakra is symbolized by a circle with a petal on either side of it. Inside the circle is a triangle that is pointed downwards. The two petals represent Ida and Pingala, the two nadis, meaning channels, which join in this chakra. Energy flows from here to the Crown Chakra.

- Location of Third Eye Chakra: Between the eyebrows

- Color: Indigo

- Associated with: Pineal gland

Crown Chakra / Sahasrara

The Crown Chakra is symbolized by a thousand-petalled lotus. Inside the lotus is a circle. The symbol represents spirituality, purity, and the realization one experiences as the kundalini energy rises to the Crown Chakra.

- Location of the Crown Chakra: Crown of the head

- Color: Violet

- Associated with: Pituitary gland

Minor Chakras and their Functions

The seven major chakras are the most discussed, naturally so as they are the primary chakras that govern overall health. However, to optimize your healing sessions you also need to know about the minor chakras, which are 21 in number. The minor chakras are linked to the major chakras, and all of these together form part of the chakra system in your body. Knowing these minor chakras gives you a better understanding of chakras and their functions.

Location of Minor Chakras

Unlike the seven major chakras, which are all aligned to the spine, the minor chakras are located in various parts of the body.

The locations of the 21 minor chakras are:

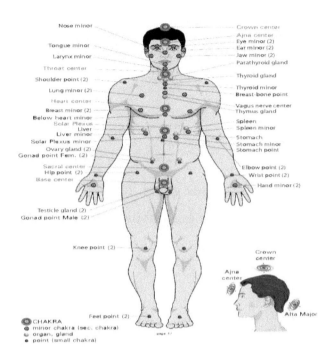

Nose minor
Tongue minor
Larynx minor
Throat center
Shoulder point (2)
Lung minor (2)
Heart center
Breast minor (2)
Below heart minor
Solar Plexus
Liver
Liver minor
Solar Plexus minor
Ovary gland (2)
Gonad point Fem. (2)
Sacral center
Hip point (2)
Base center
Testicle gland (2)
Gonad point Male (2)
Knee point (2)
Feet point (2)

Crown center
Ajna center
Eye minor (2)
Ear minor (2)
Jaw minor (2)
Parathyroid gland
Thyroid gland
Thyroid minor
Breast-bone point
Vagus nerve center
Thymus gland
Spleen
Spleen minor
Stomach
Stomach minor
Stomach point
Elbow point (2)
Wrist point (2)
Hand minor (2)

Crown center
Ajna center
Alta Major

CHAKRA
minor chakra (sec. chakra)
organ, gland
point (small chakra)

Eyes

Each eye has behind it a minor chakra that is associated with the Third Eye Chakra. These chakras improve your perception of life and fellow humans and aid in promoting consciousness.

Ears

There is one minor chakra on each cheekbone in front of the ear, where the cheekbone and the ear connect. These chakras support emotional stability, relax the face muscles, and work with the minor chakras behind the eyes to improve extra-sensory skills.

Clavicle

Located below the Throat Chakra, this minor chakra aids in treating respiratory disorders.

Thymus

A minor chakra is located in the thymus gland. Balancing this chakra is essential to improve immunity and promote emotional stability.

Breasts

Just over each breast is a minor chakra. These two minor chakras play a great role in the body's absorption of nutrients.

Solar Plexus

The Minor Solar Plexus Chakra is located below the Primary Solar Plexus Chakra. This minor chakra is associated with the major glands in this area. A balanced Minor Solar Plexus Chakra boosts circulation.

Spleen

The spleen hosts two minor chakras, one above the other. These two minor chakras strengthen the digestive system. They energize the major chakras.

Stomach

The minor chakra located in the stomach supports digestion and promotes liver and kidney functions.

Liver

The minor chakra in the liver promotes liver health. It aids in healing liver disorders and supports liver function.

Reproductive Organs

In women, each of the two ovaries has a minor chakra. In men, each of the testes has a minor chakra. These minor chakras improve fertility.

Palms

There is a minor chakra in each of your palms. These chakras, when balanced, are the channels through which you receive and pass energy.

Knees

Minor chakras in the knee joints promote acceptance and relieve fear.

Soles of Feet

Minor chakras in the soles of your feet help you to stay grounded. These chakras must stay stimulated, as they transfer all negative energies out of the body and mind to the earth.

Chapter 7: Chakras and Food Correlation

Eating is a powerful action and one of the ways our body use to breathe in our prana and use it for healing. Taking food is also one of the most integral activities in our lives that enable us to survive and live. Whether you are a nutritionist or not, you understand that foods are conduits to human growth, especially if the right food is taken.

Each chakra has a special nutritional diet that needs to be taken, and we will discuss each one of them:

1. Nutritional Food for Root Chakra

The root chakra is an excellent place to release fear around feelings of dishonesty and eating. Over-eating or under-eating might make you feel scattered. Your root chakra's work is to enable you to feel grounded so that you have a clear mind to make wise decisions and relate well with those around your life.

The best nutritional food that will enable you to be grounded and boost the purpose of your root chakra include minerals, proteins, red-colored foods, medicinal and edible mushrooms, and root vegetables.

Eating with other community members will also help your root chakra. You can also dialogue with your body to enable you to honor your body's instinct on which of these chakra works best to heal your chakra.

2. Nutritional Food for Sacral Chakra

The sacral chakra is the exact opposite of the first chakra. While the root chakra keeps us grounded and stable, the sacral chakra opens up to the movement and flow. When you are having problems with your creativity or expressing yourself, "You are not going with the flow." Eating the right food will help your sacral chakra continue with the flow.

The sacral chakra foods include seeds, tropical fruits, orange-colored foods, fats, and oils (omega-3s is one of the best), nuts, and fish.

While eating, it is important to pay attention to your senses.

3. Nutritional Food for Solar Plexus Chakra

Solar Plexus gives us the power that we need to give us the drive to achieve our goals and make wise decisions. We can also go into overdrive, and in this situation; we are bound to lose power.

However, you can harness your power and energy to be optimal by looking at the type of foods that you should take. Eat food that will assist you in sustaining your energy and try to eat them as frequently as possible.

The foods that will help solar plexus in serving its purpose include whole grains, yellow-colored nutritional foods, fiber, legumes, fiber, and complex carbohydrates.

Avoid food that will weaken your body, such as artificial sweeteners, sugars, soft drinks, and avoid drinking excessive alcoholic beverages.

4. Nutritional Food for Heart Chakra

The heart chakra gives us the ability to give love and compassion. Your heart energy will dry if this chakra is not in balance.

Food for love and compassion includes foods rich in chlorophyll, sprouts, vegetables, any green-colored nutritional food, and raw foods.

The heart chakra will also flourish if you share foods with others, express gratitude for feeding yourself and infuse love into the water we are drinking and the food that we are eating during meals.

5. Nutritional Food for Throat Chakra

The throat chakra is responsible for illuminating our truth and genuineness. It is also the pathway to our food and where several activities take place, including chewing, swallowing, breathing, and talking.

The foods that will help your throat chakra in communicating and telling the truth include fruits, juices, sea plants, sauces, and soups.

We should also not create an imbalance in our throat chakra, especially when sating our food choices—for example, avoid saying "yes" to some food choices when we mean "no."

6. Nutritional Food for The Third Eye Chakra

The third eye is the center of our intuition, inspiration, imagination, and insight. Listening to this intuition nourishes our center. We can lose sight if we allow our intellect to override our intuition.

The foods that help our third eye and stimulate our intuitive center include herbal tea, blueberries, and blackberries.

When your third chakra is unbalanced or is already in an overdrive situation, avoid food or beverages such as dark chocolate, alcohol, and coffee. These foods will stimulate and keep your moods and mind on overdrive.

7. Nutritional Food for Your Crown Chakra

Crown Chakra connects us all to life. Choosing to eat is a very satisfying form of interconnection when you feel severed from bigger things like the human race, planet, your community, or the cosmos. Eating the right nutritional food for crown chakra will enable you to get a deeper meaning when thinking about life.

Food that helps you with your crown chakra includes copal, juniper, sage, frankincense, and myrrh. Also feed your crowd chakra with clean air, unconditional love and moon-and-sun light.

Foods are excellent symbols of connection that will enable you to connect with deeper and sacred aspects of life.

8. Chakras Endocrine System and the Immune System

The endocrine system is a chemical messenger where internal glands produce hormones directly into the bloodstream during the circulatory process. The internal glands are part of different organs in our bodies, and the endocrine system helps in regulating all the organs in our bodies.

All Seven Chakras control different glands:

- Root Chakra – control adrenal gland

The adrenal is found at the top of the kidneys that produce hormones, including adrenaline, which is responsible for stimulating the "flight or fight" response. The adrenaline gland is also responsible for root chakra's survival drive, which directly ties to the base.

- Sacral Chakra – control reproductive system-including ovaries

The ovaries are responsible for controlling egg creation, sexual development, and controlling progesterone and estrogens. The drives of the sacral chakra mirror the ovaries' potential for life. The sacral chakra also links with the energies of the ovaries.

- Solar Plexus – controls the pancreas

The pancreas is responsible for hormones like insulin, which helps in our digestive systems.

Overstimulating the solar plexus chakra with things like excess blood sugar can cause various problems which can lead to diseases like diabetes. Under stimulating your solar plexus can lead to ulcers.

- Heart Chakra – controls the Heart and Thymus

The thymus is responsible for producing lymphocytes, which is an important part used for digestion and the immune system. Because of this quality, the thymus is referred to as one of the vital healing properties of your fourth or heart chakra.

- Throat Chakra – controls thyroid

The thyroid is contained on either side of the larynx, which is part of the throat chakra. The thyroid produces the hormone called thyroxine, which is responsible for controlling the rate of food conversion by the body into useful energy.

In this particular area, the throat chakra is dominant. The rate of metabolism is governed by the thyroid.

- Third Eye-Controls the Pituitary Gland

The pituitary gland is near the skull base and is responsible for releasing hormones that influence the chemistry of our body. The third eye spiritual energies are reflected by the pituitary glands and their influence on our whole body.

The third eye and pituitary gland work together in the body.

- Crown Chakra-control pineal gland

Pineal produces melatonin hormones and lies deep within our brain.

This hormone mirrors the relationship between the crown chakra and other chakras because it affects all the other glands in your endocrine system.

Crown chakra and pineal gland are part of the determinants of the entire system.

Chapter 8: Chakras and Crystals Correlation

As much as the movement of the planets in the cosmos can affect the lives of people on earth, these same elements can be used to improve the flow of energy through our chakras.

Making a small investment of time to open and realign the chakras can pay dividends to your overall sense of well-being. This chapter discusses how using specific types of crystals, gems, and stones, each one connected to a primary chakra, can help you achieve this goal by resolving blockages of energy and restoring and maintaining complete mind-body health and vitality.

How to Begin Using Crystals

Before we look at how crystals can be used to influence the chakras, this section provides a basic overview of where to find them, how to care for them, and some of the best methods to achieve balance.

Assembling a Crystal Kit

To begin with, many retailers sell chakra crystal kits online. These kits are pre-assembled and usually include seven stones, gems, or crystals—one for each of the seven chakras. Some kits contain up to 10 or more stones accommodating those who are working with alternate chakra systems. The final section of this chapter discusses the specific types of stones that are appropriate for each chakra, but most kits will generally include stones aligned with chakras according to their color:

- First chakra—red or black stone or crystal

- Second chakra—orange stone or crystal

- Third chakra—yellow stone or crystal

- Fourth chakra—green or pink stone or crystal

- Fifth chakra—bluestone or crystal

- Sixth chakra—purple or indigo stone or crystal

- Seventh chakra—violet or white stone or crystal

You may find chakra crystal kits at a variety of retail outlets both online and in brick-and-mortar stores. Often, many people prefer to hand-select their crystal kits. Visiting a hobby store or any store that sells incense or other spiritual healing tools and books is a good place to look. The process of acquiring your own set of chakra stones in itself is a worthwhile practice that allows you to spend more time contemplating the spiritual components of your conscious mind. Such efforts themselves can contribute to healing and growth. Also, by hand-selecting the crystals in your kit, they will be spiritually attuned to you, and your subtle energy body is likely to respond. If you choose to build your own set, try to select stones or crystals that are all of approximately the same size. Remember that the crown chakra crystal should be pointed at one end or "single-terminated."

Preparing Crystals

Once you have assembled your set of chakra crystals, the first step before using them in meditation is to clear and program them. Crystals constantly absorb light energy, so before use, it is crucial to cleanse the stones of any of the negative energy they may have absorbed before you.

There are many methods you can use to clear or cleanse crystals, both before and after using them. Most gemstones can be rinsed with water. Many people will soak them overnight in saltwater or bury them in brown rice—both techniques neutralize any negative energy the crystals may have retained. Some people expose the crystals to unfiltered sunlight or moonlight after clearing them so that they will be recharged with natural, vibrant energy from the universe. Be sure to clear your crystal after each use to remove any negative energy they absorbed from your body during meditation.

Using Crystals in Meditation

Preparation

As there are several methods of acquiring crystal sets and several methods of clearing them, so there are many methods of incorporating crystals into your meditation practice. Regardless of which specific method you use, you should follow a few simple steps before you begin:

1. Find a quiet, secluded space where you have plenty of room to sit and lie down on your back comfortably.

2. Make sure you have chosen a place where you will not be disturbed for 30 minutes to an hour. Please a "Do Not Disturb" sign on the door if necessary.

3. Turn off your phone and any other electronic devices. This way you will not be disturbed or interrupted, and shutting off electronic devices ensures you will not absorb any unnatural radiation or other unnatural energy while you are meditating.

4. Change into comfortable, loose-fitting clothes.

5. Program your crystals. Your recharged crystals must be attuned to your energy, so hold each one in your hand, close your eyes while focusing your energy on the crystal, and say silently in your mind or quietly to yourself, "These crystals will realign my chakras."

Laying of Stones

The practice known as "laying of stones" is derived from ancient Tantric texts in which the close placement of properly cleansed and aligned crystals near the chakra that is experiencing blockage was used to help open energy flow. Many people still use this practice today when their chakra system fails to sustain the physical body and the many spiritual and psychological demands, we encounter each day. To practice the laying of stones, follow these steps to lay the stones:

1. Complete the preparation outlined in the previous section.

2. Find a comfortable place and lie down on your back.

3. Place the crystals on your body as follows:

   a. Root chakra crystal just above the crotch

b. Sacral chakra crystal on your belly, two or three inches below your belly button

c. Solar plexus chakra crystal on your stomach, two or three inches above your belly button

d. Heart chakra crystal at the center of your chest

e. Throat chakra crystal at the center of your throat

f. Third-eye chakra crystal between your eyebrows and just above your nose

g. Crown chakra crystal on the floor or bed, one or two inches above the top of your head, with the pointed end aimed at your head

Once you are lying comfortably on your back and the stones are in place, close your eyes and take several deep breaths. You should hear your intake of breath and your exhalation as you allow the breathing to cleanse your lungs and energy body of all tension.

Next, beginning at the top of your head, and working slowly down to your forehead, eyes, mouth, neck, and throat, start relaxing all the muscles in your body. Continue through your shoulders, arms, chest, and abdomen, then down into your thighs, calves, and all the way down to your feet. Once you are completely relaxed, imagine tree roots are gently encircling your limbs and pulling you down into the soft earth. Let go completely and give yourself entirely to Mother Earth.

For the next 10 or 20 minutes, remain in a state of total relaxation as the stones work to absorb all the negative energy from your body and your chakras. Often people will have difficulty relaxing because they will be distracted by recurring thoughts. If this happens, do not try to suppress your thoughts. Instead, breathe through your nose gently and simply focus on the breath as it enters your body and exits through your nose. By focusing on your steady, quiet shallow breathing, your thoughts will recede into the background, and your mind will become still again.

When you have come back out of your deep relaxation, remove the stones in the reverse order in which you placed on your body, beginning with the crown chakra. Cleanse the crystals using one of the methods discussed above and put them in a safe place.

You should practice the paying of stones at least two or three times a week. Many people also take the time to perform this relaxation ritual every day. Laying of stones can be especially helpful when you are trying to heal from a traumatic experience, such as the loss of a loved one. It can also help alleviate physical trauma and pain, such as headaches and joint pain.

Clear Quartz Method

You may meditate with chakra crystals even if you do not have a complete set. Clear quartz is relatively easy to find, and with just two pieces of quartz, you can begin using the power of crystals to help align and balance your chakras. To use this method of chakra alignment, follow these steps:

1. Complete the preparation outlined in the previous section.

2. Find a comfortable place and lie down on your back.

3. Place on a piece of quartz just above the crown of your head.

4. Place the other piece of quartz just below the root chakra between your legs at the region of the crotch.

Once you are lying comfortably on your back and the stones have been placed as stated above, close your eyes and take several deep breaths. Focus on breathing in and out to clear your mind from distractions as you visualize the energy of your chakra system running along your spine from the base root chakra to the crown.

Feel the energy move through each chakra up from root to crown, and back down to the root. Visualize the cleansing power of the crystals charging your entire chakra system as the energy flows through you. Maintain this position for 10 to 20 minutes. When you are done, cleanse the crystals and store them in a safe place.

Crystal Point Method

This method requires the use of a specific type of crystal that has a point on one end and is flat on the other. To practice this method, follow these steps:

1. Complete the preparation outlined in the previous section.

2. Find a comfortable place and lie down on your back.

3. Hold the crystal by the flat end with your non-dominant hand.

4. Beginning at your crown chakra, rotate the crystal in a clockwise spiral over the chakra. Make nine concentric circles spiraling outward from the chakra.

5. Move the point of the crystal to your third eye. Hover the crystal above your body, drawing a line from the crown to the third eye.

6. Rotate the crystal in a clockwise spiral over this chakra, again making nine concentric circles spiraling outward.

7. Return the crystal point to the crown chakra, then hover the crystal point over your body, drawing a line from the crown to the third eye to the throat chakra.

8. Rotate the crystal in a clockwise spiral over this chakra, again making nine concentric circles spiraling outward.

9. Repeat this process for each chakra.

10. After you have covered all seven chakras, return the crystal to the crown of your head, and place it above your head with the point directed at the crown chakra.

Visualize the energy flowing from crown to root as you breathe slowly and steadily with your eyes closed for 10 to 20 minutes. After you have completed the entire cycle, cleanse the crystal and store it in a safe place.

Seven Ways You Can Use Crystals to Enhance the Healing Power of Chakras

Each chakra is responsible for exerting control and influence over different parts of our subtle energy body. As a result, each chakra requires a different type of crystal or stone to absorb the negative energy from the chakra with which it is related. Ready-made kits of chakra stones often consider this when the stones are selected. Of course, you may also choose your stones to increase the affinity between your set of crystals and your chakras.

In addition to meditation, many people find that wearing or carrying jewelry or totems associated with the healing power of each chakra helps them restore balance. The following guide shows how each individually attuned crystal can help you manifest and align each of your seven chakras:

1. Root chakra

   ○ Red jasper, for balancing

   ○ Red carnelian, for strength, cleansing, and bravery

   ○ Obsidian, for safety and the warding off of danger

   ○ Bloodstone, which is linked to warding off negative energy and building confidence

2. Sacral chakra

   ○ Amber, for the intellect and marital vows

   ○ Golden topaz, to restore power

   ○ Carnelian, to regain vitality, courage, and sexual prowess

○ Malachite, to heal sexual abuse

○ Sunstone, to remove sexual inhibitions

○ Tiger eye, to counterbalance male and female sexual energy

3. Solar plexus chakra

○ Yellow jade, to increase confidence in all areas in which you seek to exert control and influence

○ Citrine, to inspire imagination and help create a more powerful presence

○ Agate, to enhance physical strength, as well as the intellect

○ Tiger's eye, to attract fortune and prosperity and increase confidence and mental clarity

4. Heart chakra

○ Pink quartz, to promote compassion, understanding, and the capacity for calming and soothing.

○ Amazonite, to help open the pathway to divine guidance through knowledge and communication.

○ Aventurine, to support and promote your effort to create prosperity and inspired leadership.

5. Throat chakra

○ Turquoise, to protect strength, inspire strong leadership, and create a relaxed and focused mind.

○ Blue apatite, to help you achieve goals by encouraging creativity and clear communication.

○ Celestite, to effect clear communication by creating clarity of mind and inner peace.

6. The third eye

○ Sapphire, to increase happiness through the attainment of goals and resolution of conflicts

○ Lapis lazuli, to promote precise and powerful insights, wisdom, and judgment.

○ Sodalite, to strengthen the intellect and promote clarity of mental focus.

7. Crown chakra

○ Clear quartz, to magnify the properties of all other stones and open pathways to connect the soul with the cosmic source of enlightenment.

○ Amethyst, to promote healing, boost self-esteem, heal addictions, and enhance the depth of spirituality and creativity.

○ Moonstone, to open the heart to allow the energy of the crown chakra to nurture and strengthen the entire chakra system.

Whether you purchase a pre-assembled chakra stone kit or spend time searching for individual stones attuned to your psyche, including these stones in your rituals can increase your ability to function effectively in a variety of situations. This chapter has outlined several methods of incorporating stones into your meditation practice.

You may also choose to focus on any of the individual chakras by carrying one or more of the stones with you. Many people also find that jewelry made using these stones can keep them focused throughout the day. However, you decide to use stones in your spiritual practice, this chapter has provided at least seven new avenues of exploration.

Chapter 9: Imbalanced or blocked chakras

What is a blocked/imbalanced chakra?

Now because the chakra is a constantly rotating wheel of energy, there can be times when the chakra will be imbalanced, tilted or disturbed. An imbalanced chakra could be dangerous to your physical, mental, psychological, spiritual and even emotional health. A lot of times when we look around us and see that things are not going like we would like them to, what is really going on is that our chakras are not in good health. The way you nourish your body, you should also not neglect your soul. Even though the idea of the chakra is not often found in western medicine, saying that they do not exist would amount to saying that the soul does not exist just because we cannot see it.

Our lives do not always have to depend on pills, injections and antibiotics. A lot of time, what we experience as physical pain is just a product of a major tilt in our chakra and even though pills might seem to relieve the symptoms momentarily, don't be surprised that we might experience recurrence of illnesses that we have treated over and over again. The big question is "why?"

Why does it seem like we never really overcome illnesses and infections permanently? Why does it seem like we cannot take enough pills and once we stop taking the pills, the illnesses seem to come right back? The reason for this phenomenon is the fact that drugs only combat the symptoms and presentations of the true problem and not the problem itself. If we do not look after the chakras, we will end up having to take treatments over and over again. Instead of having to spend so much money on medications that are not assured or permanent, why not try something that will take care of the problem from the roots? First however, we need to look at the symptoms of an imbalanced chakra.

How do you know when your chakra is imbalanced?

Now, knowing and recognizing the cause of a problem is the first step in solving that problem. An imbalanced chakra can cause a lot of issues depending on what chakra it is that is imbalanced. So here are some tips to knowing how your chakra could get blocked.

Childhood trauma: chakra blockage or imbalance could be caused by memories buried deep within the subconscious mind from childhood trauma or events that might have brought pain and agony to us but which we have pushed to the back of our minds over a period of time. These memories, even though they have been relegated to the subconscious, actually do not go away and sooner or later, we will have to confront them one way or another. A chakra can get blocked when the subconscious mind is trying to force us to pay attention to it and give it its due. If we fight it, (which we most likely will after all the point of pushing a memory to the subconscious mind in the first place is to not have to deal with it.) We will create a conflict in our soul and our chakra will suffer for it by becoming blocked and imbalanced and thus not receive enough energy.

Abuse: Any form of abuse at all can cause a blockage in our chakra in the sense that the agony from the abuse and the hate that will result from it will make our chakra blocked and tilted, such that we will have an imbalance. Abuse creates resentment, and resentment creates a blockage, like when we are trying to force too many particles through a hose. The chakra will become burdened and blocked and not receive enough energy and thus the imbalance.

A restrictive belief or system of beliefs: we all get born into families that we do not choose. At least, we have no memories of choosing what family or religion we get born into. Some religions are all about rules and laws and restrictions so much that the soul becomes weighed down with all of these rules which would have now become like yokes or burden on the chakras and thus causing an imbalance.

Unforgiving pain: when we get wronged, as humans, we sometimes carry the resentment against whatever it is that causes us the pain for a while. Some of us let go of the resentment naturally without any external interference while some of us find it difficult to let go even when the defaulter has asked our forgiveness and has tried to atone for the sin committed against us. Over time, resentment piles up and becomes a bundle and it moves through our soul just like our chakra rotates within us. They start to clog and block the chakra and eventually start to manifest in the form of chakra imbalances.

Lack of care and attention: as funny as it may sound to you, there are a lot of people who just let themselves go through life without care. They eat anything, sleep anyhow, their hygiene is terrible, their emotions untended and a whole lot of other things just lying around in their lives and they are unable or unwilling to do something about it. Lack of care can make the soul-weary as much as the body and this can affect the chakra negatively, causing a blockage or an imbalance or both.

Now with time, pressure builds within the body from all I have listed above and more that I haven't listed here and a cycle of denial, guilt, anger, resentment, repressions, etc. will cause everything in the body to go south including metabolism, oxygenation, posture and carriage and even emotional state. Diseases will start as a result of repeatedly blocked chakra resulting from the above mentioned.

Chapter 10: Symptoms of Blockage

Chakra blockage can wreak havoc in your life. It can lead to weight fluctuations, health problems, financial problems, and relationship problems. It can lead to crippling phobias and physical issues. It can also lead to depression, anxiety, and other mental health issues.

When your chakras are blocked, you'd feel that something in your life is off. You'd have persistent worries, such as money problems, career difficulties, and fear of intimacy. If you feel that your finances, relationships, career, and everything else in your life is crumbling down, it's time to act.

Here's a guide that can help you determine if one or two of your chakras are blocked.

Crown Chakra Blockage

Your crown chakra is the gateway to wisdom and enlightenment. It connects you to the universe and everything in it. A blocked crown chakra can lead to spiritual connection, it can also lead to several symptoms including:

- Loneliness

- Lack of direction

- Inability to build a genuine connection with others

- Inability to set and maintain goals

- Nerve pain

- Learning difficulties

- Indecisiveness

- Lack of inspiration and joy

- Confusion

- Over intellectualism

- Dominance

- Nightmares

- Epilepsy

- Brain tumors

- Amnesia

- Delusions

Having an underactive crown chakra leads to confusion, spiritual addiction, catatonia, and over intellectualism. This means that if you're a "know-it-all", your chakra may be spinning too slowly.

Overactive crown chakra leads to dominance, depression, greed, headaches, and disconnection from reality. This is the reason why you should make sure that your crown chakra is balanced.

You can also say the following affirmations to help balance your crown chakra:

- I am complete.

- I am one with the Divine Energy.

- I am a spiritual being.

- I have faith in God.

- I believe.

- I go beyond my limiting beliefs.

- I am aligned with the Divine Energy.

- I am wise.

- I am open to questions

- I trust God.

- I understand.

- I am open to enlightenment.

- I am open to pure bliss.

- My consciousness is growing and expanding.

- God's love heals me.

- I let my fantasy run free.

- I am open-minded.

- I accept myself.

- I am enlightened.

- I feel pure joy.

Root Chakra Blockage

The Muladhara chakra governs your ability to connect with the world. This chakra is extremely sensitive. This chakra represents security and stability.

When this chakra is blocked, you'd experience the following symptoms:

- Kidney infections

- Tumors in the rectal area

- Reproductive health issues

- Laziness

- Addictive behavior

- Anemia

- Circulatory issues

- Bladder irritations

- Anxiety

- Depression

- Low self-esteem

- Leg pain

- Lower back pain

- Fear of change

- Materialism

- Anxiety attacks

- Lack of energy and motivation

- Insecurities

When you feel a lot of these symptoms, take time to sit down, breathe, and say these affirmations:

- I am grounded.

- I am safe.

- I am powerful.

- I am wealthy.

- I have enough.

- I am brave.

- I have enough.

- I am centered.

- I trust myself.

- I am open to possibilities.

- I am safe.

- I am loved.

- I am not afraid to change

- I am not afraid to trust people.

- I nurture my body with clean water, food, exercise, and water.

Sacral Chakra

Your sacral chakra is the center of your feelings and emotions. It is also the center of your sexuality and creativity. When your sacral chakra is balanced, you radiate sincere friendliness and warmth, without being too clingy. When you have a balanced sacral chakra, you have a strong intuition, energy, and a strong zest for life. You're also compassionate and emotionally stable.

But when this chakra is off, you'll also feel that something's not right in your life. It could lead to various symptoms such as:

- Guilt

- Lack of motivation

- Infertility issues

- Low back pain

- Low libido

- Inability to orgasm

- Depression

- Low self-esteem

- Jealousy

- Detachment

- Fear

- Lack of vitality

- Fear of change

- Diabetes

- Sexual dysfunction

- Lack of flexibility

- Diarrhea

- Weight loss

- Loss of appetite

- Chameleon personality

- Depression

- Menstrual issues

- Lack of focus

- Poor boundaries

- Bipolar mood swings

- Immobilized by fear

- Aloofness

When your sacral chakra spins too fast, you often experience jealousy, mood swings, and sexual addictions. You often consider people as sex objects and you may be overly dramatic. If your sacral chakra is underactive, you may have digestive disorders and sexual issues. You may be oversensitive and shy.

If you're overly shy or you've been acting like a drama queen lately, then you should say the following affirmations daily:

- I am confident.

- I am comfortable with my sexuality.

- I accept myself.

- I am at peace.

- I am radiant.

- I listen to my truth.

- I respect my emotions.

- I can provide for my own needs.

- I trust my instinct.

- My sexuality is sacred.

- I am enough.

- I am grateful.

- I am creative.

- I am grateful for everything in my life.

- The universe is filled with beauty.

Solar Plexus Chakra

When your solar plexus is balanced, you have complete control over your thoughts and emotions. Your small mind or ego won't influence your actions. You fully accept your place in the universe. You love and appreciate yourself and others. You can also easily see the uniqueness and importance of the people around you.

When this chakra is balanced, you have a healthy self-esteem. You have good relationships.

If this chakra is unbalanced, you're overly critical and judgmental. You'll easily find fault in others. You may be demanding and may have extreme emotional problems. You may be rigid and stubborn. You are also more likely to engage in a codependent relationship. You'll also experience the following symptoms:

- Diabetes

- Binge eating

- Constipation

- Lack of self-control

- Gallstones

- Hepatitis

- Inability to lead others

- Stomach ulcers

- Self-esteem issues

- Allergies

- Pancreatitis

- Reflux problems

- Obesity

- Inability to reach goals

- Stomach ulcers

- Growing addiction

When your solar plexus chakra is not balanced, you can say the following affirmations:

- I am strong and powerful.

- I am empowered.

- I make my own choices.

- I treat myself respectfully.

- I trust myself.

- I am worthy of love and kindness.

- I am authentic.

- I direct my own life.

- I am at peace with myself.

- I am responsible for my life.

- I release my desires and appetite to the universe.

- I accept my responsibilities.

- I make my own choices.

- I am successful.

- I am in control.

Blocked Heart Chakra

Holding a grudge or a traumatic event may block your heart chakra. Repressed feelings can also negatively affect the function of your heart chakra and can lead to:

- Heartlessness

- Fear of getting hurt

- Loneliness

- Social anxiety

- Shyness

- Holding grudges

- Inability to give or receive freely

- Fear and suspicion in romantic relationships and friendships

- You are extremely self-centered.

- You feel unworthy of love.

- You feel embarrassed about your failures.

- You easily lose patience.

- You have difficulty breathing and you have allergies.

- You have heart and lung issues.

- You may experience insomnia.

When you have an overactive heart chakra, you are unable to say no to others. You try your best to please others and you are desperate for other people's love and appreciation.

When you have an underactive chakra, you feel like you're cold, shy, and resentful.

The heart chakra controls most of your emotions. So, if you want to achieve emotional stability, it is important to keep this chakra balanced. If your heart chakra is not working well, you can say these affirmations:

- Love is all there is.

- I am worthy of love and respect.

- I love myself just as I am.

- I forgive myself and I forgive others.

- I trust in the power of love.

- My heart is filled with love.

- I open my heart to unconditional love.

- I love my life.

- I am compassionate.

- I openly receive love.

- I am not afraid to love.

- I am compassionate and forgiving.

- I am grateful.

- I embrace love.

- I open my heart to love.

These affirmations will help heal emotional wounds. If you have problems giving and receiving love, say these affirmations in the morning after you wake up and at night before you fall asleep.

Throat Chakra

This chakra governs our ability to tell the truth. So, habitual lying is not just a character flaw, it is also a symptom of blocked throat chakra.

Throat chakra blockage has also several other emotional and physical symptoms such as:

- Extreme shyness

- Social anxiety

- Inability to express thoughts

- Inconsistency in actions and speech

- Social anxiety

- Detachment

- Stubbornness

- Inhibited creativity

- Detachment

- Chronic sore throat

- Laryngitis

- Frequent headaches

- Mouth ulcers

- Thyroid problems

- Neck pain

- Hoarseness

People with blocked throat chakra are deceptive, manipulative, domineering, anxious, and insecure. So, if you're constantly insecure or envious, take time to say the following affirmations:

- I have a voice.

- My opinions matter.

- I speak the truth.

- I uphold the truth.

- I am free of all delusions

- I claim my voice.

- I am speaking my truth.

- I let go of the chains that are holding me back.

- I have a beautiful voice.

- I am not afraid to speak my feelings.

- I listen to others with others.

- I am content and truthful.

- I value honesty.

- Important.

- I am not afraid to speak up.

Third Eye or the Sixth Chakra Blockage

Sixth chakra blockage can wreak havoc to your health. It could disrupt your day and it could lead to serious mental issues. It's normal to feel crazy on some days. But, if you're feeling crazy too often, then you may have a blocked third eye chakra.

This chakra governs your psychic abilities and intuition. So, if you feel that your intuition is out of whack or you get deceived easily, you may be experiencing sixth chakra blockage.

If your sixth chakra is blocked, you'll experience these symptoms:

- Poor vision

- Seizure

- Migraines

- Sciatica

- Inability to focus

- Oversensitivity

- Delusions

- Depression

- Paranoia

- Anxiety

- Fear of success

- Lack of clarity

- Paranoia

- Cognitive problems

- Psychotic behavior

- Severe retardation

- Lack of discipline

- Pride

If your third eye chakra spins too fast, you're proud, dominant, manipulative, and you may be living in a fantasy world. If it spins too slow, you're often confused, undisciplined, afraid of success, oversensitive, and unable to focus.

So, if you have an imaginary fiancé or you're experiencing other third eye chakra blockage, then you must take action by saying these affirmations:

- I see clearly.

- I have a strong intuition.

- I have an open sixth sense.

- I am important.

- I am intelligent.

- I am open.

- I am ready to see the truth.

- I am wise.

- I trust my intuition.

- I forgive myself for my past mistakes.

- I accept myself.

- I am open to bliss and inspiration.

- I am at peace.

- All is well.

- I release my past.

When you feel that something is off in your life, one or two of your chakras may be unbalanced.

Chapter 11: Basic chakras healing methods

Massage

There are various massage techniques that people can use to improve their focus and connect with their chakras. There are several massage techniques you can try, such as:

1. Deep-Tissue Massage

Practicing this form of massage on your back is the first step you should take. The deep-tissue practice is not necessarily deep but rather slow and specific to a particular part. The main goal is to massage a particular muscle in a focused and slow manner using a broadening stroke or lengthening stroke meaning with or across the fiber, respectively.

When performing a deep-tissue massage, the biggest advantage is focusing on the fascia or connective tissue. According to research, the connective tissue is the wiring of the energy flow in the human body. The fascia, on the other hand, acts as the conduit through which the energy in our body flows. This will enable us to focus on the erector spinal muscles with the determination to work with prana or chakra energy.

Practice lengthening strokes on your iliocostalis, longissimus, and the spinal. Also, practice broadening strokes on the gluteus media, which will enable you to open the flow of the energy that connects prana with the legs. Also, practice broadening stroke on the longissimus.

Reflexology

Another technique is the "chakra" foot reflexology massage. The reflexology practice focuses on two chakra aspects: Chakra's physical location and the endocrine gland that is associated with each chakra either through proximity or related function. The physical locations are situated along with the head reflex points on your feet and along the spinal as well.

The root chakra is located at the sacrum, and the root chakra reflex in your foot is in the sacral reflex on your foot. The seventh chakra reflex is found on the big toe's distal portion. The chakras are associated with the main endocrine glands.

All the other chakras are positioned in the feet as well. Also, other places connect to the chakras such as the sciatic nerve which connects with the root chakra, uterus connects to the sacral chakra, and the solar plexus and heart reflex connect to the third chakra and fourth chakra respectively.

2. Energy Work

Another technique is the chakra energy work. The light touch is the focus of the energy work over chakra while also focusing on the intended purpose. Focus on the connection and intention as well. Focus your visualization on two aspects, including working with the right (visual, intuitive) and left (analytic, logical) sides of your brain. Visualize colored energy in a spinning wheel on each part of the chakra (on the right brain).

3. Life Energy Massage

It is one of the most popular techniques. The main focus of the life energy massage session is the advanced healing energy to clear the body. The cleansing involves getting rid of old feelings or habitual thought patterns. The session will enable you to clear negative thinking, clear past traumas, expansive feelings, improved sleep, increase energy, etc.

It's a gentle hand-on kind of session.

4. Chakra Foot Massage

In this form of chakra massage therapy, start by preparing a tub, foot bath, a small basin or a large bowl here bot your feet can fit comfortably. Lay a towel beside you to set and dry your legs and protect your floor. Add several teaspoons of sea or Epsom salt (you can also use coarse sea salt which is readily available in many grocery stores). Fill the very hot water, but it should not be too hot to hurt burn your legs. You can wait for the water to get cold for a few minutes.

You can also add few drops of recommended essential oil and an oil blend, perform massage on both feet, one at a time. When you are done with massaging one foot, put it in water as you massage the second one. After massaging both feet, place them in water and let them stay there for 10 to 15 minutes as long as the water is still hot. That's why it is still important to prepare very hot water. Breathe in and exhale smoothly. You can perform this form of meditation while listening to cool music; the use of chakra affirmations is also great. You can also prepare an inspiring statement that you can be reading while practicing this meditation.

For instance, if you are practicing root chakra, you can say, "I am grounded, I am safe, and the process of life is trustworthy."

You can also use the color that represents the chakra you are trying to heal. For your root chakra, use a red towel or blanket and so on for the rest of the chakras.

The main difference between getting a chakra massage and other types of massages like the regular massage is the knowledge about the chakra locations by chakra professionals massage providers. The expert giving you chakra massages will be able to facilitate your body's connection with your wisdom. They will be able to connect with you as a client or their patient properly, their main focus will be to balance or heal your chakra, and they will be able to align the healing process with your intentions for concrete solutions. They will prepare the room and make sure it's warm and has a receptive environment to enable the quality meditation process and effective healing.

5. How Different Chakras Can Be Healed or Balanced Through Massage Therapy

Root chakra: With this chakra regarded as the foundation of the whole chakra system, its good health is required just like the rest of the chakras. A professional chakra massage therapist will recommend the stimulation of your back through reflexology and balancing massage.

Solar Plexus: Located above the navel and below the heart, it is also regarded as the power center. Our power center can experience imbalance in situations such as the transition from adolescence to adulthood, dealing with a job loss or transition of your career. A professional chakra therapist will recommend deep-tissue massage in your back to realign the chakras.

Throat Chakra: This chakra is represented in throat and neck areas. A chakra massage expert will not just master the massage practice and perform it on you but will master the communication practice as well. They will help with massaging your neck and throat areas to help you have a relaxing and comfortable expression and communication.

Crown Chakra: This is a chakra that helps connect with the higher purpose and relate to your wisdom. When this chakra is in good condition, you will be able to enjoy the full joy of our universe and feel blissful. The use of aromatherapy and deep-tissue massage will greatly in giving you this desirable feeling.

Use of Clockwise Circular Stroke

You can also practice this form of massage using water medicated and soluble oils alongside with the herbs. The root chakra can be massaged on the coccyx using dashmool oil, which is formed from a blend of 10 herbs. The sacral chakra regulates creativity, sexual functions, and water balance. Dilute essential oil used for sacral chakra and massage the sacrum or the lower abdomen. For solar plexus, massage the navel area with ginger oils and peppermint.

The heart chakra is massaged at the upper back and the center of the chest using diluted basil oil. The throat chakra is massaged on the throat using oil that is infused with calamus. The third eye can be massaged with Triphala or oil infused with a rose at the center of your forehead. The crown chakra is massaged at its chakra point as well, which is at the top of the head.

Massage therapies are an excellent solution when looking for a way to balance and heal your chakras. In most cases, when one chakra is not allowing energy to flow freely either because of imbalance or blockage, massages will be of great help. Massages are applied to the correct places and will help you restore their correct energy. It is also easy to correct your chakra, especially if you are new and trying to heal or balance the chakra because you will identify with exact chakra points and master their locations. It is also advisable for you to combine massages with other practices such as health and the right diet, exercise, and meditation.

When there is a smooth flow of energies through your chakras, you will have stable and balanced mental, physical, emotional, and spiritual health. Chakra massage therapy is an excellent technique which does not only helps you realign your chakras but also makes you feel better, relax, and rejuvenated after the chakra massage sessions.

Essential Oils

One method that a lot of people like to work with to clear out their chakras includes essential oils. These oils are so amazing for the whole body and since they are all natural and there are so many different kinds, you are going to be amazed at how well they work and how many different ailments they can help you out with. If you have ever been curious about working with your chakras, it is time to bring in some different essential oils.

There are a few different methods that you can work with when it comes to using the essential oils. Some people invest in an infuser and will put the essential oil of their choice into it. Then they just need to sit in the room for some time and let the wonderful smells from that oil go around them in that room. Another option is to choose to put the oil on the skin or the area that is bothering them. This works well if you would like to work on the throat or the crown chakra, but make sure that you combine it with a carrier oil because the undiluted essential oil can make your skin itch and can even burn it.

The method that most people are going to stick with includes taking a bath in the essential oil. This will allow you to reach total relaxation while getting to have the essential oil work on your skin and through your nose. Make sure that you are using the right amounts of the chosen essential oil right from the beginning to make sure that everything works the way that you want and that you get the best results.

As you can see, there are many different types of treatments that you can use that will help to heal the chakras and make them as strong as possible. The important part is to learn more about the chakras and then focus some of your energy on them to make yourself feel better. You can choose any of these methods that you would like, and sometimes you may have to work with a few of them to get the best results.

Chapter 12: Crystal healing

Chakra Healing with Crystals

As with all things regarding our chakras, finding the right crystals to help you is going to take patience. Your mind needs to be clean and quiet. This can make choosing the right crystals quite time-consuming. However, putting the effort in will ensure that you end up with the correct tools for the job at hand. Noticing what different characteristics a crystal holds can make the decision easier. When holding it in your hand, does it make you feel calmer? If so, this could be the perfect crystal for helping to heal your levels of anxiety.

Our intentions toward chakra healing can be intensified when we work with crystals. Our connection to the earth is commonly made tangible by using crystals. Their physical forms contain vibrations that help provide energy to our chakras. If you have been struggling to find the energy you need to clear a blockage, using the right crystal can help you achieve your desired goal.

When you are working to heal your chakras with the aid of crystals, the intention is everything. It is your starting point and if it is used in your daily practice, your intention will become part of the energy of the crystal. Using crystals as a source of added energy to your chakras is extremely beneficial and can help to quicken the process of chakra healing.

If you understand the challenge that you are currently facing, it can make it easier to choose the right crystal. Knowing which crystals are related to which chakra can help. There will be a plethora of information on crystals provided to you in one of our future books. It is important that if the issue at hand is the mental confusion, it could be an excellent option to improve your levels of concentration. As you can see, there are different crystals for different ailments. It will take time, concentration, and dedication to learn everything you need to know to use crystals to your advantage.

Once you have found the crystals that you were going to use, you need to cleanse them and put your intentions into them. Crystals have natural abilities, but if you're using them for a specific purpose, they need to be aware of it. It will allow them to promote you in the job you have at hand. Upon pushing your intention into your crystals, you remember exactly what you are striving for every time you pick up that particular crystal.

To cleanse a crystal, there are a variety of different methods that you can use. One of the most common methods is to run them through the smoke of a sage stick as it burns. Frankincense is also oftentimes used to cleanse a crystal. Other options are to bathe your crystal in the light of the sun for at least a few hours. It depends on what your desired outcome is. If grounding your root chakra is what you are looking for, then burying your crystal in the earth may be the best course of action. This is because the crystal will be able to absorb the energy from the earth.

After you have cleansed your crystal, you will then want to hold it in your hands with your eyes closed. Focusing on your breath, you will want to think about what you want this crystal to help you accomplish. This is what we mean when we say pushing your intent into your crystal. Doing this during meditation can truly help charge your crystal to its highest level.

After you have pushed your intent into your crystal, you will then use it on top of the area of the chakra that is experiencing a blockage. This will, oftentimes, require you to lay down. Adding a charged crystal to a session of meditation can truly help to clear blockages more quickly. You will notice the difference in how you are feeling after your meditative state is much improved as compared to meditating without a crystal.

The uses of crystals vary widely. Clear quartz, for example, is an excellent crystal for beginners. It helps to improve your intention while meditating. It is considered to be key to any collection of crystals. Also, it is extremely versatile. Its vibration will help to magnify any stones or crystals that are also being used during meditation. Clear quartz is also used when you are trying to add energy to two other crystals. Over time, the energy within our crystals will be depleted and needs to be added back in. Clear quartz is an excellent choice for doing this.

We talked a bit about amethyst but know that it is, oftentimes, used for its spiritual properties. It is frequently kept around the house not only because it is beautiful, but also because it promotes strength and protection within a home. The energy that this crystal emits is truly calming. The more amethyst you keep around you, the calmer you will find that your life is. Besides, it is fantastic when you are trying to focus on yoga and meditation as you need a calm mind to participate in these practices.

As noted, this is only a small step into the world of crystals. Healing your chakras, as well as your mind body and spirit, should include the use of crystals. Gaining information is critical. There is such a plethora of different crystals available to you learning the basics is advantageous. Sometimes, it's hard to know where to start, but since there is so much information on crystals available, it should not be hard to work them into your routine.

Be aware that you can buy crystals just about anywhere. That does not necessarily mean you should buy them anywhere. Ordering them online may save you time and money; however, you may not be getting the crystals that resonate with you. Taking some time away from your busy life to go on a crystal hunt is the best way to ensure that you get ones that are particularly meant for you as an individual.

Crystal healing is truly an art form. Once you find the good vibrations and energies that they can add to your chakras, you will never be able to live without them. They will become a critical element in your daily routine. Heightening your awareness and bringing positive energy into your life is work. However, it is work that you will find to be well worth the trouble. The investment into some healing crystals does not need to be one that is major. Figuring out where your imbalances lie and what crystals are going to help you is the first step toward crystal healing.

At the end of the day, crystals, meditation, and yoga are all advantages that you can use in healing and opening your chakras. Once you can focus your mind on the transfer of energy from your root chakra to your Crown chakra, you will start to notice the major improvements made in your mental, physical, emotional, and spiritual health.

Hopefully, this book has allowed you to gain insight into the importance of your chakras and the role that they play in your daily life.

Chapter 13: Meditation

How to balance chakras

Six Simple pieces of advice to Balance Your Chakras

1. Eat properly: sometimes when the chakras misalign and malfunction, it is either because we are not eating enough natural chakra balancing meals or we are eating too much of it. It would be very helpful for the sacral chakra for example to eat properly to avoid constipation and the unpleasant effects that come with it.

2. Be tidy: chakras are sensitive to almost everything in our life and even things that seem inconsequential such as the state of our environment can influence the activities of the chakra. So, grab some brooms and mops and clean your home from top to bottom. You will be surprised at the change of air that will happen almost immediately.

3. Chakra bath: you could have a chakra balancing bath where you would light up the bulbs all around the bath and meditate right there as you wash your skin.

4. Exercise and stay active: physical activities not only help the body to get rid of toxic waste and tone our body, they also help unblock the chakra and help the chakra to become active again. Exercises such as belly dancing, hula hoops and lunges would help in this regard.

5. Meditation: spending quality time with meditation will help your chakras to be open and you will be able to notice even the slightest of changes fast and fix them too. In the long run, chakra meditation is more or less the most actively effective of all the chakra opening techniques.

6. Know your chakras and know their needs: If you make yourself familiar with the chakras, you would be able to know how to go about things when your chakras start acting up. Life as a self-aware person is way different from life as the opposite. Strive to know more details about your chakras now and you will be glad you did.

What is mindfulness

If you wish to achieve and sustain spiritual balance, you need to master the art of self-observation. You must look within yourself and recognize the imbalances that may form at any given moment. The sooner you can recognize imbalances, the easier it will be to correct them and move forward.

You can come to understand yourself, physically and spiritually, by practicing mindfulness. This is a word that is used a lot these days, but we need to focus in on a very particular definition. Mindfulness is an understanding and acceptance of the present. It is about quieting the active mind so that you can experience the world as it is, not the warped world we see after we have colored everything with our preconceptions. It's about looking inside yourself and accepting what you find.

Many people are unable to solve their problems because they do not understand themselves. It feels like we should naturally be equipped to understand ourselves, but it's often the case that we are in the worst position to make sense of our circumstances. If you have been taught to believe things that aren't true about yourself, then you will naturally have a distorted understanding of yourself, which will be holding you back from achieving true peace and balance.

Knowledge of self is especially important when you consider the nature of the chakras. While there are some overlapping qualities, in many respects each chakra is unique and requires special treatment to achieve balance. If you aren't able to pinpoint the source of your issue, then you will be poorly equipped to address it.

Achieving balance requires the constant use of a two-step process. The first step is looking within and identifying spiritual imbalances. The second step is taking action to address the imbalance. It's not an overly complicated system; what's important is that it is practiced with commitment and consistency.

We must once again return to the idea that achieving spiritual health is a lot like achieving physical health. You would never jog once around the block and announce that you were suddenly a physically fit individual. But on the other hand, many people attend one yoga retreat and believe that they have "achieved" balance.

Balance is something that must be constantly worked towards. We live in a world filled with negative energy that we must always process, and most people create their toxic forces even when the world gives them a break. This means that life is a never-ending struggle against the forces of negativity. We must constantly endeavor to counteract these forces and work toward a balance that we understand to be temporary, but worth the effort.

Once again, entire books have been written on the spiritual mindset. It's a topic that's worth a lifetime of study, but in this chapter, we will provide you with a foundation that you can start working on today and build on for the rest of your life.

We'll be looking at the two pillars of a spiritual outlook: mindfulness and positivity. The ideas seem simple in theory, but as you put them into practice, you will come to appreciate their full complexity and power.

What is meditation

Meditation is a reliable technique to get in touch with your spirit and ask your greater self for assistance. It is a terrific method to stay in today, release trapped or undesirable energy and undesirable blockages, to welcome brand-new and favorable energy, and to stabilize your chakras. While any type of meditation is a fantastic practice to open your chakras, specific assisted meditations to activate your chakras are the best.

Brief History description of meditation

Meditation History:

Meditation is a word derived from the Latin word "meditatum", meaning "to ponder". When people meditate, they are looking to find a more concrete connection with themselves and the world around them. It allows us to be more present to the moments that occur around us every day rather than simply letting them pass by. It promotes awareness and gets us better in tune with our emotions.

Many people ask how long meditation has been around and that is a difficult question to answer. Honestly, it's been around for basically, ever. Regardless of what part of the world you are researching, you will find that meditation is present. Some of the earliest forms were found in China and India, however, it is been used across the globe for generations.

Some of the earliest texts recorded about meditation came from the traditions of the Hindu people. It was part of the school of philosophy and was regarded as one of the paths to enlightenment spiritually. The exact origins of meditation have been debated for an exceptionally long time and, likely, that will never nail down exactly where it started.

Meditation, in today's world, is extremely popular and most are happy understanding that the roots of it started long before the written text was even a thing. As with all things, meditation has adapted over time. Depending on your culture and where you live, meditation practices will be quite different. Learning the origins and roots of other cultures can help broaden your knowledge of this ancient practice.

Before written documentation, there was wall art that depicted meditation images. They show people sitting in meditative postures and appear to be in a state of true relaxation. These paintings or found in India.

Hindu traditions make us aware of the fact that meditation in caves was also predominant with the yogis of that time. It is important to note that many of our modern traditions today in meditation come from this line of practice. This includes movement techniques based on the Hatha Yoga practices. These Yoga practices are not at all what we think of today, they were a different set of movements and thought patterns. It has truly developed over time.

Meditation and Buddhism go hand in hand. Most images of the Buddha have him sitting in a meditative position. In the Buddhist language, the word meditation is actually "Bhavana", which means, mental calmness. The practices of Buddhist meditation are quite different than others. As they were developing, so were their counterparts in places like India, China, and other areas around the globe. While all of them focus on clarity and calmness, the teachings and practices varied.

Meditation did not crop up in the West until approximately the 1700s. Through philosophy texts, the techniques of meditation and the practice is involved in them were translated into a variety of different languages. After the translations, meditation was typically a simple discussion between intellectuals. In roughly the 20th century, it became more predominant as an actual practice and not just a discussion.

By the late 1960s, spirituality had been much removed from the practice of meditation and studies on it went more towards outcomes in psychology. Meditation was found to help reduce stress, increase mindfulness, and it truly was found to have a way of helping to correct negative issues in a person's life. As this information was discovered more and more, people took to the practices of meditation.

As time went on, the mindfulness piece of meditation was combined with a variety of different types of therapy, including cognitive-behavioral therapy. The results were amazing. People started flocking to the practices of meditation more and more because of the fantastic results that people were having when practicing it.

Today, meditation is known across the globe and is practiced frequently by a plethora of people. Regardless of your position in life, meditation can be helpful. So many people have found it makes such a true difference in their life, it is not surprising at all that it is gained such popularity. While there may not be a true science behind meditation, the results will speak for themselves.

Meditation can benefit anyone's life in a huge variety of ways. Some find that it can help reduce pain, stress, and anxiety. It can help to improve the health of your heart an even boost your body's levels of immunity. Meditation promotes relaxation and this can help us in so many ways. It helps to free our minds and our bodies from whatever is weighing us down.

Chapter 14: Meditation practices

Pranayama meditation

Pranayama uses the breath to help you align and focus your energy and is commonly associated with a variety of yoga practices. It has been studied and shown that these yoga-style breathing exercises will help to improve your mental state, sense of calm, health, and spiritual groundedness. Breath helps to align and balance your channels of energy and will spurn the Kundalini force to open and awaken with greater ease.

There are a few, main types of Kundalini breath that you can use to help you get acquainted with your pranayama practice:

1.   Breath of Fire: a forceful, rapid breath that uses your diaphragm and abdominal muscles to rapidly pulse air in and out of your lungs. It is considered to be purifying, cleansing and invigorating and can sometimes feel like you are jogging, or running, with this kind of breath.

2.   Long and Deep Breath: when you draw air in at a long, slow pace (count of ten), hold for a while (count of ten), and exhale for a long, slow period (count of ten), then you are engaging in a long and deep breath. This breath style is good for meditating on your energy centers and can contribute to a more open third eye and crown chakra. Usually, with this pranayama, you would press your tongue to the roof of your mouth while you inhale and exhale, only breathing through the nostrils.

3.   Breath Between Nostrils (Alternating Nostril Breathing): this pranayama helps create a deeper calm and be a great way to prepare for more challenging breath techniques you will find if you are practicing more advanced Kundalini work. Essentially, you plug one nostril with a finger or thumb and breathe through the open

one. Before you exhale, plug the open nostril you just breathed through, and exhale. From here, breathe into the open nostril, and then switch sides to exhale. Doing this several times is incredibly enriching to the Kundalini energy.

4.   Mantra Breathing: in yoga and other practices, there are sometimes simple mantra words that can be expressed aloud, or internally, as you breathe in and out. A common phrase for Kundalini pranayama is "so-hum". When you breathe in, you intone, or think, "so". Exhale with "hum" and repeat as needed. Incorporate the long and deep breath with your mantra breathing or try it with any of the other pranayama styles if it feels right.

Bija Mantra

Bija mantras are the mantras that are chanted to clear, heal and open your chakras. 'Bija' is the Sanskrit word for the English word 'Seed'. This seed empowers you to implant the most important energy or vital force in your body. It enables each chakra to align itself with the other chakras to achieve the desired harmony and balance.

You can choose to chant these Bija Mantras or Seed Mantras individually to strengthen a particular chakra or they can be chanted as a series that empowers you to balance your seven chakras. How you want to chant these Bija Mantras is up to you. You may choose to chant these aloud or in your mind, depending on your preference. Want an added dose of energy? Visualize the location, color and positive impact of each chakra as you chant the corresponding Bija mantra.

•   To chant the Bija Mantra, start at the root chakra and recite the sound LAM. Let this sound be emphatic and short ('m' should not linger).

- Now, move up to your sacral chakra by reciting VAM.

- Next, stimulate your solar plexus chakra through the chant of RAM.

- Move to the heart chakra now using the sound YAM (this is pronounced as 'yum')

- Open your throat chakra by the chant of HAM (this is pronounced as 'hum')

- Now, stimulate your third eye chakra with the sound of OM.

- And finally, open your crown chakra through an extended sound of OM or complete silence.

Throughout the process, visualize caring, loving energy traveling through your body into the universe. Tell yourself that you can feel this positive energy traveling from your root chakra to your crown chakra and then into the universe.

If you choose to chant these mantras in a series, you can replace the OM or the silence of the crown chakra with "SO HUM" which implies "I am that" – this is used as a positive affirmation that you ARE these chants, you ARE this energy, and that you ARE perfect. Don't forget to visualize yourself in great health as you chant these mantras.

Practicing this chakra chant for a few minutes every day leads to harmony and happiness. You can chant everywhere – in your car, during lunchtime, while doing the dishes, while folding your laundry, while baking and cooking, while walking or running, while traveling, as a part of your meditation or yoga practice or even while bathing! Chant these Bija Mantras during peak traffic time and experience the magic these bring into your life – you will feel relaxed and calm in no time! Stressed out at this moment? Try the Bija Mantra chant, it will work wonders and you will notice your stress melt away in seconds.

Treat your body as the most marvelous orchestra and strive hard to maintain the perfect rhythm.

Affirmation mantra

Mantras are an excellent way to open yourself as much as unconditional love and empathy. You can utilize them throughout a meditation or your day duplicating them out loud or in your mind. Like mantras, positive affirmations can increase favorable energy in your body.

Yoga meditation

Kundalini yoga is an excellent practice to help your life-force awaken. This style of yoga was created specifically for that purpose and it will engage in you in a full-body, chakra alignment journey if utilized regularly. Other forms of yoga have similar poses and postures; however, Kundalini yoga focuses more on your "subtle" body, or chakra energies, to help you align your electromagnetic field with your whole being. It is a highly cleansing and empowering practice that includes all of the following aspects:

1.   Meditation to open the chakras, relieve stress, and conjure the life-force energy within.

2.   Pranayama to improve control of energy and bring it into deeper focus (see the previous section)

3.   Asanas to bring your body into poses and positions that will allow for a wider opening of your energy channels.

4.   Bandhas are physical acts that will "lock" a muscle group to help inflate or increase the pranic energy flow. This can help release physical, emotional, and mental toxins from the body.

5.   Mantras help to create a sound channel, whether the words are thought in the mind, or intoned aloud, to bring your energy and purpose into focus.

6.   Mudras will bring your hands into classic positions of opening, to ask for the energy of you to be brought through, out and in. There are several types of mudras to explore, specific to Kundalini.

7.   Kriyas are an aftershock of awakening your energy and can feel like tremors, spontaneous muscle jerk or flinch, tingling and shaking, and even a change in the way your body smells, as a result of your energy shifting.

Visualization

Visualization techniques are important aspects of any meditation practice, as well as a chakra work routine. Visualization techniques are used to master the art of controlling the mind. If we can successfully clear the mind and create visualizations intentionally, then we will be able to work with our chakras more efficiently. Visualizing colors, mandalas, images, and scenarios allow us to train our mind and can also offer spiritual insight if properly used.

While visualization is a simple concept, mastering the techniques take a lot of time and most importantly, dedication. It is very easy to get distracted. The human mind is chaotic, and often, it can seem impossible even trying to control it. But it can be done. The more you practice calming and clearing his mind, the easier it will become. We must train our mind to respond to our methods the way we want it to, instead of wandering through memories and images.

The art of visualization is found in every culture around the world. These practices are used to communicate with spirits, see into the future, or even diagnose diseases. The holy men of ancient cultures relied heavily on shamanistic visualization techniques, dedicating their entire lives to the practices and their communities. There are many visualization techniques, we have chosen some are suitable for beginners that pertain directly to chakra work as well.

Let's look at a few practical methods which can get you started.

Visualization Method #1

1. Sit comfortably in your practice space.

2. Close your eyes and breath normally, letting any thoughts or images roll pass. Do not let them distract you.

3. Fill your mind white light. Let it fill all the visual space in your mind, become immersed in this light.

4. Try and maintain this immersion for as long as possible, not letting any other images enter into your mind.

Visualization Method #2

This technique is similar to technique #1, but instead of white light, you can choose the attributed color to the chakra you're working with.

1. Sit comfortably in your practice space.

2. Close your eyes and breath normally, letting any thoughts or images pass by. Do not follow them or let them distract you.

3. Fill your mind with the chosen chakra's color. Let it fill all the visual space in your mind, immerse yourself in this colored light.

4. Try and maintain this visual space as it is for as long as possible, don't allow any other images to enter your mind.

Visualization Method #3

This technique is much more advanced than the previous two, and it will be a practice in itself to master. Many spend years focused on this technique to hone their visualization skills.

1. Get comfortable in your practice space.

2. Close your eyes and clear your mind using the white light practice in technique #1.

3. Now visualize your hands in front of you. Turn them and analyze them.

4. Visualize that you have an orange or other fruit in your hands. Smell it, and feel its peel. Be aware of its temperature and firmness.

5. Begin to peel the fruit. The flesh is getting under your fingernails, the skin not cooperating with your efforts. Continue to peel until the fruit is ready to eat.

6. Now break apart the slices one by one. Eating each one as you go. Note the flavor and texture.

7. Finish eating the fruit and wipe your hands clean.

By building this visualized narrative, we can take control of our mind, this can be done using a wide variety of narratives, but start with the fruit story.

Visualization Method #4

This technique is the seven-chakra visualization. It is simple and effective to learn about your chakras and to work with them directly.

1. Sit comfortably, close your eyes, and clear your mind.

2. Focus on the serpent-like Kundalini energy at the base of your spine. This can be symbolized by a snake or a colorless energy, pick whichever you prefer.

3. Move the energy around, awakening it casually.

4. Now move the energy upward along your spine, being sure to connect each chakra for a short duration of time. Note the colors and feelings that come as you practice this technique.

5. Once you are making your way to the upper chakras stop at the third eye chakra and spend adequate time there. Can you see with your third eye?

6. Once you feel it is right, quickly move the energy to the crown chakra, breaking through your crown and rising to the heavens as white light.

7. Let the energy fall back down to the base of your spine, perhaps even falling like rain around you, then repeat from step one.

Chapter 15: Chakra meditation

Meditation gives you the power to transform your mind. It is meant to help positively change your emotions, improve your concentration, and bring you a sense of calm. Through different meditation practices, you can train your mind to new patterns. With chakra meditations, you will be focusing your mind on your chakras to help clear them of blocked energies.

Root Chakra Meditation

This mediation is a tried-and-true method of creating a connection with your root chakra.

1.   Find a comfortable position, either laying down or sitting, and take in three deep and slow breaths. With each inhale, imagine the breath sending energy to your perineum; this is the space between your anus and genitals. With every

exhale, release whatever you are holding in this area. This could be pain or fear. It could even be what you think you should be feeling while in this meditation.

2.   Begin to gently tap at the top of your pubic bone or on either side of the lower parts of your hips. This will wake up the connection you have with your root chakra.

3.   As you continue to breathe in and out through your nose, direct your breath to your chakra. Picture a red glowing light growing and pulsing in your lower pubic area. For people who identify mostly as male, the light should spin clockwise. For people who identify mostly as female, the light should spin counterclockwise.

4.   As you fall further into your meditative state, talk to your root chakra to see what it needs. Take some more breaths to notice if you get any feedback. This feedback could be a word, intuition, color, image, song, sound, or feeling. Act upon the feedback you receive. If nothing comes up, you don't need to worry about it. You will get something as you continue to practice.

5.   If you didn't receive a message but you start to feel a new awareness in your root chakra, something like a pulsating in the lower hips and down through your feet, you have made a connection to your root chakra.

6.   As your meditation comes to a close, take three deep and slow breaths. Direct your inhales towards your feet so that you are grounded, and then slowly open your eyes.

7.   Make sure you take things slowly as you start. This will take some time and practice so be patient. If you end up feeling any sort of pain in your legs or lower back, you are trying too hard. Take a break and go back to it later.

Remember that even seasoned meditators will sometimes find it hard to shut off their mind. Take this moment to observe these thoughts without judging them; let them go and gently refocus your mind.

Sacral Chakra Meditation

1.   Find a comfortable position, either laying down or sitting. Take in three deep and slow breaths. With each inhale, imagine the breath sending energy to the space right below your belly button. With every exhale, release whatever you are holding in this area. This could be pain or fear. It could even be what you think you should be feeling while in this meditation. You can place your hand on this area while you meditate if you would like.

2.   Begin to gently tap the area below your bellybutton with two fingers. You can also gently massage the area in a circular motion.

3.   As you continue to breathe in and out through your nose, direct your breath to your chakra. Picture an orange glowing light growing and pulsing in your lower abdomen area. For people who identify mostly as male, the light should spin clockwise. For people who identify mostly as female, the light should spin counterclockwise.

4.   As you fall further into your meditative state, talk to your sacral chakra to see what it needs. Take some more breaths to notice if you get any feedback. This feedback could be a word, intuition, color, image, song, sound, or feeling. Act upon the feedback you receive. If nothing comes up, you don't need to worry about it. You will get something as you continue to practice.

5.   If you didn't receive a message but you start to feel a new awareness in your sacral chakra, something like a pulsating in this area, you have made a connection to your sacral chakra.

6.   As your meditation comes to a close, take three deep and slow breaths. Direct your inhales towards your feet so that you are grounded, and then slowly open your eyes.

7.   Make sure you take things slowly as you start. This will take some time and practice so be patient. If you end up feeling any sort of pain in your lower abdomen, you are trying too hard. Take a break and go back to it later.

Solar Plexus Chakra Meditations

1.   Find a comfortable position, either laying down or sitting. Take in three deep and slow breaths. With each inhale, imagine the breath sending energy to the space right above your belly button. With every exhale, release whatever you are holding in this area. This could be pain or fear. It could even be what you think you should be feeling while in this meditation. You can place your hand on this area while you meditate if you would like.

2.   Begin to gently tap the area above your belly button with two fingers. You can also gently massage the area in a circular motion.

3.   As you continue to breathe in and out through your nose, direct your breath to your chakra. Picture a yellow glowing light growing and pulsing in your upper abdomen area. For people who identify mostly as male, the light should spin clockwise. For people who identify mostly as female, the light should spin counterclockwise.

4.   As you fall further into your meditative state, talk to your solar plexus chakra to see what it needs. Take some more breaths to notice if you get any feedback. This feedback could be a word, intuition, color, image, song, sound, or feeling. Act upon the feedback you receive. If nothing comes up, you don't need to worry about it. You will get something as you continue to practice.

5.   If you didn't receive a message but you start to feel a new awareness in your solar plexus chakra, something like a pulsating in this area, you have made a connection to your solar plexus chakra.

6.   As your meditation comes to a close, take three deep and slow breaths. Direct your inhales towards your feet so that you are grounded, and then slowly open your eyes.

7.   Make sure you take things slowly as you start. This will take some time and practice so be patient. If you end up feeling any sort of pain in your upper abdomen, you are trying too hard. Take a break and go back to it later.

Heart Chakra Meditation

1.   Find a comfortable position, either laying down or sitting. Take in three deep and slow breaths. With each inhale, imagine the breath sending energy to the center of your chest. With every exhale, release whatever you are holding in this area. This could be pain or fear. It could even be what you think you should be feeling while in this meditation. You can place your hand on this area while you meditate if you would like.

2.   Begin to gently tap your chest with two fingers. You can also gently massage the area in a circular motion.

3. As you continue to breathe in and out through your nose, direct your breath to your chakra. Picture a green glowing light growing and pulsing in your chest. For people who identify mostly as male, the light should spin clockwise. For people who identify mostly as female, the light should spin counterclockwise.

4. As you fall further into your meditative state, talk to your heart chakra to see what it needs. Take some more breaths to notice if you get any feedback. This feedback could be a word, intuition, color, image, song, sound, or feeling. Act upon the feedback you receive. If nothing comes up, you don't need to worry about it. You will get something as you continue to practice.

5. If you didn't receive a message but you start to feel a new awareness in your heart chakra, something like a pulsating in this area, you have made a connection to your heart chakra.

6. As your meditation comes to a close, take three deep and slow breaths. Direct your inhales towards your feet so that you are grounded, and then slowly open your eyes.

7. Make sure you take things slowly as you start. This will take some time and practice so be patient. If you end up noticing your heart is racing uncomfortably, you are trying too hard. Take a break and go back to it later.

Throat Chakra Meditation

1. Find a comfortable position, either laying down or sitting. Take in three deep and slow breaths. With each inhale, imagine the breath sending energy to the notch of your throat. With every exhale, release whatever you are holding in this area. This could be pain or fear. It could even be what you think you should be feeling while in this meditation.

2.   Begin to gently tap the bone at the notch of your throat with two fingers. You can also gently massage the area in a circular motion.

3.   As you continue to breathe in and out through your nose, direct your breath to your chakra. Picture a blue glowing light growing and pulsing in your throat. For people who identify mostly as male, the light should spin clockwise. For people who identify mostly as female, the light should spin counterclockwise.

4.   As you fall further into your meditative state, talk to your throat chakra to see what it needs. Take some more breaths to notice if you get any feedback. This feedback could be a word, intuition, color, image, song, sound, or feeling. Act upon the feedback you receive. If nothing comes up, you don't need to worry about it. You will get something as you continue to practice.

5.   If you didn't receive a message but you start to feel a new awareness in your throat chakra, something like a pulsating in this area, you have made a connection to your throat chakra.

6.   As your meditation comes to a close, take three deep and slow breaths. Direct your inhales towards your feet so that you are grounded, and then slowly open your eyes.

7.   Make sure you take things slowly as you start. This will take some time and practice so be patient. If you end up feeling any sort of pain in your neck, you are trying too hard. Take a break and go back to it later.

Third Eye Chakra Meditation

1.   Find a comfortable position, either laying down or sitting. Take in three deep and slow breaths. With each inhale, imagine the breath sending energy to the space between your brows. With every exhale, release whatever you are

holding in this area. This could be pain or fear. It could even be what you think you should be feeling while in this meditation.

2.   Begin to gently tap the area between your eyebrows with two fingers. You can also gently massage the area in a circular motion.

3.   As you continue to breathe in and out through your nose, direct your breath to your chakra. Picture an indigo glowing light growing and pulsing in the area between your brows. For people who identify mostly as male, the light should spin clockwise. For people who identify mostly as female, the light should spin counterclockwise.

4.   As you fall further into your meditative state, talk to your third eye chakra to see what it needs. Take some more breaths to notice if you get any feedback. This feedback could be a word, intuition, color, image, song, sound, or feeling. Act upon the feedback you receive. If nothing comes up, you don't need to worry about it. You will get something as you continue to practice.

5.   If you didn't receive a message but you start to feel a new awareness in your third eye chakra, something like a pulsating in this area, you have made a connection to your third eye chakra.

6.   As your meditation comes to a close, take three deep and slow breaths. Direct your inhales towards your feet so that you are grounded, and then slowly open your eyes.

7.   Make sure you take things slowly as you start. This will take some time and practice so be patient. If you end up feeling like you are getting a headache at the front of your head, you are trying too hard. Take a break and go back to it later.

Crown Chakra Meditation

1.   Find a comfortable position, either laying down or sitting. Take in three deep and slow breaths. With each inhale, imagine the breath sending energy to the top of your head. With every exhale, release whatever you are holding in this area. This could be pain or fear. It could even be what you think you should be feeling while in this meditation.

2.   Begin to gently tap the top of your head two fingers. You can also gently massage the area in a circular motion.

3.   As you continue to breathe in and out through your nose, direct your breath to your chakra. Picture a purple glowing light growing and pulsing at the top of your head. For people who identify mostly as male, the light should spin clockwise. For people who identify mostly as female, the light should spin counterclockwise.

4.   As you fall further into your meditative state, talk to your crown chakra to see what it needs. Take some more breaths to notice if you get any feedback. This feedback could be a word, intuition, color, image, song, sound, or feeling. Act upon the feedback you receive. If nothing comes up, you don't need to worry about it. You will get something as you continue to practice.

5.   If you didn't receive a message but you start to feel a new awareness in your crown chakra, something like a pulsating in this area, you have made a connection to your crown chakra.

6.   As your meditation comes to a close, take three deep and slow breaths. Direct your inhales towards your feet so that you are grounded, and then slowly open your eyes.

7. Make sure you take things slowly as you start. This will take some time and practice so be patient. If you end up feeling any sort of pain in your head, you are trying too hard. Take a break and go back to it later.

Chapter 16: Mindfulness meditation

This kind of meditation is done with your eyes open. Again, take the same kind of seated stance and get your breathing into a rhythm, thinking only of the breathing. When you have achieved that rhythm, open your eyes. Observe what is in front of you, but do not let your observation lead to other thoughts. Mindfulness is awareness. That's all it is. Be aware of what is around you, observe it without any kind of judgment and then dismiss it. Keep your mind occupied with observation without moving out of the meditation position. If you want to help yourself to be able to achieve this kind of meditation, place something inspirational in your meditation space. A vase of fresh flowers with scents is ideal because what you are doing is opening up your senses. Feel the atmosphere of the room, observe it and then dismiss it. Enjoy the scent of the flowers and then embrace all of the goodness that surrounds you. This is a great way to meditate in a wonderful place that fills you with inspiration and awe. The beach at sunset or sunrise is perfect.

My particularly favorite place is on the top of a hill that overlooks the countryside. It helps me to feel humbler but at the same time tells me that my belief in goodness and in God is justified. It gives me a sense of wellbeing. The sights, sounds, and aromas are all part of your appreciation of life. If you find your thoughts wandering to other places, acknowledge the thought and then dismiss it without judging the thought.

You may be wondering at this time how this helps your chakras. However, once you have incorporated mindfulness into your life, you won't ask that question anymore because your mind and body will feel better. You will feel complete and in harmony with life because you are putting away the thoughts about any other moment and simply living in the moment you find yourself in. That helps you to feel peace and tranquility and that, in turn, helps your chakras to be open to energy flowing through them.

Simple Meditation

If you are just getting started with understanding meditation, you may be worried that this is going to be too hard for you to handle. Meditation is an ancient idea, one that has been around for many years and through many different religions. This may make some people feel like they are never going to be able to get meditation down or understand what is going on.

The good news is that meditation doesn't have to be complicated or too hard to work with. Meditation can be really simple and you are going to love how great it can make you feel. Many people have reported improvements in their energy levels, lower stress and anger levels, and so much more. Even if you aren't working on improving your chakras, you are going to see some amazing results when you work on meditation in your daily life.

Working on meditation is easy to do. You first need to set aside about ten to fifteen minutes to work on meditation at least once or twice a day. You also need to work on finding a place that is nice and quiet, one where others are going to leave you alone and there won't be a ton of distractions that go on around you. It is really hard to concentrate on your breathing and do the deep concentration if you have someone interrupting you all of the time or if there are a lot of distractions around you.

Next, you need to make sure that you are comfortable. You need to have your back nice and straight to help the breathing come easier. You can use a pillow to help keep the back as straight as possible as well or use a chair, as long as you don't slouch down.

When you are ready, close your eyes and start working on some of the deep breaths. You want to slow down the breathing and get it down to a relaxed rate rather than the fast-paced one that you are dealing with from work, school, and other stressors. While you work on calming down and doing the deep breathing, you also want to make sure that you are trying to clear out the thoughts that are in your head. There are likely to be a ton of thoughts that run through your head all of the time and most of them are about the worry and stress that can cause harm to your body.

In the beginning, it is going to be hard to quiet down all of the thoughts that are going through your head regularly. You are used to having the mind focus on the stress and the worry, and it is going to be hard to make that stop. Just be gentle with yourself during this time. If you get all mad because you can't quiet the thoughts that you have, you are just going to make it worse. So instead of getting angry, you will simply need to push the thoughts back to being simple and relaxed without judging or getting mad at all.

If you are having trouble with keeping your mind clear for this part, you can try a few other techniques. Some people like to have gentle music in the background that they can listen to, instead of their thoughts. Some people enjoy adding a bit of guided meditation to help them have something to focus on during the day. And still others will want to use the visualization technique because it gives their mind something solid to focus on during the whole meditation session.

When you are done with your session of meditation, you will slowly get up and then go on with the rest of the day. This is a pretty simple process that you will go through, and after just a few days, you are sure to notice the big differences it is making in your life. Try to stick with this each day, either right away in the morning or right before you go to bed at night, and you are sure to see the good results that you want in no time.

Doing Meditation for the Chakras

Meditation can be good for the whole body. Whether you are looking to reduce your anger, reduce the amount of stress that you are feeling or to help your body in some other way, working on meditation can help you out so much. Many people who are working on enhancing their chakras will choose to work on meditation to make this happen a bit more. Meditation helps you to focus just on the chakras a little bit, focusing on what is so important for your overall health.

If you are interested in using meditation to help out with your chakras, there are some important steps that you can take to make this happen in your life. First, decide if you would like to work on all of the chakras in a session or if you just want to focus on one or two. This meditation technique is going to be the most successful if you can fit in all of the chakras at once because this helps you to feel the best, but if you are short on time or want a little bit of practice first, working with just one of the chakras at a time, perhaps one each day, will be just fine. This demonstration is going to look at how to work on all of the chakras in one session so you know how to do it, but you are more than welcome to work on just one at a time if you would like

So, when you are ready to work on your chakras, follow some of the same instructions from above. You will want to start with finding a nice quiet place where you can be all by yourself. If there are a lot of noises around you or other distractions, you are going to have a hard time working on the chakra that you would like. So, go to a room that is comfortable and where you can be alone for some time, to get the deep concentration that you need.

Next, make sure that your posture is nice and strong. You want to make sure that the chakras can line up well together when you are working on this part, and if you are slouched over and uncomfortable, this is just not going to happen. The best thing that you can do is to sit up nice and straight, adding in a pillow to your butt if it helps to support you a little bit. If you have some troubles with sitting on the floor, you may want to consider using a chair to sit on, just make sure that you are sitting up as straight as possible.

When you are ready, close your eyes and start concentrating on the deep breathing that you need to calm down. Going straight into this from a hard and stressful day can be hard on you and will bring more challenges in getting things done. So, spend a minute or two working on some of the deep breathing exercises that were discussed before and then your heart rate and your concentration will be right where they should be.

At this point, it is time to start concentrating on the chakras. Start with the root chakra and move your way up as you go through this process. The main color that comes with the root chakra is red so this is the one that you will spend your time concentrating on.

Each chakra has a different color, with the first three being the warm colors, the red, orange, and yellow, and the top ones are going to be the cooler colors like green, blue, indigo, and purple. You will be able to use these colors as you move through all of the chakras.

But for now, you are just going to concentrate on the root chakra, and nothing else; you can get to the other ones a little bit later. Think about the color red while you are doing your deep breathing. It is probably going to come in as a dull color in the beginning, but you will want to concentrate on giving it some power and making it a bit stronger. As you concentrate on the chakra and the color red, it is going to become brighter and brighter until they burst out and are as bright as you can handle. When you get to this point, you know that the root chakra has gotten some of the attention that it needs and you can move on to the following chakra.

You will keep going through this process from the root chakra to the crown chakra, allowing each of them to have some time to get nice and strong on their own. You may find that some don't need as much attention as the others so don't feel bad if you take a bit longer on one of them and then the next one is going faster. Each person is going to take their amount of time on the chakras so go at your own pace, don't rush things, and just relax while you are getting it all done.

As you can see, going through all of the chakras can be a lot of work for some people and if you don't have that much time available to get it done, it is fine to work on one or two chakras a day to help keep them strong. When you are all done with working on the chakras for the day and you feel like you have given them some of the cleansing that they need, you can slowly get up and out of the meditation, and then go on with the rest of your day, feeling so much better and more fulfilled than ever before.

Doing meditation for your chakras can be an amazing way to take care of your body and your spirit. While many people spend that time reducing their stress levels and such, many are finding that this is also a fantastic way to work on their chakras. The work for doing this is not that hard, but it does take a little bit of time and effort to get it done. But if you can follow some of the techniques that are in this chapter, you are sure to strengthen your chakras and make them feel better than ever.

Journaling

Journaling is dubbed as a mental exercise. It requires being mindful as you have to recall your actions, emotions and thoughts the day before. However, it doesn't usually cover awareness of your chakras' conditions. This activity will make you feel more connected and in control of your energy centers if you write about them as part of your regular journal entries.

Start your journal entry by contemplating on what chakras seem to be off when you woke up earlier. Next, reflect on what happened during the day. Describe the environment that you're in and discuss your thoughts, emotions and actions. Assess which among your chakras are experiencing problems as evident in the way you think, feel and behave.

Journaling with chakras in mind is advantageous to the seven main chakras. Through this activity, you can pinpoint which among your energy centers need some healing. You can avoid the factors that worsen the chakra's condition and carry out healing practices.

The activity also offers additional benefits for the third, fifth, sixth and seventh chakras. Remember how the solar plexus chakra helps you deal with major life changes. Journaling keeps you aware of the causes and impact of such changes. Such awareness strengthens your control of your third chakra.

As for your throat chakra, the mere act of writing every day enhances the way you communicate. It trains you to organize your thoughts. It also teaches you the value of backing up your statements. When you write a journal entry, you just don't discuss what you think, feel and do; you're supposed to tell why as well.

Journaling also helps you keep your thought processes in check. Your train of thoughts can either supply positivity or negativity to your third eye chakra and crown chakra. Being conscious of the way you think helps you avoid going the negative route.

To make journaling an effective way to assess your chakras' condition, do it before bedtime. If you find journaling every day a bit dull, bullet journaling or scrapbooking may fit you. Aside from writing, you can exercise your sketching, painting and collage-making skills in those activities.

Affirmation

Affirmations can help heal chakra blockages. Chakra blockages are caused by certain emotional and environmental issues. Heartbreaks and financial problems can cause chakra blockages.

If you're experiencing problems that are associated with chakra blockage, recite the affirmations. You can also recite the following affirmations:

- Crown chakra – "I am one with God."

- Third eye chakra – "I am wise and I truly understand life."

- Throat chakra – "I express myself clearly."

- Heart chakra – "I give and receive love unconditionally."

- Solar plexus chakra – "I am proud of who I am."

- Sacral chakra – "I am radiant."

- Root chakra – "I am humbled and I am enough."

If you're experiencing problems that are associated with chakra blockage, recite these affirmations every morning upon waking up and at night before sleeping.

Music

Like color, sounds carry vibrations. This is the reason why good music can treat various conditions such as autism, mood disorders, and chronic body pain. It can also heal unbalanced chakras.

Chapter 17: Everyday Practices

You now know how to start your mindfulness meditation practice, but you might be wondering how you can bring mindfulness into your everyday life. You also may not be interested in adopting a meditation routine, but you can still bring mindfulness into your life with a few simple actions.

As you have learned, humans tend to go on autopilot, and this happens more often during the everyday tasks we have to do. These are the moments when you need to become more mindful. You don't have to clear your mind of everything, just become aware of what you are doing, and notice how it feels. Here are some activities where you can become more mindful.

- Taking a shower

When you are on autopilot you are vaguely aware of how the water feels when you are showering. You battle trying to get the water right, trying to hit that right temp, but then your mind wanders off thinking about what you watched on TV, or what you have to do today. You aren't in the moment.

Instead, start to think about how warm the water is and how it feels as it slides down you. Think of how your shower gel, shampoo, conditioner, or soap smells, and how the bubbles feel on your skin. Once you become used to noticing these things, being more mindful will become easier.

- Brush your teeth

When you brush your teeth you probably don't think about what you're doing. You've been doing it for years and it's not that hard. You stare at your reflection and focus more on how your skin looks than what you are doing. You may even have to run through your house with the toothbrush sticking out of your mouth.

Instead, start thinking about the texture and taste of the toothpaste and brush. Think of how the brush feels as you move it in your mouth. Think of how the floor feels under feet and your arm feels as it moves. Be mindful as you brush each of your teeth.

- Drive to work

You slide into your car, bus, or train and you sit there mindlessly staring out the window. Even when you're driving, you don't focus on what is going on around you, you're thinking about what you are going to have to do. The man sitting next to you on the bus feel asleep on your arm and you don't even notice until you have to get off.

Instead, pay attention to the people around you. Whether you drive yourself or take public transportation, look at what's around, how they look and smell. Notice how the ride feels, is it bumpy or smooth? What kind of things do you pass by? Notice little details that you normally would have overlooked.

- Wash dishes

Most people have a dishwasher now, but when you have to wash dishes by hand you moan as you approach the sink because of the menial task. You robotically scrub, rinse, and dry; over, and over again.

Instead, notice how it feels. Feel the water on your hands. Notice how the scrubber feels when you rub it against the dishes. Notice the difference between how the dirty dishes feel and the clean dishes feel.

- Stand in line

There are lots of times where you will find yourself standing in line; the grocery store, shopping mall, DMV, wherever. You stand there, trying not to make eye contact, and groaning about the time that it's taking.

Instead, start looking at things, noticing them. Notice what the area looks like. Look at the people around you, don't stare, they may take offense to that. Notice the smells, hopefully, they are pleasant. Take advantage of this moment to notice your surroundings, and to become more aware.

Beyond making sure that you notice things about normal tasks you do every day, you can start adding other actions into your life that will, over time, make you more mindful. Here are a few.

1. Mindfully eat

When you sit and eat without thinking about what you're doing, either by being on your phone or watching TV, you miss the joy of eating. You don't taste how the food tastes. You don't smell the food. It can also keep you from feeling full and satisfied.

This is because your mind thinks you have missed out on eating since there weren't any other sensory triggers. Try not to do fifty things while you are eating. When it's time to eat, sit down and focus only on your food, and not everything else.

2.   Mindfully Walk

Walking may just seem like something you have to do to get from place to place, but it's more than that. When you walk, don't just walk, notice how it feels. Notice how your body moves and the things around you. Take note of the way your feet touch the ground and the muscles that it takes for you to pick up your feet. Observe the sounds and sights that are around you as you walk.

3.   Take Note of Your Breath

Breathing is rhythmical and a natural occurrence. When you take the time to notice it, it will bring your mind to the present and end, for a moment, the wandering thoughts in your head. You are free from your thoughts for a few minutes. In that moment, as you think about your breath, you have no fears or worries about anything, you are just there.

4.   Please Your Senses

Involve all of your senses; sight, touch, sound, smell, and taste. These give you away into the moment. When you are only in your head your senses don't get to work for you. You've heard the phrase "stop and smell the roses", well, that's what you need to do. Notice the smell of the coffee you're drinking. Smell the salty air at the beach. See the color and diversity of the flowers around you. Take notice of the smell and taste of the pizza you eat. Feel how your clothes move across your body. Smell and feel the clean sheets on the bed. Feel the warmth and comfort of your significant other's kiss.

Notice the feel of grass under your feet. How the water feels when you take a bath or wash your hands. Use all of your senses as you go throughout your day.

5. Take Pause during the Day

Take a moment and stop what you are doing and just listen to your surroundings. Listen to how the phone sounds like when it rings. Take a moment to notice how your bodyweight feels in the chair you're sitting in. Take a moment to feel the door handle before you open the door. Taking moments out of your day to pause and ground yourself can make you more aware and mindful. It also gives you a chance to clear your mind and can give you a boost of energy. Picture it as if these pauses are bookends to begin and end tasks throughout your day.

6. Listen with Your Heart

We as humans tend to not listen to what people say when they are talking to us. They are either absentmindedly thinking about what they are going to do, or something that just happened to them. They could also be judging what the other person is saying or just lost in a daydream. The next time you are talking to somebody, make sure you listen to what they are saying. Don't let yourself get lost in thought. If you notice you are straying from their words, bring yourself back. You don't have to worry about what you are going to say in response because your mind will know what to say, and it's okay to pause for a moment after they finish before you begin.

7. Lose Yourself in What You Love

Each of us has things that we love doing. They are what help us connect to our spirit and help us feel completely alive. It could be swimming, cooking, building things, dancing, painting, hiking, gardening, singing, or writing. It doesn't matter what it is. When you participate in these activities, you'll find that you will lose yourself in them.

This doesn't mean you go into autopilot. In these tasks, you lose the part of you that is constantly worrying about things. It quiets your mind because you love doing it and you are solely focused in that present moment. Start doing more of the activities during the week, and your happiness will improve.

8.   Daily Meditation

Meditation has lots of benefits, many of which we have already covered. You will have more energy, inspiration, peace, and happiness. You don't have to have a lot of time to meditate. 10 minutes a day can positively affect your day to day life. This will also boost your mindfulness, so it will become easier to use mindfulness during your day.

9.   Mix up Your Day to Day

There are lots of reasons why you feel so happy during the holiday season. When you travel to different places your mind will automatically become more mindful. This happens because there are new smells, sights, and sounds to experience. The senses naturally take over and it frees your mind so you can live in the moment. If you don't have time to travel somewhere, that's okay. You can get the same effect by switching up your normal day to day routine. Instead of driving the same way to work every day, change up your route. Try a different coffee shop. Shop in places you have never been in, or participate in some local adventure, or learn something new.

10. Take Notice of Emotions and Thoughts

You've heard me say this before; you are not your thoughts; you only observe your thoughts. Since you can listen to what your thoughts are, that proves they aren't you. You're separate from your thoughts. Simply acknowledging them and observing them without any judgment allows you to become more present in your life. This keeps you from getting caught up in the constant flow of your thoughts. When you take notice of your thoughts, avoid letting them carry you away. Think of the thought like a train. You're standing on the platform and you just watch as the trains come in and as they leave. You don't try to jump on them and let them take you to some unknown place.

Traits of the Mindful Person

Mindful people are going to live their life differently than the autopilot person. Here are some ways to know if a person is a mindful person.

They take lots of walks.

It's easy in our crazy world to become burnout and exhausted, and the mindful person knows how to solve that problem. Through walking. They know that they can go on a walk to clear their mind and to help them calm their thoughts. A walk can give them more awareness and a new perspective. Also, being in nature and seeing all the greenery might be good for the brain and send it to a meditative space. Studies have shown that walking outside gives you the ability for involuntary attention, which means that your mind can focus on the present and you can also have the chance to reflect.

Daily tasks are done mindfully.

Taking notice of the little things that happen during your normal tasks is a good way to be mindful. Noticing how things feel, taste, and smell brings you into the moment.

They create things.

Mindfulness can boost your creative ability. Mindful people will naturally start doing more creative things during their day. The act of creative work can help you place your mind in a meditative state. If you are having problems in regular meditation, doing something like drawing, cooking, or singing can help you meditate.

They listen to their breath.

I've covered this a lot. Mindful people notice everything about their breathing. They don't breathe on autopilot.

They don't multitask.

Multitasking will keep people from being able to focus on things that they are doing. It is the enemy of mindfulness. Most people, though, multitask throughout their whole day. Some studies have discovered that when a person's attention is divided between tasks, it will take them 50% longer to finish the task. Errors are also more likely to happen. You need to make sure that you only focus on one thing at a time. Interruptions will happen, but you have to bring yourself back to the one task at hand.

They check their phone at the right time.

People who are mindful keep their relationship with electronics healthy. This could be making sure that as soon as they wake up, they don't reach for their phone to check their e-mail. The same goes for bedtime too. They may even go so far as to keep their phone in a completely different room than the one that they sleep in. They may even turn it off on the weekends or vacations

 so that they can unplug. The biggie is that they turn off their phones when they are with family and friends. This allows them to mindfully interact with the people around them.

They look for new experiences.

Mindful people are open to new things. People that prioritize peace of mind and presence will enjoy savoring the little moments and big moments in life. Having new experiences will make you more mindful as well.

They venture outside.

Making time to experience the outdoors is a powerful way to reboot your mind and give you a sense of wonder and ease. The outdoors can help you to relieve stress and boost energy and attention. You will find that your memory will become better after you have spent some time outside.

They know what they are feeling.

Contrary to popular belief, mindfulness isn't solely about being happy every moment of the day. Instead, it's about accepting what happens and how you feel. If you are constantly preoccupied with being happy, you are only hurting yourself in the long run. You will constantly focus on the fact that you are not happy, and that only causes you to be unhappy.

They take the time to meditate.

This has been talked about a lot. Meditation plays a large role in being mindful, and mindful people know and understand that.

They know the mind and body.

People tend to shove food in their mouth without thinking about how it tastes, or if it's making them feel full. Mindful people will make sure they notice everything about what they eat and how their body responds to it.

They don't take themselves seriously.

People like to worry about everything they have done and the problems they have. A mindful person doesn't do that. They keep their sense of humor even when problems are going on in their life.

They allow their mind to wander.

Mindfulness is about being present, but letting your mind wander is also important. Mindful people can find that happy medium between mindful and autopilot. If you stay constantly present, you may miss out on connections between your mind and the world. Using your imagination may even help your mindfulness in the long run.

PART 2

REIKI HEALING

Chapter 18: Introduction to Reiki

This book will help you on how to heal your energy through reiki. Many newbies to the world of Reiki energy and natural healing may choose to work with a professional for their first few sessions. It is important to remember that Reiki sessions only restore the natural flow of wholesome energy through your body. You may be aware of the sensations of energy as they fill you, but you typically notice the benefits after the session. You will notice the benefits in the way that you interact with the negativities of the world around you. You will also notice how the healing energy helps heal you from ailments and complaints, but this happens over time. Reiki stimulates the body's natural healing process. Though many people have Reiki experiences that they refer to as 'miracles,' the reality is that the body and the energy flowing through it cause the healing—not the session itself. Often, it takes time for the effects to begin.

The Science of Reiki

The research on Reiki is fairly new, though this should not come as a surprise since Western medicine has only started to scratch the surface of more holistic, alternative treatments. While some studies have disputed the presence of this energy, it is believed that Reiki works because of the overall relaxation and healing environment that it provides to the body. By allowing the body to exist in a more relaxed, stress-free state, it encourages the body's natural healing processes. This can be seen in the many stories of miracles of Reiki and how it has healed people—whether their pain was physical, emotional, or mental. Reiki promotes all-over body wellness, unlike Western medicine, which relies on the treatment of symptoms rather than trying to heal the body and encourage long-term health and healing.

History of Reiki

The beginning of Reiki goes back to early Tibet, a long time past. This method of healing was revived by Dr. Mikao Usui of Japan, towards the end of the 1800s – the beginning of the 1900s. The practice of Reiki was passed by word of mouth from experts to experts and from apprentice to apprentice. Historians seemed to have added many embellishments to how the practice began, perhaps to highlight the marvel and splendor of the myth of Dr. Usui.

In earlier days, Reiki masters circulated some tale to their apprentices. As years passed, fresh details have appeared on how Reiki began, including the story behind Dr. Usui, his schooling, and other facts about his life and practice. In the main, this new information has helped to put the records straight, to not mislead the Western practices of Reiki therapy practitioners.

A story passed on by Hawayo Takata tells how Dr. Mikao Usui learned Reiki therapy, though much of it has been regarded as imaginative.

The story of Reiki revolves around its originator, Dr. Mikao Usui, who is occasionally referred to as Usui Sensei. He was the offspring of an affluent Buddhist household and was born in 1865. Dr. Usui was given comprehensive schooling that existed in those days. His education in a Buddhist convent included martial arts like swordsmanship and the Japanese version of Chi Kung, known as Kiko.

During his schooling, Dr. Usui was motivated to study the medical sciences, psychology, and divinity. These study engagements led him to seek self-healing for himself and others through placing hands on the body.

Dr. Usui went to many places, learning various kinds of cures. In the process, he worked in many occupations – in journalism, administration, missions, civil service, and security. Eventually, Dr. Usui occupied a Buddhist minister's position and stayed in a convent.

Over time, he learned some Reiki practices and spread to his disciples.

Reiki in Japan

After the time, Hawayo Takata came with traditional Japanese Reiki to Hawaii. The healing system had reached several nations of the west and had gone through many changes. These adapted Reiki earned the name, "western Reiki" to differentiate it from the traditional Japanese Reiki.

Therefore, the method employed in the usual practice of western Reiki differed from that obtainable in Japanese Reiki. Individuals sometimes attempt to learn what differentiates Japanese Reiki and the western Reiki based on their forms. The only way anyone could learn the dissimilarity in the practice of Reiki in Japan and in the west is simply to learn how people live their lives in the two cultures.

For a westerner to truly employ the Japanese original system of Reiki, he or she should learn how the Japanese people live and practice Reiki, to fully grasp the way this method is used in the Japanese culture. I believe this explanation brings more understanding to those who live in other cultures different from Japan to learn the original system of Reiki to improve their practice.

I hope that the work I have done in this book would help you grab the idea of how it works. My thinking is that "Reiki adherents everywhere" would be exciting to learn and experience. Lastly, there are concrete evidences about Dr. Usui and his work and practice of Reiki that are not mere fiction.

At first, Dr. Usui's concepts were novel, and most people resisted them. However, after careful studies and thinking about Dr. Usui's background on Reiki practice, there has been a wider acceptance of what he taught about the system. These recent clarifications came from documented interactions with the Japanese Reiki individuals and have fortified western practitioners of Reiki with authentic background evidence of Reiki's validity. These clarifications have also fostered a better understanding of all who practice Reiki all over the world.

Reiki in western countries

Reiki's system of healing has progressed evolutionarily since Mrs. Takata arrived in the western nations with the practice in 1938. Here comes an interesting part which makes people astonished while they read and study the history of Reiki. It was a sudden turn it the practices of Reiki, and it has been said that that was also a turning point in the teaching practices of this method.

Takata was the only Reiki practitioner in the whole world after World War II. Consequently, any individual who desired to acquire the knowledge of Reiki had only one person to learn from. At the beginning of her Reiki training institution in 1970, Mrs. Takata demanded $10,000 from every individual who wished to be a Reiki expert.

Owing to the negative circumstances resulting from the crisis with Japan and the situations in her Reiki classes, Mrs. Takata maintained a strict method of teaching. She did not permit any of her students to try anything, except to engage themselves in what she told them. She made the clarification that they would not be practicing Reiki if anyone deviated from the method she was teaching them. Thus, she dissuaded them from inventing and developing any fresh method in the practice of Reiki.

This practice of Mrs. Takata not only stopped the way to the progress of the practices but also transferred only those Reiki practices which she was aware of. It also deprived the poor classes of the society of learning and practicing it as the fee she was charging at that time was a gross amount that everyone was not able to pay and get started.

So, in the western world, the Reiki which they initially learned was all about the knowledge of Mrs. Takata. All her students used to think on the same lines, and it kept the process of evolution of this healing technique at bay for a long time.

The words "Western Reiki", often used by Reiki experts and trainers of the practice, were coined by Japanese personalities like Jikiden Reiki and Gendai Reiki Ho, who invented the system. Also, this method applies to similar Reiki experts and trainers mainly concerned with the knowledge about the way Mikao Usui and Chujiro Hayashi adapted and trained on the Reiki system during their times.

When looked at carefully, the words "Western Reiki" could be explaining the ways western Reiki got affected by the Japanese Reiki. Consequently, it is frequently unclear what the words "Western Reiki" mean to practitioners of today. However, it is apparent that most of those who make use of these words are most likely of the opinion that Reiki remains the "only widespread living force." To them, there is nothing like "Western widespread living force" or even "Japanese widespread living force". Considering that nowhere on the planet can be referred to as "widespread", the word "Western Reiki" is not meaningful at all.

Chapter 19: What is Reiki?

Reiki is a very powerful healing energy than can be used to heal the body, mind, and soul. It was discovered by no one other than Mikao Usui, who was a Buddhist monk who was able to understand this energy and channel it to heal himself and others around him. Usui was born into a wealthy family in 1865; he had access to a well-rounded education and chose to study psychology, theology, and medicine. Through his years of learning and training in the monastery, he eventually decided to start his training, taking place in a cave of Mount Kurama. For 21 days, he meditated, fasted, and prayed continuously and on the 21st day, in his vision, he saw Sanskrit symbols which helped him develop his system of healing. He names this system 'The Usui Treatment Method for Body and Mind,' or what is currently known as Reiki.

The word 'Reiki' is made out of two Japanese words, 'Rei' and 'Ki.' If we were to translate these words into English, then the meaning will be rather twisted since an exact spiritual translation is rather difficult. 'Rei' is defined as a ghost while 'Ki' is defined as vapor, these definitions only point in the direction of what we are looking for, but it is not the whole picture.

In a spiritual context, 'Rei' is interpreted as the Universe or also known as the Higher Intelligence, which guides every living thing, spirit, and functions the universe. Rei can also be defined as subtle wisdom which permeates everything the living and the dead. This wisdom guides the development of life, the creation, evolution, and the unfolding of many galaxies. This power is extraordinary and big, but if you look at it more on a human level, this energy acts as a source of guidance which will help us any time we require assistance in life. This infinite nature is constantly around us and it is always available to help us. It is also called 'God' in many cultures and religions, but either way, this nature is all-knowing.

'Ki,' on the other hand, is a non-physical energy that inspires, animates, and encourages everything that is living. This energy is everywhere, in humans, animals, and even plants. Those who have a high Ki are confident and strong; they can take on whatever life throws at them with no doubts. But when this energy is low, their strength is replaced with weakness and may even get sick. Ki is also known as the life force, odic force, bioplasma, and orgone by many religions and cultures. This so-called life force leaves when the body when it dies. Although it is unknown what happens after death, many religions believe that the soul or life force moves on by reincarnating, going to heaven, or going to Summerland which is the spiritual world on the other side. Either way, this energy still lives on.

Combining the two words, Reiki can be described as the non-physical healing energy that guides your life force by the Higher Intelligence, also known as God or Deity. Many refer to it as spiritual guidance and spiritual healing for your body, mind, and soul. However, this is only a technical definition; Reiki itself is so much more. Many of those who practice Reiki and the Reiki healing practice agree that this energy or force has an intelligence of its own; it can understand what one needs and where this healing is required. Reiki cannot be controlled, which is why it is not limited by the ability and experience of those who practice Reiki.

Reiki is a power. This power liaises and activates the central healer. The central healer, in this case, is that inner part of you which has the record of what exactly needs to be done for you to be well. Reiki is lead by the spirit and therefore, it forms its basis on love with Godly aptitude that is ever humble and very beneficial. The purpose of Reiki is to mend and bring together every power system in our bodies.

The power systems are mental, emotional, spiritual as well as the physical organizations of our bodies. It digs deep into a specific attribute that requires healing at the time of its initiation. Therefore, the root of the problem could reside in any of the mentioned systems of the body. There are examples of asthma and allergy.

These conditions are mainly brought about as a result of unregulated emotions. Whenever you are exposed to any medical curative procedure, it is not automatic that the procedure will lead make you heal. Instead, they are the systems that will team up to agree that the root of the problem has been eliminated.

Many are times where medical attention alone has failed to yield to the permanent healing of an ailing person. That is where Reiki comes in. You are left feeling relaxed and peaceful, able to take up life at large. It is the prime role of your central healer to obtain results more directly and in an ideal mode; therefore, Reiki kindles as well as enhances the inner healer.

How Reiki Works

When the power of life flows through us, we are kept alive. We also refer this to as life-force. There are passages for this force within our bodies, namely: nadis, chakras, and meridians. The movement within our bodies also takes place in an energy zone referred to as the aura.

It helps to maintain the body organs as well as body cells, enabling them to work well. The flow must be free from any form of interference; otherwise, it will lead to a breakdown in either one or many tissues and body organs within the physical body. In other words, the force reacts to our feelings and thoughts. The flow feels disturbed every time we agree with the negativities in our feelings or thoughts concerning our bodies.

These negative thoughts will later join with the power field, thus, leading to a breakdown in the smooth running of life force. In the end, this will lead to a general breakdown of the normal functioning of the body and its organs. It is at this stage that Reiki finds a basis for operation. It heals by running through the energy field that is mostly affected by pumping-in the right energy.

It goes deeper to find where the negative thoughts are being harbored; then, it creates the level of positive energies around them. The harmful energy is replaced by the right and helpful energy. Therefore, Reiki will clean, make straight, and then heal the pathways. This, in turn, leads to a smooth flowing of life-force naturally and healthily.

Reiki Levels

Reiki has got levels in which it operates in. They are often referred to as degrees. We will take a look at three major levels basically; level 1 or first degree, level two or second degree and lastly, level three or third degree.

Reiki Level 1: The First Degree

The first level is known as a 'beginner' level; it is open to anyone. Everyone and anyone has the power to perform Reiki on themselves. The goal of this level is to open the energy channels, where Ki flows. It permits the student to channel the Reiki energy on a physical level with the use of only one initiation, the Usui Tibetan system. After this initiation, the student will start to feel the energy flowing into and through their hands which can be perceived as tingling, heat, buzzing, coolness, or any other sensations within your hands or throughout your body. For some people, those sensations within the hands or body sometimes don't happen straight away, but rather sometime after the initiation has been performed.

When the energy is released, it harmonizes and balances the seven main chakras, which are the major energy centers located and spread throughout the top of the head, down the spine, and to the bottom where the tailbone resides. This level is open to anyone with or without experience; the teaching of this method often takes one weekend to teach. However, this connection can never be undone; it is permanent and can be used whenever the student wishes.

The amount of this energy that has been channeled after the initiation varies differently, but when Reiki is used more and more, that energy becomes more constant. The energy on the physical level consists of 80% to 90%, with the other being located within the emotional, mental, and spiritual levels.

Reiki Level 2: The Second Degree

Before moving on to the Second Degree, the student must first complete the First Degree. It usually takes around twenty-one days and up to three months to practice and perfect the First Degree, with regular self-treatments and practices throughout the weeks. In the Second Degree, the central channels have been expanded and opened to a greater level with an increase in the channeled energy. This is also where the Reiki healing is expanded and practiced on others. With that in mind, the student also receives three Reiki symbols, the Power Symbol, the Distance Symbol, and the Mental/Emotional Symbol. Reiki symbols are used to draw the qualities and energy of those symbols to connect more deeply to the universe and succeed in the Reiki energy channel.

Due to the attunement process and intensity of the Second Degree, there has to be at least twenty-one to a full three months passing period on the level one Reiki before moving on to the next level. There is usually one attunement required in the second degree with the focus on the heart chakra and opening the central channel.

Reiki Level 3: The Third Degree

This level increases the student's capacity once again. The student also receives the Usui Master Symbol, which will help him make contact with his inner truth and work on a more spiritual level. This level is also known as Inner Master because it enables practitioners to recognize that everyone is a master of their path, destiny, and each person is responsible for their own life. The Third Degree also helps the student find its life path and the required changes to live the life that the student wants.

Reiki Level 4: Reiki Master

The Reiki Master is considered to be a teacher of Reiki, with a lot of energy and knowledge to be able to teach new Reiki practitioners and attune them to Reiki at the beginning of their journey. There is also a Reiki Master attunement that needs to be received with its corresponding symbol to feel confident and comfortable when it comes to attuning others. The one who chooses to follow this level will also learn a variety of techniques to be able to attune and initiate others. Reaching this level also demonstrates a deep commitment to the Reiki practice with the knowledge and skills to be able to perform and teach others of Reiki healing and self-discovery.

Chapter 20: What Is A Reiki Master?

Given the idea of the ace level and the energies that become accessible to us, being a Reiki ace can be a progressing procedure including consistent self-improvement. With the ace attunement and the utilization of the ace image, we get the chance to open increasingly more totally to the boundless capability of this art and to create within each of us the characteristics that are held within the vitality of Reiki.

Consider every one of the parts of Reiki vitality - other than the possibility to mend all disease, it likewise contains boundless love, delight, harmony, empathy, astuteness, bounty and significantly more. We know these are the characteristics of Reiki because individuals experience them when giving or accepting Reiki medications. They are particularly evident when we think about the wellspring of Reiki. When doing as such, many are lifted into a protected spot where they feel thought about and become mindful of the superb potential outcomes that can emerge out of inside.

When we mull over these things it is anything but difficult to move toward becoming overpowered with good faith and a certain comprehension of the fact that any, and all, difficulties of the world can be overcome and that our existence could be a great encounter. The Japanese term of the highest degree in Reiki is Shinpiden that signifies "Puzzle Teaching." The riddle that is talked about is the secret of God's adoration, shrewdness, and power.

It is a riddle since God has no limits; every one of the qualities of God including marvel, excellence, and elegance reaches out a long way past our capacity to understand. Regardless of how created in this life or any future degree of presence, we will never completely get it. This is the reason it is and will consistently stay a superb secret.

When we get the Usui ace image and the attunement that engages it, it makes the likelihood for us to end up mindful of the Ultimate Reality. This is communicated in the meaning of the Usui ace image that demonstrates that it speaks to that piece of the self that is as of now totally illuminated! When we utilize the ace image, we are interfacing with our own edified selves. This truth be told, is the genuine wellspring of Reiki vitality - it originates from the most profound and most significant piece of our inclination, our very own illuminated self. Even though we might be under the impression that this phenomenon is originating from afar and descends to use through the crown chakra, the fact of the matter is that it is merely a hallucination and just shows up along these lines in light of our restricted mindfulness.

The healing energy that is summoned in Reiki is bestowed upon by the creator. It is therefore this energy that leads us to heal and opens us up to greater self-understanding and enlightenment. However, improvement doesn't happen naturally. Reiki regards our through and through freedom and doesn't compel advancement on us, yet on the off chance that we look for it and expect it, and use Reiki for this reason, at that point absolutely, we will be guided into a more prominent recuperating background. Attempt this analysis. Begin by conducting Reiki on your self-utilizing our ace image in the hands within an agreeable position. (On the off chance that you aren't an ace at Reiki but rather at the first or second level, attempt it in any case without the ace image.) Then ruminate over this insistence. "I give up totally to the Reiki vitality and the source from which it comes." Repeat this assertion again and again, at that point as the Reiki vitality keeps on streaming, with your inward eye, search for the wellspring of Reiki, either inside yourself or above.

By doing this, you will have numerous significant encounters. These are probably going to incorporate ending up progressively mindful of the way Reiki functions inside you and sensing that its astonishing characteristics. New conceivable outcomes for self-awareness will be exhibited and you will be welcome to partake in life in a progressively important manner. As your mindfulness draws much nearer to the actual source, you will wind up mindful of stunning bits of knowledge and have regularly expanding encounters of happiness, security, and harmony. This is a superb exercise and justified even despite the time. We recommend you do this regularly and as you do as such, these encounters will end up more grounded. At that point, on the off chance that you acknowledge the mending changes that are displayed, profound recuperating will start occurring and you will likewise start accepting direction about how to improve your life. While this contemplation is basic, it is additionally exceptionally ground-breaking and can lead you into a cheerful and sound perspective, making enduring changes that will shape the establishment of an increasingly advantageous life.

Reiki can manage you in approaches to make its recuperating power progressively advantageous and to mend all the more profoundly. What's more, simultaneously, one can assume that this discipline will direct you to additional mending strategies that are directly available for your use notwithstanding Reiki. You may likewise get direction about changes you have to make that expect you to make a move. Your capacity to settle on choices can improve, making it extremely simple to choose precisely what you need, who to connect with, where to work, and so on and this could bring about a new course for your life!

When you are engaged with the recuperating procedure, a great method to decide your advancement is to utilize your external world as a sign of your internal improvement. This works since we show our whole experience through our contemplations and goals - both cognizant and oblivious. When we experience something in our lives, it because some piece of our being has made it. When we acknowledge this thought and assume total liability for what happens in our lives, we enter an extremely amazing spot. We would then be able to get rid of the things which do not provide any benefit and make every part of our lives better.

If your external world contains positive encounters, and you are making a mind-blowing most, this implies your internal world is in a comparative state. The turnaround is likewise valid, thereby when we go through agonizing experiences and circumstances, or are disillusioned or experience by situations that cultivate dread, stress or uncertainty, this is additionally because some piece of our inward being is out of parity and necessities recuperating. On the off chance that something upsetting, or undesirable happens in your life, instead of accusing other individuals or conditions outside yourself, direct your consideration internally and search for the piece of yourself that has made this terrible occasion. At that point utilize your Reiki mending abilities to support and recuperate this part. When you do this, the disagreeable encounters will stop and be supplanted by sound positive encounters.

As we proceed on our recuperating way, we will end up mindful of a degree of cognizance that lives profoundly inside every one of us that can bring a great better approach for living. It makes another disposition that is positive and carries with it the capacity to take care of numerous issues and make positive outcomes that beforehand we didn't think conceivable.

What Are the Roles Of A Reiki Master?

Understanding the job a Reiki Master plays in taking an interest in your mending is significant for everybody included. Understanding what a Reiki Master does and doesn't do impacts a mending session and otherworldly and self-awareness. For the customer, however for the Reiki Master healer as well.

So, what does a Reiki Master do precisely? It might shock you, yet a Reiki Master isn't required to fix your medical issues! From my encounters working with customers through the world, I have seen that numerous individuals don't completely comprehend the job a Reiki Master healer plays with regards to mending. There is a constant flow of customers who go to a Reiki Master with a rundown of desires.

Reiki Master Healers just associate you with The Source. Regardless of whom your Reiki Master healer is, their job is to associate your body, being and vitality with the vitality of The Source. From here, it is up to The Source what gets mended in you and what doesn't. The aftereffects of a Reiki treatment are not the duty of the healer. Some portion of the duty rests with the customer and the rest with The Source. So how open the customer is to being mended, the amount they have confidence in the capacity to recuperate, and that they are so associated with God, The Source, are a portion of the numerous elements that decide the achievement of a mending session. It is the job of your Reiki Master to associate your vitality with the vitality of The Source. From that point, a customer's mending is about their more profound association with The Source.

The principal obligation is to oneself, to sustain and create from inside, and to discharge any cynicism from inside.

Regularly in this day and age, we run over a clash that we can decide to either accept or smoothly resolve. We may get malady that we are to mend from comprehensively. We are tested with negative passionate responses that we should relinquish. We are tested with remaining negative feelings from quite a while ago, sentiments; for example, stress, outrage, low self-esteem, we are not to enable these emotions to rot and develop however to release them and recuperate. Most importantly, we need to deal with ourselves, living by the Reiki Principles as given by Mikao Usui, the originator of Reiki, and permitting ourselves Reiki mending each day. All things considered; we are not very useful to any other individual if that we are ourselves a wreck! I find that for myself and other Reiki Masters, this first duty is the hardest to complete. It is a continuous exertion that gets simpler with long stretches of training. The key is to prop up back to the lessons of Usui with a receptive outlook and humble soul.

The subsequent obligation is to individuals who come to us for Reiki. There are individuals from the open who want treatment and understudies who seek commencement and education.

When somebody seeks a treatment with Reiki, my instructing was to disclose to the customer that Reiki is a comprehensive vitality, going to where it is most required, and to urge the customer to comprehensively deal with their wellbeing. Reiki works uniquely in contrast to allopathic prescription. While allopathic drug fixes the side effect, Reiki mending is aimed at the entire individual. For example, if a customer came griping of knee torment, it might be that the knee is focused on because the hip is twisted. The hip may have turned into that path to make up for a shoulder being twisted. This may have occurred because of worry in the individual's life. On the off chance that this pressure is as yet progressing, the Reiki is probably going to mend the pressure first. This bodes well, as leaving the worry there may prompt further bear hip-knee misalignment and further knee harm! Some portion of the duty of the Reiki Master is to make the customer mindful of this all-encompassing procedure and the requirement for a few sessions. This allows the Reiki to recuperate the side effects just as the hidden causes.

At the point when an understudy seeks commencement and educating, this is the start of a profound, passionate, mental and physical adventure. The Reiki Master needs to consider the street went before this point and above all, bolster the understudy on their energizing new venture with Reiki.

A significant number of us have come into Reiki from a foundation of physical or passionate agony. For a few, there was a profound void to fill. A decent Reiki Master will be delicate to the necessities of their understudies. This implies staying away from natural aggravations in the class to think about understudies with compound sensitivities. It means relinquishing injurious comments given by furious spirits. It means being firm yet delicate with understudies from a sincerely despondent life. Most importantly, in the class, the Reiki Master ought to guarantee the understudy feels needed, regarded, acknowledged and adored. After the commencement and educating, the Reiki Master can bolster their understudy by making accessible and focusing on the requirement for ordinary contact and supervision. The rest is up to the understudy and what feels directly for their advancement with Reiki.

The third obligation is towards friends and family and every single other animal; to put it plainly, our condition. Our mending incorporates thinking about this condition.

This doesn't mean enabling an injurious relative to manhandle us or adding to social wrongs since every other person appears to! It means being capable, cherishing genuinely, and enabling recuperating to stream any place it is required and with the consent of the healer. For example, a Reiki Master can begin every day by asking that they are a channel, or course, for Reiki vitality and enabling it to stream any place they stroll in nature. A Reiki Master can buy earth amicable items. A Reiki Master can be accessible for relatives for recuperating as feels fitting and be a power for good. A Reiki Master living by the Reiki Principles will win their living truly, respect their educators and older folks, and be charitable to each living thing.

One of the most normally looked for after administrations I offer to customers is relationship mending. Regardless of who the individual and what kind of life they live, everybody has associations with individuals. Regardless of whether with an accomplice, a companion, a relative or a business associate, a huge piece of life comes down to the connections we have with others. So, relationship recuperating is a prevalent region that individuals frequently need assistance with. Anyway, numerous individuals expect a Reiki Master to do something amazing and power two individuals together in 'amicability'. This is a remarkable inverse of concordance. Indeed, utilizing vitality to constrain two individuals together is more much the same as dark enchantment than mending. No Reiki Master should utilize vitality diverting to control the Will of someone else. Regardless of what the goal might be. There are significant explanations behind why individuals meet up. There are similarly significant purposes behind why individuals part. Inside this uniting and separating of connections are numerous significant open doors for self-advancement and otherworldly development.

So, the job of a Reiki Master isn't to conflict with the regular progression of the Universe. The job of a Reiki Master is to help the individuals in a relationship to make harmony with their connections, to comprehend the message, if conceivable, and to enable them to mend and proceed onward if that is the regular course that relationship should take. The best job a Reiki Master could accept that is turning into a channel and manual for assistance individuals comprehend the more profound importance of their connections.

The specialty of Reiki and profound recuperating plans to enable the individual to rehearse it. By figuring out how your condition communicates with you, and how you cooperate with your condition, you can start to utilize your musings, goal, feeling, and vitality as instruments of progress. Now and again, numerous customers have an ordinary Reiki Master healer who mends them, yet they don't wish to learn Reiki themselves. We have a couple of customers who feel this way. Anyway, there are various hindrances to this that customers ought to know about.

The job of a Reiki Master is to recuperate, enable and improve their customers. If a co-dependent relationship creates among healed and healer, this can be counter-productive for the development and advancement of the customer. By not figuring out how you make vitality at each minute, how you channel it into your life, and how your life turns into an impression of that vitality you channel, you will never arrive at the purpose of being responsible for your heading throughout everyday life. Acknowledge how vitality streams and you can accomplish self-dominance. There is little reason in a Reiki Master Healer expelling a negative vitality hinders from inside you if your considerations, expectations, and activities are more than once re-making those equivalent blockages. When you figure out how you make these vitality squares yourself, and you find how to discharge them yourself, there is no compelling reason to contract a Reiki Master to recuperate you. Since you can do it without anyone else's help. The best job a Reiki Master can take is spurring you to change. Since without change, there is no genuine advancement. The vitality of Reiki itself will help change to happen naturally. Anyway, by learning Reiki, you enable that change to turn out to be a lot further and unquestionably increasingly significant.

Chapter 21: Benefits of Reiki

1. **Reiki promotes balance and harmony.** Reiki is extremely effective at promoting balance and harmony within an individual. It has relaxing effects that help people return to a state of balance, where their emotional and mental energy is restored. While the primary focus of Reiki is its healing ability for the physical body through the use of energy, it also helps promote overall wellness in terms of mental and emotional states. It works deep on problems to restore balance overall and does not simply mask or relieve symptoms as some medicines may do. When we speak about the mental and emotional balance found through Reiki, we often refer to equilibrium in both sides of a person's brain as well as balance in the male and female aspects of our personalities. We also go further to seek balance in the good and bad things that happen to us and the positive and negative things in our lives, not labeling any of them too much.

2. **Reiki helps relieve stress and promotes relaxation.** Stress is the main source of all diseases, and Reiki has a great ability to relieve any stress in an individual which helps lower the risk of them obtaining more symptoms caused by a reduction in Ki levels. Many people find Reiki to be relaxing and stress relieving because it allows them to be fully immersed in the present moment. Instead of 'doing', they are simply 'being'. Many clients have reported feelings of clarity and peace in themselves after Reiki treatments. They also report feeling more relaxed and physically lighter (a feeling that tends to come as a result of letting go of the mental weight we are carrying).

Reiki allows a person to become more aware of their physical body and the inner dialogue going on in their minds, like what happens during meditation. This enables people to listen to their bodies more and make any important decisions concerning them from a more grounded place. This added benefit helps relieve future stresses or worries that have been lingering.

Allowing yourself time to be more present can help calm the mind and quieten the noise that tends to get in the way of clear thinking. Being present helps us tap into the unlimited wisdom that we all have within.

3. **Reiki improves balance and energy.** Reiki can help us discover a more calm and peaceful state within ourselves. We can find a place in which we are more adjusted to deal with stressful situations. Having an improved

mental balance through Reiki can also improve other related aspects of life such as our ability to learn new information, our ability to retain that information, and our mental clarity. Reiki has the power to heal mental and emotional scars and it also combats negative emotions like fear and anger. It can also help to reduce the level and frequency of mood swings as emotional regulation improves. Another knock-on benefit to this is improved and strengthened personal relationships.

4. **Reiki can be used to detox.** Reiki is an excellent way for the body to get rid of any toxins. As our bodies spend a large amount of time in stress, also known as fight-or-flight mode, toxins such as cortisol are released and can build up to dangerously high levels. When the fight-or-flight phase becomes your normal state of being, it is very dangerous to your health. Energy is given to the extremities for survival and is thus taken away from the immune system. We need to have our immune system functioning properly if we wish to remain healthy. Reiki reminds the body to access the parasympathetic nervous system. This is more commonly known as the healing mode. We access this system when we are in a relaxed state. It is responsible for healing the body and protecting the vital organs.

This resting mode does not mean being active is a bad thing. The opposite is true. Moving around and being regularly active throughout the day is important, but our heart rate should remain below the stress-inducing threshold. Being in this resting phase improves our sleep and our ability to digest food. These are two key factors in keeping the body healthy and maintaining vitality. The more time you can spend in the parasympathetic state, the more energy you will have to be active and productive throughout the day. It will also lower your chances of reaching states of stress, exhaustion, or burnout.

5. **Reiki helps improve focus.** Reiki is great for clearing the mind, and this induces a new level of improved focus. The grounding effects of Reiki are a huge benefit in helping us feel more centered. When grounded and centered, we can think much clearer and our focus becomes much sharper. We act much more concisely and purposefully while being in the present moment. Our brain has a better ability to focus when it is no longer concerned itself with thoughts of the past or worries of the future. It also gives you an increased ability to accept what comes your way and focus on a solution to any problems that arise, instead of getting caught up in all the potential consequences if something goes wrong as well as all of the unnecessary emotions that accompany those consequences. You can react and deal with people and situations in a more productive and supportive way rather than in a defensively or negatively.

6. **Reiki helps improve sleep.** One of the most talked-about benefits of Reiki is its ability to make us feel more relaxed. Many people never take the time to switch off from their busy lives and thus do not acquire enough sleep each night as their brains are still working in overdrive. Reiki makes us feel more relaxed, which helps improve the amount of sleep we get as well as the quality of that sleep. The benefits of receiving adequate and good quality sleep are endless, but the main ones include improved memory,

improved mood, and increased healing in our bodies. Reiki is so effective at helping people relax that many who come into a Reiki session sleep-deprived often fall asleep during the session itself!

7. **Reiki helps improve self-healing.** Reiki has the amazing ability to improve the body's ability to heal itself naturally. By removing the blockages in Ki and increases the energy flow throughout the body, Reiki can provide huge benefits to overall physical health. Reiki helps return your body to its natural state by getting the right amount of Ki flowing through it. This results in improvements in your blood pressure, heart rate, and breathing. Breathing longer and deeper breaths is one of the primary steps of the self-healing process. With improved breathing comes a huge host of benefits including a more relaxed mind and body. Breathing deep and slow breaths indicate to the body that you are in a relaxed environment and not in a stressed state. As such, the body reacts by kicking into the parasympathetic nervous system and thus starting the healing process. This is where your body is primarily meant to be functioning.

8. **Reiki is excellent for relieving pain.** Reiki can relieve not only emotional pain but also physical pain. By working at the deepest level and unblocking the accumulation of negative energy, Reiki can result in the alleviation of pain in the body. By encouraging your body to get its primary functions back on track, such as breathing, digesting food, and sleeping, it helps the body return to its natural state for healing.

Reiki is known to aid in relieving migraines. It also helps with fatigue, insomnia, and asthma.

9. **Reiki enables emotional cleansing.** Reiki can improve your spiritual growth by helping you deal with emotions that are holding you back. You do not need to be a spiritual person to receive these benefits from Reiki. We all have underlying emotions affecting our everyday thoughts and decisions, whether we realize it or not. Reiki can help get to the root cause of these emotions and pull out the negative ones for us to see. Negative emotions act as weeds which inhibit positive ones (which act as plants) to grow and flourish. To develop into the person you wish to be, you must get rid of the negative emotions holding you back from letting your positive light shine brightly. Reiki focuses on addressing the whole person and not just the symptoms of pain. This can lead to profound shifts in being from deep within.

This can lead to a whole new perspective on life and a whole new identity of yourself. It enables you to see yourself more clearly, both the positive attributes and the imperfections. It gives you the ability to take action based on what you see and choose a path for yourself based on what you desire.

10. **Reiki compliments alternative treatments.** Reiki acts as an excellent complement to traditional medicinal practices. It often acts to relax the patient which puts them at ease during other forms of treatment such as surgery, which

can naturally put the body in a state of stress. As we know, putting the body in a state of relaxation promotes the effects of healing and accelerates the process. People also sleep better following Reiki treatments, which also aids in their recovery from things such as surgery.

It does not interfere with surgical operations as it can be administered non-intrusively. Many Reiki practices involve the practitioner not needing to physically touch the body. If a Reiki master is present during surgery, it would not be wise for them to have to share the same physical space as the operating surgeon.

Reiki is safe to use despite any condition you may have, whether it be diabetes, heart problems, or epilepsy. People undergoing chemotherapy may also receive Reiki treatments, and they often do to help aid in recovery and for pain relief. Even pregnant women can receive Reiki treatment to aid them through the different stages of their pregnancy.

Chapter 22: Mental and Emotional healing

One of the many benefits of using Reiki is to heal our mental health. This level of healing, however, requires being a second-degree student of the art. This area of healing is where we focus and can work with the conscious level of our thought process. Through this level we can recognize, alter, and improve upon our judgments, patterns, habits, and behaviors.

Because, as was discussed with performing Reiki on others, Reiki only applies as much healing as is necessary and the person is ready and willing to accept, this means that you cannot heal your mental health any more than you are ready to. So, although it seems nice, you will not be able to become a second-degree Reiki student and instantly become enlightened. It will still be a gradual process that occurs with each new step of growth along the way.

There should be no concern over the efficacy or security of healing your own or anyone else's mental health, it cannot be manipulated for negative purposes. It does not resemble or act like any type of dark manipulation like hypnosis or spells. Again, it is merely the life source of the Universe correcting an imbalance, even in a mental capacity.

If you are interested in working with your mental wellbeing in general, you can do so by simply focusing your energy on a mental level. No need to have a specific goal in mind or challenge to overcome, but the mere act of channeling the life energy to improving your mental health will accomplish this. Through Reiki, you are activating the efforts and "muscles" of self-improvement, introspection, mindfulness, and self-care to encourage energy flow through these areas of your life. Much like physical exercise, creating a routine is crucial in building up your effectiveness and outcomes, even in Reiki. Through the repeated mental focus of energy you will be more able to recognize patterns that you have, conscious or unconscious, reflect upon how those patterns are serving you, decide if that is something you want to change, and then brainstorm how and why you would change that.

You can also focus on specific problems in your mental capacity. This will require a clear understanding of exactly what you are trying to work through to best focus your energy there. The amazing thing about Reiki is, although you may notice an area you want to change, you do not have to know exactly how to change it or what the solution is. Because Reiki provides exactly what is needed in exactly the way it can be best accepted at that time, the Universe's knowledge will be all that you need. You can help channel more energy by using tools like the symbols; you will need to become a second-degree Reiki practitioner to learn how to best activate these triggers. You can also combine these tools with the use of chanting, affirmations, or mantras. All of these can be done either silently inside your mind, or you can say them aloud. Either will work, but studies show that there is an extra element of healing vibrations that occur within yourself when you speak or chant aloud.

To become advanced in your Reiki practice, it requires a certain level of mental healing in this way. Because the channeling and focusing of the Universe's energy requires a certain level of enlightenment and connection with the Universe, this cannot be done with a closed mind. You must begin any Reiki practice with a certain level of self-awareness to harness the life force. One cannot possibly humble themselves enough to attempt to sue the source energy of the world without this base level of mental aptitude and introspection necessary to heal one's mind. The focus of our energy is reflected and manifested in our thoughts. Therefore, the more in control and focused your mind is, the more in control and focused your energy practice will be.

The Five Reiki Rules

There are generally five accepted rules to follow to get your mind the proper place for Reiki. These are general tenets that, much like mindfulness, are more about the journey of attempting them, rather than subscribing successfully to them at all times.

Today only, I will...

1. Not be moved to anger.

2. Not worry.

3. Humble myself.

4. Work honestly.

5. Use compassion in all that I do.

Today only, I will...

To begin with, all of the guidelines begin with the phrase, "Today only, I will..." to serve as a reminder of our mindfulness practice. The only time to focus on is the moment happening right now, and therefore, when it comes to our guiding principles, it only makes sense to focus on what is in our control, which is today only. Setting a goal that is too grand or too large to accomplish will only serve to discourage you from attempting it. If a task seems too insurmountable to be completed, at the first sign of difficulty, you will have no reason to pick yourself, dust yourself off, and give it another try. Rather, these guidelines are built to do the opposite; they give you the very small, very manageable goal of not worrying about any other day. Not worrying about any streak of days going unbroken. Not worrying about cheat days or weekends. No, with these guidelines, you only have to focus on following them today. Yesterday is gone and tomorrow you can do whatever you want. Just worry about trying these things today.

Not Be Moved to Anger.

Anger is a reactionary emotion. Anger is not something one comes to after a lot of thought. It bubbles up inside of you uncontrollably, trying to take over our nervous system, our energy, our thoughts, and our reasoning. That is why the first tenant is to do our best to overcome this. We cannot experience life at our highest energy vibration if we are stuck in anger. This emotion usually arises from a disconnect between what you want to be happening and what is happening. Fortunately for all of us, we cannot control everything--or much of anything--so this is a responsibility we should take off our plate. Think about it like this: to be angry about something that you cannot control is the ultimate example of fruitlessness. That is a lot of energy spent on nothing.

Not Worry.

Worry is an emotion-based in another time. Either you are worried about something in the past that has already happened that you cannot change, or you are worried about something in the future that has not happened and that you cannot change. Both of these instances mean you are not living in the present moment, which is the only time that matters, and is the only time that applies to Reiki healing.

Humble Myself.

To be grateful is to be humble. You cannot fully appreciate the gifts that are given to you if you fancy yourself so important that occurrences are rendered a nuisance. For that reason, you should try to humble yourself to utilize the massive force that is Reiki and be grateful for the energy flowing through you.

Work Honestly.

Integrity means doing the right thing all the time, even when you will not get noticed or recognition for doing so. It is that little voice inside of you telling you when you are veering off course, and it will not let you settle until you get right with it. To work honestly means that your integrity is in line with your conscious, telling you that you can sleep easy knowing you did your best. Truly, the only way to learn and become better is to be honest about where you are, where you want to go, and how you are progressing. The Universe does not have time for your ego-stroking illusions. It only knows and cares about the truth, so you should meet it on its level.

Use Compassion in All That I Do.

The ultimate requirement in Reiki is to have compassion. The life force energy that we are attempting to manipulate unites us with every other thing in the Universe. That means we truly are all one. The only way to use Reiki is positively, and the easiest way to feel the love and understanding you share with others is by showing them compassion. To honor and respect every other being's journey, struggles, triumphs, and energy is the most holy thing a human can do, and that is what Reiki asks of all of us.

Chapter 23: Physical healing

Physical healing is one of the benefits of Reiki that people seem to be most skeptical about. They do not understand how something that restores energy can help relieve the symptoms of their physical condition, whether it is a simple headache or a chronic illness. Those who doubt this method have often been healed using a Western form of medicine, which commonly focuses on treating the ailment directly instead of using a full-body approach. This is one of the reasons that people turn to alternative or holistic medicine when a more scientific approach has healed them. In many cases, the results have been a complete turnaround. There are even anecdotes of people who have turned to Reiki healing and other alternative medicines and had success in healing cancer, relieving chronic pain, and fighting off severe illness.

The following is a description of hand positions while treating different diseases. Place your hands on the parts of the body indicated, while sending the energy directly there.

Here are some of the main techniques:

- TANDEN is an energy center located between the top of the pubic bone and the navel

- TANDEN-CHIRYO – technique for detoxification. Place one hand on the tanden and the other one on the back on the same level. Hold your hands until you feel the effect is achieved. Fold your palms in Gassho. Tanden's healing is used as the main technique for creating energy. This technique can also increase willpower - both yours and your patient

- GENETSU-HO: a technique for lowering body temperature - the forehead along the hairline, temples and top of the head, the back of the neck, throat, crown, stomach and intestines. In this case, the main work is carried out on the head

- BOGEN CHIRYO: treatment of the cause of the disease - forehead along the hairline, temples and top of the head, nape, back of the neck, throat, crown, stomach and intestines. In this case, the main work is carried out on the head

- HANSHIN CHIRYO: a technique for treating half of the body - muscles, tendons of the back of the neck, shoulders, spine, thighs, buttocks

- GEDOKU-HO: another detoxification technique. Keep your hands in the position of TANDEN CHIRYO for 13 minutes, imagining how all the toxins are removed from the body

Spirituality

The flow of energy that you experience with Reiki can help you notice the interconnectedness between all the life forms of earth. As you connect to all that is living around you, you will feel a greater connection to the divine. You will also feel as if you are part of something greater than what exists in your immediate world. For many people, this creates the feeling of being connected to something great and powerful. It offers reassurance that you are present in the Universe and you know that you are loved by and connected to the spiritual beings, both living and non-living that you may encounter through your day.

Anxiety

It is not just basic levels of general or acute stress that Reiki has been proven to assist with. It is also a complimentary service to treat more intense feelings of anxiety and depression. Of course, with more serious cases, Reiki should not be used as the only form of treatment, but many doctors suggest using Reiki in conjunction with their other forms of healing regimen.

While anxiety is a form of and a result of stress, it is different in quite a few ways. It often manifests itself in the form of sleeplessness, being irritable, irregular heartbeat, chest tightness, sudden feelings of fear, nausea, feeling out of control of their emotions, and headaches. The thing that classifies it as anxiety is its recurrence frequently that allows it to disrupt your regular life.

Reiki is especially important in helping to eliminate worry. While worry and anxiety are different things, they are related, and therefore Reiki will be a logical solution to the more elevated, exaggerated, and overwhelming version of anxiety. Keep in mind the second rule of Reiki, "Today only, I will not worry." Worrying is a mindset that you can control, and although it may seem automatic, that is only because you have not yet mastered the ability to stop yourself short and redirect your thoughts. Much like worry, anxiety is your mind and body telling you that something is not right and that you want something to change. While you may not know exactly why or what it is that is causing your anxiety, you do not need the source to treat it with Reiki. The simple solution is to take action by using Reiki! Something needs to change, and it could be something as simple as focusing on your energy. That is a change! You do not need to try to push the anxiety out of your mind, as this will only make it stronger and more powerful because it gets to live in the shadows and mystery. Instead, you can simply redirect your thought from how overwhelmed you are feeling to allowing your energy to wrap around, though, over, and under those anxieties and let them melt away. This may take some practice before it becomes an automatic trigger, but over time it will become easier and more automatic.

Depression

Depression is, unfortunately, a rather common mental illness. The most mainstream treatments include various medications to stabilize the mood, increase chemical secretions in the brain, and in more severe cases antipsychotic medications. Most depression treatments are also accompanied by psychiatry and also therapy.

Common symptoms of depression include:

- Sadness

- Guilt

- Lack of interest

- Eating too much or too little

- Low self-esteem

- Sleeping too much or not enough

Depression can be triggered by an event such as loss of a loved one, loss of a job, or another traumatic event. In the worst cases, depression can lead to suicide, complete disability, mental break downs, institutionalization, and sometimes outwardly violent tendencies that endanger others.

If left untreated, depression can completely disrupt life and quality of life. In more recent years with depression treatments, Reiki has become accepted as a complementary therapy alongside traditional depression treatments.

Benefits of Reiki for depression include:

- Mental and physical balance

- Relaxation

- Returns control to client/patient

- Connection to another person

- Stress relief

Many people suffering from depression feel disconnected and out of control. Offering a physical connection to them through Reiki and having them participate in a proactive treatment for themselves can return a feeling of connection and control that may be lacking.

Infertility

It is sad to think that many couples still struggle with infertility. The idea of wanting to have a baby and being unable to conceive is just devastating. The process of fertility treatments and IVF can be painful, emotionally draining, and disheartening if desired results are not achieved.

Unfortunately, that pain, emotional stress, and depressed feeling only negatively contribute to infertility. It is a horrible cycle that many prospective mothers can get into.

Sometimes they are looking for relief from the pain and sadness, other times they might be looking for an alternative therapy to help increase their chances of conceiving or achieving IVF.

What we know of the energetic anatomy says that the Sacral Chakra is most closely related to female reproduction. Often, women who are struggling with infertility have blockages and low energy levels in the Sacral Chakra. This block can be formed by old emotional wounds or traumas that have built up over the years.

Since Reiki enhances and complements other medical treatments, using it in congruence with fertility treatments can give increase a woman's chances of conceiving a child or producing viable eggs for IVF. Also, it can help battle the more debilitating pain and emotional stresses that can accompany long term fertility treatments.

Releasing mental, emotional, and energetic blocks have yielded some surprising results for women going through fertility treatments. Reiki isn't a cure-all and different clients may experience different results, but from the stories of many women who have used Reiki with fertility treatments and their success, there is no doubt that Reiki can help!

Since Reiki releases blocked energy and balances the body and internal as well as energetic systems, the reproductive system is given the leeway to function on a more balanced scale, thus leading to better results or increased chances of conception!

Chronic pain or Crohn's Disease

Crohn's disease is a somewhat well-known autoimmune inflammatory disease that can cause serious abdominal pain, irregular bowel movements, and can affect the digestive system anywhere from the mouth down to the rectum.

It is a highly researched disease with no cure, and most who suffer from it are in and out of the doctors for the rest of their lives. There are lots of medications, treatments, and even surgeries to help manage the symptoms as well as dietary restrictions. However, that does not mean there will be long term relief or even a cure.

Sometimes the body can be acting completely normal, and then there will be a flare-up. These flare-ups can be intense, painful and debilitating. A lot of people who suffer from Crohn's disease have limited their lives, like avoiding long term travel, going abroad, or committing to long term programs or experiences. They fear being away from their doctors if a flare-up occurs or not being able to complete a program due to intense symptoms.

Reiki is about restoring balance to the body. Autoimmune diseases are essentially an overactive immune system that begins to attack the body trying to restore health. That seems very out of balance! Additionally, the intestines and stomach are the roots of the immune system in terms of energetic anatomy.

Restoring balance to the digestive system, reducing the overactivity of the immune system, and shifting the energetic vibration and frequency in the body is how Reiki can help relieve Crohn's disease symptoms.

Additionally, the emotional benefits can provide a much-needed boost in morale. Reiki can be performed at a distance. Offering distance sessions may even give your clients the confidence and security to try a little travel if Reiki reduces their flare-ups. This gives your clients back some control of their lives and their health.

The power of touch alone is immense, especially in clients who feel disconnected or are suffering from a painful or debilitating disease. Reiki sessions offer a gentle touch that can create connections, relieve pain, and provide clients with something they may very well be missing in daily life. It is such a gift to be a Reiki practitioner and know that you can use touch as a healing method.

Chapter 24: Symbols of Reiki

You might be aware of a Reiki session from a self-practiced session, or you might just hear about it. Reiki is an ancient healing method based on the energy transformation in the body. It is a great mental, physical, and emotional healing process, which has an amazing amount of health benefits.

The most amazing and significant features of Reiki are its symbols. These symbols allow people to continue their healing sessions and experience the energy of the universe. In most of the cases, the symbols only affect the involuntary actions of the body. However, the Reiki symbols work in a different method. These symbols change and modify the functioning of mind and body. The Reiki practitioners envision of Reiki's symbols and loudly say their names draw them in the healing process. If you are utilizing your intentions in the initiation process, then you will experience success for your efforts.

Therefore, it is significant to know about the symbols of Reiki and their actual meaning. These symbols have always been kept in secret; however, the research and exposure in the past few years influenced the symbols, and we have collected quite a lot of information. Here is the most important information regarding Reiki's symbols.

The Power Symbol: Cho Ku Rei

The powerful symbol of Cho Ku Rei is utilized to boost or reduce the power depending on the specific direction. The purpose of this symbol is to illuminate the light switch, which represents its capability to brighten up our spirituality. It is quite similar to the coil, which is believed by Reiki practitioners to increase and limit the energy flow in the human body. The power could be in different forms in Cho Ku Rei. This symbol is highly effective in the physical healing and purification of the soul. It can also be utilized in drawing attention and the focus of an individual.

If you are thinking to enhance or decrease your power, then Cho Ku Rei is the perfect symbol for you. It can be recognized by portraying a coil, which can be in clockwise or counterclockwise, representing chi that is the movement of energy from the body. You can think about a switch for imagining the power symbol. When this switch is activated or on, then a Reiki practitioner has a higher capability to brighten up the energy channel in your body.

Effectively Utilization of Cho Ku Rei

Cho Ku Rei is normally utilized at the beginning of a Reiki session. It assists in enhancing energy and power at any point in the ongoing session. One of the most common ways of utilizing Cho Ku Rei is while healing a wound or injury. It can be highly effective in dealing with common to severe pains or injuries.

In theoretical terms, Cho Ku Rei can be great in clearing out negative thoughts, energy, and feelings from your body that could be an obstacle in your Reiki session. If you are dealing with negative energy in your body, then Cho Ku Rei is the solution to your problems. It helps in taking the symbols out of your body and assist in filling it with light and positivity.

Cho Ku rei can be highly beneficial in improving the strength of your relationships. Moreover, Cho Ku Rei can be effective in getting a job or working on getting a job or relationship with your loved ones. It can also provide protection against different misfortunes, which happens because of having unclean energy in the body. Therefore, utilizing Cho Ku Rei could be a great boost in improving your energy system. On the other hand, if you are thinking to give a natural advancement in your nutrition, then Cho Ku Rei is the solution for removing negativity from your food and system.

The Harmony Symbol: Sei he ki

This symbol represents harmony. The primary purpose of this symbol is a purification for improving the mental and emotional healing process. This symbol is identical to the beach wave, which has the natural capability of washing and sweeping negative feelings. Different Reiki practitioners utilize this symbol while treating patients of depression and addiction. It helps in improving the natural balanced state of the body. It can also help treat the patients to recover from the emotional or physical state of disturbance. The symbol of Sei he ki is highly important in unblocking the creative energies of our system.

If you have been looking to purify and balance your emotional and mental health, then sei he ki is the perfect solution for you. The symbol of sei he ki is quite similar to a wave getting ready to crash the bird's wing or the beach. The symbol is extremely beneficial in establishing a balanced state between right and left-brain. It also serves as the protection symbol. You need to establish a healthy balance in your brain to perform your daily tasks perfectly.

Effective Utilization of sei he ki

Have you been looking to remember new information for taking a test or improving your memory? Then sei he ki is the perfect solution for you. You can draw a symbol of sei he ki on your book during reading or studying for improving your memorizing power. You will remember the information for years. If you just utilize this symbol of Reiki during visualization, you will experience a boost in your information.

Moreover, if you have been struggling to quit some habits like drinking or smoking, then turning to sei he ki could be highly beneficial for you. Remember, people adopt bad habits after experiencing some bad energy. If you utilize the symbol of sei he ki around you, then you can reduce negativity and spread positivity to get rid of bad habits.

Having headaches could be another form of dealing with depression or poor mental and emotional health. You can consult sei he ki for getting rid of your headaches as well. You can eliminate your headaches and the habit of consuming different unnecessary medications. Sei he ki also helps in giving you protection from negativity. This symbol removes negative from your body. Even better, it can enhance your positive affirmations. If you write affirmations daily, then try drawing sei he ki next to them. You will experience great positive and motivational energy within your body.

The Distance Symbol: or Hon-sha-ze-sho-nen

This symbol is highly effective in sending qi over large distance locations. The intention of this symbol is timelessness. It contains a tower-like appearance, which provides the basis of its second name as a pagoda. The primary function of this symbol is to bring people together over different time or space. Distance symbol can change itself for unchaining the Akashic records, which is believed to be the fundamental source of human awareness. Reiki practitioners consider this an ideal tool in dealing with previous life issues and the inner-child state of customers.

The idea of this symbol is a little difficult to understand as compared to other symbols of Reiki. The primary meaning is having no present, past, or future. This symbol is utilized for sending energy and power of Reiki in different space and time. Moreover, this symbol cannot change your past; however, it provides healing to deal with past traumatic situations.

It can help in the identification of actual life experiences and getting over old wounds and injuries. The symbol can help to turn an awful incident into a learning experience. The symbol helps Reiki practitioners to send the energy in the future that could result in some bad news of exams, jobs, or tough communication with our special loved ones.

Effective utilization of distance symbol

A little different than utilizing the other symbols of Reiki. One of the most powerful symbols of Reiki; however, correct implementation is required for getting results. This symbol works effectively on the subtle body than that of a physical body. Therefore, Reiki practitioners recommend utilizing this symbol regularly for successful healing of past, present, and future.

The Master Symbol: Dai ko myo

This symbol represents the whole concept of Reiki. The primary purpose of this symbol is to bring enlightenment to the body. Reiki masters only use this symbol while initiating the attunement. This symbol allows healing by bringing the power of healing. It is one of the most complicated forms of symbols to be drawn with hands during a Reiki session.

All power to the wonderful symbol of daily ko myo, which is also the master symbol. This is responsible for bringing nourishment and enlightenment to the body. Therefore, this is also known as the holiest symbol of Reiki. It brings the great forces of vibration and provides the awesome transformational power than all the other five symbols of Reiki. The healing powers of dai ko myo consist of the upper chakra by involving the soul in general. Dai ko myo is the representation of empowerment and represents the meaning of 'bringing shining light' in the body. This process of spiritual empowerment through dai ko myo helps in getting closer to God with the help of Reiki practitioners.

Utilization of Dai ko myo

You can utilize different methods to visualize, think, and draw the symbol of dai ko myo for getting it to your third eye. You can meditate with dai ko myo for receiving and nourishing your soul or body. It releases amazing power to help yourself and the world.

On the other hand, if you are thinking to improve your relationship and establish awareness to get better spiritual insight, then dai ko myo is the most significant symbol for you. Utilizing this symbol along with other symbols of Reiki can do wonders for you. Dai ko myo is an excellent way of improving the health of your immune system. Dai ko myo helps in improving the energy flow in your body. It helps in removing blocked particles that could be affecting your immune system. If you are taking any homeopathic medications to improve your health, then considering dai ko myo could enhance your capability to avail from the benefits and improving your well-being.

The Completion Symbol: Raku

Raku is the symbol used during the last stage of a Reiki attunement. The symbol intends to ground the person. Practitioners utilize the symbol once the Reiki treatment is coming to an end. It helps to calm the body and contain the new active Ki within. The lightning bolt symbol is drawn in a downward motion, symbolizing the healing session coming to completion.

Where the Raku symbol originated is unknown. It was not part of the original Usui Reiki. Multiple theories are claiming Raku's origin. Some say it is a Tibetan symbol that was used by a Reiki Master named Iris Ishikuro. They claim that one of her students named Arthur Robertson brought the symbol to the West.

Aside from grounding and sealing the attunement process, the symbol also separates the energy between the master and the student after the attunement process is complete.

This symbol can also be used for healing. It is excellent for removing kidney stones. It is often imagined as a pink laser that can be focused on the area in need of healing. It is also used to get rid of blood clots from the body. A person should always be attuned to this symbol first before using it.

Chapter 25: Reiki Tools

Reiki tool is a holistic alternative treatment practice that involves the use of various tools and resources. Reiki Tools are meant to facilitate the process as well as ensuring that the client or yourself is kept as comfortable as possible throughout the treatment process. Furthermore, some of the tools and resources are also meant to facilitate the creation of the most ideal environment for a typical Reiki treatment. This is because; Reiki treatment is a fairly delicate process that should be handled by uttermost care. This section will discuss one of the common Reiki tools and related resources. Keep in mind that these tools are preferred but not required. Reiki is a practice that can also be done in the comfort of your home and your mind.

Massage Table

Perhaps the most vital tool that must be present in every Reiki treatment room is the massage table. The Massage Table is the area where the client or yourself will lie throughout the Reiki Treatment session. Since the amount of time that a client is expected on the table can be quite long, it is important to take several measures to ensure that the table is ideal for the treatment. First and foremost, the table should be as comfortable as possible. In light of this fact, you should consider using extra padding for the top surface to maximize the client or yourself comfort. Secondly, the table should also have strong support to accommodate clients or your own of different weights and sizes. Finally, the color of the table should be bright enough and one that resonates with the overall setting of the room.

However, if you are studying Reiki to heal yourself and/or your friends or family, you can always use the couch, the floor, or the bed for your practices. If it will become something continuous, make sure that you pick a sacred spot within your house that will continue to be used for your reiki practices. That way, the Reiki energy will always be floating within the room.

Reiki Pendulum

A special pendulum should be used in conducting the Reiki treatment process. The pendulum can be used as a diagnostic tool when analyzing the energy levels in the body. The Reiki pendulum must be infused with universal healing energy to make it an appropriate device for treatment. A typical Reiki Pendulum can consist of a charged crystal suspended by a string that is equally charged.

Reiki Symbol Stones

Reiki Symbol Stones are special stones that are used in the Reiki treatment process. The stones contain several images that are the cornerstone of Reiki treatment and healing. There is a stone for the Master Symbol, one for the Power Symbol, Harmony Symbol, and finally, a stone containing the Completion Symbol. The Reiki Symbol Stones can be used at various points during the treatment session to ensure that there is maximum energy channeled to the client or yourself while at the same time, establish the appropriate connection with external forces.

Reiki Treatment Cards

Just as is the case with the stones, Reiki treatment can also be enhanced with the use of special cards with each card having a specific role in the process. For instance, the set of cards contains one that is designated as the listening card. This card is meant to enable the client or yourself to listen to their internal rhythm and connect with a force higher than them. Similarly, there is another card referred to as the *Freshen up Card*. The second card is vital in facilitating body purification making it easy for the client or yourself to rejuvenate and regain lost energy.

Timer or Stop Watch

Reiki is a rather precise practice that involves subjecting the client or yourself to different types of treatment meant to handle specific ailments that the person is having. Each treatment is precisely timed, and thus, it is important to know when to switch from one treatment position to another. For instance, the first position treatment that involves cupping the client's or your face with your arms must take place for a specific period before switching to the second position which is the sides of the head. A timer or stopwatch can be set for each treatment position to ensure that the practitioner can spend adequate time on each treatment. The timer will, therefore, enhance the overall effectiveness of the treatment.

Reiki Energy Pendant

The Reiki Energy Pendant is essential in enabling the practitioner to invoke the much-needed Universal Life Force that is the basis of any form of Reiki treatment. The Pendant is worn by the Reiki Practitioner as a symbol of power and energy.

Reiki Symbol Poster

Despite the emphasis on bright colors, it is important to ensure that the treatment room is not an entirely dull affair. You should have some appropriate fittings and even literature that help your clients or yourself connect with the treatment. The Reiki Treatment Poster is perhaps one of the most commonly used tools or resources to make the Room appealing to the client or yourself. It is a poster that can be placed on the wall and it contains the images of several Reiki Symbols. You can get a good artist to make you a nice poster with unique bright colors that will improve the overall aesthetics of the treatment room.

Reiki CD

Having some audio material playing on a CD player is also very important during the treatment session. The audio CD contains a lot of information that can enlighten and empower the client or yourself throughout the treatment process. The Reiki Treatment CD is even more effective than the literature material such as Magazines since the client or yourself can listen to it at all times, even while concentrating on something else. All in all, several tools must be used in every Reiki treatment session. The overall effectiveness of any treatment session will depend largely on the availability of all these tools that each play a unique role in ensuring the entire treatment process is indeed a success. You can also consider putting on some soft and light melody in the background to help you focus more.

Chapter 26: Reiki Body Energy

Everything is about energy, which means that healing also ultimately involves energy. In Reiki, energy helps promote healing through enhancing the flow of energy and correcting any disturbances that occur in the "human energy field," also called the aura. This aura permeates the body and surrounds it. When the body experiences the flow of energy, the body will have the capacity to heal by itself.

Energy healing works on the basis that your body is made up of various patterns of energy. When you work directly with body energy, you will influence the mental, physical, and emotional level. Using energy healing in Reiki is seen to be holistic.

This is why it is vital that when your body or mind experiences disturbances, everyone wants to address these levels. However, energy healing doesn't work on its own; rather, it supports other healing methods that we use in daily life. Reiki healing focuses on the energy of which your body, mind, and emotions are made up of.

At the center of the human field are seven primary chakras that are supported by thousands of other smaller meridians and chakras. The seven chakras are placed vertically along your spinal column, and it begins on the pelvic floor. The first one is the Root chakra that is at the level of the pelvic bone, and the one at the top is the Crown chakra. Each of the chakras works as its own transmitter as well as the recipient of the energy. When the chakra receives the energy, it will direct it to corresponding organs as well as the endocrine system within the body.

The Energetic Bodies

In addition to the chakra, the human body uses the human energy field to make it work perfectly. The energy field is made up of smaller energetic bodies, which include the mental, spiritual, etheric, emotional, and physical bodies. All these allow you to relate with and experience the environment in different aspects.

When all the chakras and energy bodies are in harmony and are working well together, you will be full of vitality and have a sense of wellness. On the other hand, when the energy centers are not balanced, you will become sluggish, and you will experience confusion, fatigue, and illness at all times. You need to work with a healing practice that can identify the problem areas. He will do so to release the blockages then create a positive flow of energy in the body so that he can make you heal. Healing can happen immediately, or it can take time.

The 5 Layers of the Human Energy Field

The human energy field is composed of 5 layers that we explore below:

Physical Energy

This is the layer that we look at to be the physical part of ourselves. Although we look at the body as a package that consists of the skin, flesh, bones, and organs, they also have energy, similar to the other layers of the body that you can't see, or you cannot sense such as the mind.

Etheric

This word is derived from the word "ether," – which is a layer that sits from one quarter to one half of an inch, but not any more than an inch, from the location of the physical body. The practitioners that have sensed this body describe it as a gray feeling. It is like a spider web, and it can stretch, and it is usually seen as the blueprint of the physical layer.

Emotional Energy

This is the third layer from the outside. It is at the center of all the five layers that we have looked at. The emotional layer is the layer where fears and feelings reside. It can be very volatile when we have emotions. It comes into play whether you are experiencing both low and high emotions.

Mental Energy

This is the layer where our ideas and other emotions spring from. It also forms the store from which the belief system gets stored. This is the space where our thoughts are stored then sorted out, and it is where people store their truths or any perceptions that are based on experiences.

Spiritual Energy

This is the final layer, where higher awareness and consciousness is stored. It is the layer where our past lives are tied as well as the universal consciousness that is common to all people.

Chapter 27: Reiki Meditation

Meditation may seem very complicated or difficult to do, which pushes people away from ever giving it a try. In reality, it is one of the easiest things to begin doing, although true greatness comes with practice and patience. At its core, meditation is simply a process in which you sit with yourself and use various techniques and tools to focus the mind and bring about a sense of calm and peace.

Through sitting with yourself, often in silence, you allow yourself a moment to disconnect from the hectic world around you and to really focus on your

thoughts and feelings. You can see what is stressing you out, what is hurting, what emotions you are overwhelmed by, and what persistent thoughts are attacking your mind. As you allow all of this to flow in, you acknowledge that it exists, and then you simply let it go from your mind, body, and soul.

Learning how to meditate is easy and accessible to anyone who would like to try it, although being able to engage in it for long periods does take practice. We are so used to our minds constantly being stimulated and engaged that it can be difficult to motivate ourselves to simply sit and exist.

Why is Meditation Fundamental to Reiki?

Meditation is a core aspect of Reiki because it allows both the practitioner and the client to get in touch with their energy and experience. Most Reiki practitioners will engage in a quick form of meditation before beginning any session, and they will also often use meditation in their day to day life. Meditation allows us to connect with ourselves, but it also welcomes divine energy into us. It can allow us to understand a higher truth, but it can also calm our minds and prepare them for any healing that is about to come our way.

Meditation is all about transformation, and it is through the process of meditating that we participate in transforming our lives and our experiences. We begin to have a grasp on our minds, and instead of being controlled by our thoughts, we learn to control them. You can learn how to replace anger with compassion, sadness with gratefulness, and anxiety with excitement. You will energize yourself, learn to truly love yourself, and ultimately be comfortable within your truth.

When you pair these benefits with Reiki, you are given a practitioner who is more attune and more aware. They not only understand the divine energy, but they also understand their energy and how it functions in their bodies. They can make the practitioner more at peace and clear their mind of their problems before they work with a client. By purifying themselves through meditation, Reiki healers can offer more pure healing, as there is no risk of transferring their negative energy onto someone else.

Even if you are not a practitioner, meditation can be used in conjunction with your Reiki treatments to continue the benefits that were seen in the session. Reiki can help heal you at the moment, but it is up to you to maintain that, and through meditation, you can tap into that healing energy and feel it working inside of you.

If your mind is constantly talking to you, give it a break, and try meditation. Learn to thrive inside the silence, and welcome the break from the fast-paced world that we live in. The only true way to achieve ultimate inner peace is by incorporating meditation into your everyday routine. You will gain real control over your mind and thoughts, experience a deeper calmness and mental clarity, and be more in touch with the spiritual energy that runs throughout you.

And meditation is not simply a spiritual technique, but rather something that is backed and endorsed by science and medical professionals. Constant stress is very harmful to us, and if we don't find ways to cope with and master that stress, then we can end up sick or worse. Meditation is great for removing that stress from our lives, as well as teaching us better coping strategies and making us realize that we don't have to succumb to the stress but rather that we can transform it into something positive.

When Dr. Mikao Usui came to understand Reiki, he learned that simply healing a person's energy wasn't enough to create long term change. Instead, after encountering individuals whose bodies he had healed and seeing they were still struggling, he understood that healing the mind was the second piece of the equation. This is why Reiki and meditation are so closely linked, for true healing only comes when all parts of us are at peace.

Learning How to Meditate

When you first start out learning to meditate, you must be patient with yourself as well as the process. Most of us are not accustomed to sitting still in silence with nothing to distract us, and that is one of the many excuses people use as to why they cannot meditate. Some of the common excuses also include:

- I don't enough time to meditate

- Meditation won't work for me

- My brain refuses to shut off

- I'm uncomfortable with silence

- I get bored too easily

- I get too distracted by other things

- I can't stick with it

- I'm not doing it right

- I don't want to be alone with my thoughts

But in reality, none of these excuses are valid ones, because all of them can be combated through meditation. Let's break a few of the excuses and see why meditation is beneficial instead of something to be avoided.

"I Don't Have Enough Time to Meditate"

We all lead busy lives, where we most likely work or go to school as well as having family and household commitments on top of it. Adding in meditation may seem like an impossible task, as there simply isn't enough time in the day for everything. But meditation doesn't need to take long, as it can be done anywhere at any time. From quick 5-minute sessions, to longer 30-minute ones, these are all easy to fit into the day if you want to. Maybe you wake up 15 minutes earlier so you can meditate before your shower. Or maybe you take 15 minutes before bed to just sit quietly and practice. No matter when you choose to do it, it still leaves you 23 hours and 45 minutes each day for everything else.

"Meditation Won't Work for Me"

There isn't anyone on this planet that meditation doesn't work for, and that is because it isn't some crazy concept or spiritual activity that requires special education or a certain belief system. Instead, all it is giving yourself a moment to relax and exist without having to do anything else. Even if all you do is sit quietly and breathe, you're automatically reducing your stress levels and calming your mind without any extra effort. By the time the 15 minutes are up, you will feel relaxed whether or not you want to.

"I Get Bored Too Easily"

This is a pretty valid excuse, but not in the sense that it should prevent you from meditating. If you get bored so easily that you cannot go 15 minutes without being distracted, then you could benefit from meditation even more so. With social media and television and all of the gadgets we interact with, there is almost no time in the day where our brains aren't stimulated and distracted. But this prevents us from spending time alone with ourselves and getting to know our minds on a personal level. Instead of shying away from boredom, embrace it. After a while, you will come to love your personal, quiet time, and instead of being bored, you will simply be calm.

"I Don't Know How to Do It, and I Can't Do It Right"

There is no right or wrong way to meditate, only suggestions, guidance, and various techniques. When we break meditation down to its basics, we see that it simply, you spending time with you. You can do it sitting, standing, or lying down and you can do it for as little or as long as you like. You can play music in the background, follow a guided tutorial, or sit and think of nothing at all. You may think about various things, you make become distracted, you may feel bored, you may be completely absorbed in it, or you may just focus on your breathing. All of this is fine, normal, and part of the meditation process.

So, if we remove these excuses from our minds, what are we left with? How do we begin meditation, and how exactly do we learn to do it? Follow these steps to try meditation for the first time:

1. Find a time in the day where you can set aside five-minutes without being interrupted

2. Go somewhere quiet where you won't be bothered by anyone, such as your bedroom

3. Sit comfortably, or lay down, and then set a five minute timer

4. Close your eyes and begin breathing normally

5. As you breathe, begin focusing on your breath and feel each inhale and exhale and how it affects the body

6. If you begin to think of something else, simply return your mind to your breath

7. When the timer goes off, you are done

And that is all there is to it. This is meditation at its simplest form, and there is no need to get extravagant or make it into something more complicated than it is. As you get accustomed to doing five minutes a day, you can start to increase the time. Move to ten, fifteen, and even thirty-minute sessions. So long as it is helping you, then you are doing it correctly.

Once you feel accomplished with the very basics of meditation, there are numerous variations that you can try to unlock different parts of your mind. Next, we will look at different meditations, how to do them, and what the benefits are of each.

Different Meditations to Try

We know that meditation can offer numerous health benefits, but did you know that different meditations are depending on what you are trying to achieve? Some people go their entire lives only doing breathing meditation, and if that works for them, then it is perfect. But others find that breathing meditation doesn't go deep enough, or they enjoy variety, and so they seek out other techniques to satisfy these needs. Let's look at some of the various ways in which we can meditate to benefit our mind, body, and spirit.

Concentration Meditation

The basic meditation is a form of concentration meditation, but it is only one version of many. This technique is used to develop our concentration skills, and to give yourself a focal point in case you find yourself getting distracted during your practice. Instead of simply focusing on the breath, you can choose to focus on anything that you like. Maybe you play a mantra or music, maybe you light a candle and watch the flame, maybe you hold a crystal in your hand and focus on that, or maybe you identify one of the chakras and keep that in your mind's eye. Whatever it is you choose, make sure it has meaning to you and is the subject of that meditation. Don't pick a dirty sock on the floor, unless you are trying to manifest the willpower to keep your room clean. Meditation is always about intention, so find what you are attending to achieve, and every time your mind wanders, bring it back to that focal point.

Mindfulness Meditation

This type of meditation is quite different, as you no longer have a focal point, such as the breath. Before, when the mind would wander, you would bring it back to the center, but now we want to encourage the mind to wander. In mindfulness meditation, the point is to be mindful of our thoughts and feelings and to let them float across our minds. As each thought comes you will acknowledge it, and then let it drift past as a new thought or emotion fills you. The purpose of this is to begin to understand how we think and feel, and to detect the patterns in our mind. There is no judgment on your part or even any involvement, you simply are observing how your mind works.

Over time you will learn how you think, why you think that way, and be better equipped to handle your thoughts and take control of your mind.

Reiki Zen Meditation

Coming back to having a sort of focal point, this type of meditation is all about your Chi, or life energy. As you get into a meditative state, you want to seek out and find the energy that is flowing through your center. Once you can find and feel it, expand your experience, and notice how that energy pulsates out from the center and through your entire body. Trace the course of that energy as it moves from chakra to chakra, limb to limb, and simply allow it to envelop you. There is no need to use it as a focal point, but instead, simply acknowledge it and enjoy it.

The Center Finger Technique

Sometimes having a mental focal point isn't enough, and our minds will wander too far without us noticing and bringing them back to the center. Before you realize it, the timer is going off, and you have spent the last five minutes thinking all about what you are going to get to the grocery store later. To combat this, the center finger technique uses a physical feeling to pull your mind back and prevent it from wandering off. To do this, bring your fingertips together so that each one of the hands is touching its counterpart on the right hand. Now, focus completely on the middle fingers and the sensation of them pressed together. When your mind starts to wander, keep pressing the fingers together so that the physical pressure is enough to make your mind take notice.

Reiki Specific Meditation

During your Reiki education, you will be taught various forms of meditation that incorporate the healing hand movements with the focus of the mind. To practice these, however, you need to be taught by a Master so that they can show you the proper technique and so that they may attune you with the energy needed to conduct a session properly. Two of the most common Reiki specific meditations are:

- Joshin Kokyu Ho (Level 1)

- Hatsurei Ho (Level 2)

While you will not be able to learn these without taking the corresponding classes, you can incorporate some of the hand positions in your regular meditative practice. The most common hand position that people use is called "Gassho," and it simply involves bringing the hands into a prayer position and placing them against your chest. This helps to bring energy into your heart chakra, and also helps focus and calm the mind. Adding this to your meditation can connect you to a higher focus, create added stillness, and increase our intuitive nature.

These are only a handful of the various techniques that are available to you, and once you have mastered the basics, then it is encouraged that you explore all of the different options available. If you are having trouble getting started, then there are also plenty of guided meditations that you can use by playing while you meditate. Whatever feels best for you, is what you should do.

Chapter 28: How to Learn Reiki

Welcome to the practical aspect of our journey. Now that you know the theoretical points of the subject matter, we will take you through a series of steps that you can utilize to learn how to practice Reiki.

There are higher levels of universal energy. We may not be able to take on all of them because it requires a lot of training, but what you will receive here is a solid foundation and a good start for your Reiki practice.

The system that you will be exposed to is the same one used by Dr. Mikao Usui. Through this system, you will experience amazing improvements in your personal, emotional, and spiritual well-being. You can also observe changes in the lives of the people you share this process with. Hence, it is a great way to introduce Reiki into your relationships.

The variants of Reiki have been used worldwide by holy men, healers, and Rishis. They used to believe that everything in the world was made up of vibrational energy. The system also works because it improves the energetic make-up of the body, which makes it possible for the root causes of the problem to be handled.

When you heal with Reiki, three things can happen to you:

1. Your body's energetic blueprints are improved.

2. Your body adopts the new state causing much healing.

3. You can tap into the universal energy flow.

The first step that you can take towards the mastery of Reiki is your choice to focus on the entirety of your system while inviting the grace to heal, clear all the mental barriers in your head, and believe in the efficacy of the steps that will be shared below.

You must read everything carefully because you can use them to apply Reiki healing into your life.

Steps for Learning Reiki

Step 1: Reiki Energy

Universal energy is the building block for reality, and it is everywhere. It explains the discovery made by scientists that the universal energy field genuinely exists all around us. Reiki healers tap into this energy pool and then channel it to provide life-changing benefits for us and their patients.

For you to tap into the universal energy, your consciousness needs to increase to a higher level where you can tune yourself into the realities that exist beyond the physical world — a realm of emotions, love, thoughts, and heightened spirituality.

Some people are always skeptical of this first step because they erroneously believe that they don't have the "gift" to form this secure connection with the energy source. Well, those Reiki masters who have access to the highest forms dedicated their lives to studying and practicing. If you have the diligence and determination to settle with each step and practice for a long time, you will surely have a success story to tell. But first, you must handle this initial stage before perfecting the others.

Step #1 entails that you must make a connection with the universal energy, which has a consciousness. To begin this process, you must clear your mind and ask for permission to be used as a healing channel first.

Speak the Reiki invocation out loud or think about it. The words have to be in line with your beliefs. You can say simple words, such as "I ask the power and wisdom of universal energy to allow me to become a channel for infinite love and healing..."

The invocation above is just an example. You can create yours, but the point is that you need to ask the universal energy for its help so that it can channel its gift to you. By acknowledging that you need assistance, you will be giving up any claim you may have had in the past to the power of your own.

Next, you need to visualize the energy entering your palms. Visualization is so powerful because it allows you to connect with the energy (you will observe as we make progress that visualization cuts across almost all the steps). Numerous visualization processes will help you connect with universal energy, but you can utilize the one that's known as INFINITE LIGHT:

- Close your eyes and breathe in.

- Exhale and visualize the beams of white energy all around you.

- Feel the energy from its infinite field.

- Inhale and when you exhale this time focus on your palms while using your will to call on the light around you.

- Visualize the light entering your body and flowing into your palms.

- Feel your palms as they radiate energy.

The most critical part of this step isn't getting every aspect of it right but feeling the energy, and this is what a lot of people haven't got right. By practicing the concept of universal energy visualization, you will be able to feel and sense it all around you.

When you visualize the connection taking place, you will be focused on your will that makes the link happen and then your thoughts, willpower and everything else that comes in contact with this energy flow will cause the Reiki reality to take shape.

You have a grasp on how to get in touch with universal energy. The next step will teach you how to detect negative energy present in your body.

Step 2: Aura scan

One of the beautiful things about Second Degree Reiki is the ability to scan or sense aura. This is one of the reasons why I particularly don't recommend that anyone who just receives Reiki begins to heal everyone they meet. When you have attained your Second-Degree attunement, you can now scan your client's body using the palm of your hand to determine what part needs healing by scanning their energy field. You would also be able to scan the client's healing aura, which would enhance the client's ability to receive the healing.

To do this, have your client lay down flat. Rub your hands together for about 15 seconds to awaken them. As you rub them together, as Reiki to show you the areas that need healing. Close your eyes and gently, with your non-dominant hand, place your hand above the body (at about 15cm-20cm). Start at the head and very slowly make your way down the body. You can move in both directions to each shoulder just make sure you keep your hands at the same distance you began with.

As you do this often, Reiki will lead you into knowing what each sensation you feel means. These sensations will vary from person to person but trust Reiki to guide you in this. Sometimes you may feel the distortions as slight heat, pressure, coldness and sometimes it may a pulling on your hand. Trust Reiki, you would be guided to the right spot – that place that needs attention.

Once you have found the area that needs attention, you could deal with it directly or keep a mental note of that area as you continue scanning the body for other affected areas. To treat that area, keep your palms facing downwards and using both hands, channel Reiki into that spot until you feel the flow on Reiki subsiding.

As you practice this, you may notice a few changes. One major thing many notice is their heightened sensitivity and intuition. They can know the cause of the problem and what to do to facilitate the healing process. After the healing session, speak to the client with love and care and tell the client what they can do to avoid being in the same position again. It is not advisable to give medical advice if you are not a medical doctor so limit the recommendations you make.

Step 3: Set Your Intention

Setting your intention is as simple as stating what you want. By knowing what blockages or disruptions you are experiencing, you can trace this back to the root problem. By using a targeted approach and directing Reiki energy, you can heal specific ailments. Some examples of problems commonly healed during a Reiki session include:

- Achieving Spiritual Balance

- Reduction of Pain

- Reduced Stress

- Promote Healing of Trauma

- Promote Healing of Obesity

- Restoration of Relationships

- Improved Sleep

- Connect to a Higher Purpose

- Ability to Overcome Addiction

- Increased Positivity in Emotional State

You can think of your intention as a message. You are communicating with the aura, whether your own or another person's. This communication states your desired outcome and by directing your energy to that outcome, it strengthens the results. For your message to be heard, it must be clear and strong. As the Universe grants this request, the aura reflects that intention and heals the body and/or mind.

Setting your intention can be greatly improved by using Reiki techniques in combination with visualization. As you are focusing on your intention, visualize the outcome. Visualize how the outcome will change your life. Feel yourself becoming happier and focusing on more positive things, like going out dancing with your friends or having more time to spend with your significant other. Focus on the pain going away or on resolving whatever is holding you back.

For visualization to work, it must be incredibly vivid. Imagine how you would feel if you intended to come true. Feel the relief of pain, whether emotional or physical. Imagine how you would look and feel if you were able to overcome your weight loss struggles or how refreshed and invigorated you would feel if you were able to get a full night of sleep. If you are healing someone else, visualize the changes that may come about and how they would feel if you were able to heal them. Combining visualization with setting your intention can have profound benefits and increase your Reiki healing power.

Step 4: Reiki Symbols Activation

Reiki symbols are symbols that you create with your hands that improve your ability to heal, transmit energy, and more. There are several symbols commonly used during Reiki, depending on your intended purpose and whether you are practicing on yourself or someone else.

To learn how to tap into Reiki power on a deeper level, it can be helpful to learn these symbols. While they will be described here, it would be impossible to describe how to do them in writing. You can find tutorials, charts, and other guides online that will help you with activating Reiki symbols the proper way. You could also take a class or speak with a Reiki teacher about learning these symbols. The most commonly used Reiki symbols include:

- Cho Ku Rei (Power Symbol) - The power symbol can amplify many things. It is commonly used at the beginning of a Reiki session to help amplify healing energy, as well as provide spiritual protection that people need when they are connecting to the aura of others to heal them. It may also be used to empower other symbols or infuse food with energy.

- Hon Sha Ze Sho Nen (Distance Symbol) - This symbol is about enlightenment, peace, and unification. As it unifies, healers typically use it when they are healing someone across a distance. It can also be used to send attunements across distances, allowing people to open their chakras and be receptive to the wholesome, healing energy of the Universe.

- Sei He Ki (Mental & Emotional Reiki Symbol) - This symbol is ideal when you are trying to heal yourself (or someone else) mentally or emotionally. It is attuned to the energies of love and wellbeing in the universe. Not only does it create a calmer mental state, but it may also be used to help someone release negative energies or remove addictions.

- Dai KO Myo (Master Symbol) - As the name suggests, the Master Symbol is the most powerful in Reiki. Often, it is only Reiki Masters that can connect with this symbol. It is used to create wondrous life changes, to heal the soul, and to relieve the body of disease and illness in the aura.

Step 5: Guiding the Energy

Now, this fifth step is a culmination of all the other steps you read through up to this point. You may know that, as a healer, your hands can be positioned correctly to guide energy into the aura and chakras that need healing.

Despite that, the hand positions will not work by themselves. You need to manifest the healing by creating a secure connection with steps 1 to 4.

These steps, when used together, lay the foundation for your healing session and enable you to channel energy and use it for the right purpose. With the hand positions alone and a weak energy connection, you may be able to get a small amount of healing, but you can get so much more combining all the steps. You can harness the potential that lies within Reiki and allow it to manifest the changes you desire in your well-being.

So, this is how you can become better with Reiki: by using the system created by these steps to aid the realization of your healing intention. After laying the right foundation, you can then go further with aura cleansing, reiki breath, chakra balancing, etc.

With step 3, you set your healing intentions and formal message that is sent to your aura. This message details the kind of positive changes you want to see, and you transmit it by guiding the universal energy to your will.

While on the process, if you discover other issues while going about your aura scan, repeat steps 3 to 6 until the issues are taken off.

Now, you are going to learn how to close your Reiki connection safely with the next step.

Step 6: Closing the Connection

Reiki sessions shouldn't end without you taking this step. Reiki masters say that while they work with patients, they absorb the negative emotions of the patient and feel it lodged in their system.

You should ensure that the emotions are released from your body so that you can continue to enjoy a heightened state of energy. Again, you will have to rely on visualization to get this done by visualizing the energies being pulled out of your body through your palms and freeing your system.

Wash your hands afterward in cold water, so they are purified and ensure that all residual energies are out entirely. Also, ensure that you are not in any way attached to the healing session emotionally. Believe that the energy is gone and take the last step below.

Step 7: Expand Your Energy Channels

Now, you have to consistently increase the channeling of your energy in between sessions so that your healing ability can be better in terms of effectiveness. This way, you will also be able to perform advanced techniques and progress to higher Reiki levels.

So, how can you expand your energy channels?

Firstly, you can utilize Ki exercises, which are meditations that you can practice by cycling energy through your system. These exercises open your chakras to allow more universal energy to get into your body and channeled towards healing.

Secondly, you can use attunements, which help you become harmonious with something. It is the primary way of advancing from the level of Reiki you are already into another one. Attunement is like a radio dial; you only get a station when you turn into its frequency.

Most people can practice the primary forms of Reiki, so you need these exercises to be able to go over and beyond the fundamental level.

There will never be a better time to discover true happiness that happens as a result of the alignment you attain with your higher self. You know yourself best, you know the challenges you encounter daily, so if you want to experience some peace, now is the time to get on with Reiki healing.

You can use the ideas proffered in this chapter to embark on the most profound healing experience that will enable you to define your existence and live to your most accurate potentials.

Still, how does a Reiki session work? Do you know all about the positions of the hand and how distant Reiki treatment is done?

Chapter 29: Beginner's Reiki Meditation Session

How to Create the Best Self-Reiki Practice

Now that you have learned the various levels of Reiki healing, it is time to get into the swing of things. You will find it easier to run the life the way it needs to be run, and you will be able to enjoy your tasks each day. However, you need to come up with the right schedule so that you can incorporate Reiki into your daily routine. The good thing is that all you need to enjoy Reiki self-healing is yourself – nothing else. Here are a few tips to get you running:

Start Small

For you to enjoy the benefits of Reiki, you should start small. You might choose to do 30 minutes a day after the first meeting with the practitioner, but you will find this to be hard. Our busy lives don't allow us to do this. Make sure you set a time duration that you can stick to. If you choose to do 10 minutes a day, then be it. If you feel you can only handle 5 minutes, then go for it. Just make sure you start small then build upon what you have started. Gradually build up the time, and soon, you will be able to do more.

Make it a Daily Routine

The more consistent you are to self-healing practices, the easier it will be for you. Make sure you are consistent in all you do and believe in what you are doing to make sure you achieve your goals. Consistent daily sessions will give you a better result than long term sporadic sessions. Just the way you set a routine for going to the gym, you will find that setting a specific time of day for you to perform the self-practice will work better than if you decide to do things anytime you feel like. You will also find that getting a particular spot in the house of the task will make it ideal for you. Set up the spot in the same space each day so that you remember that you have a task to do. Early in the morning or late in the evening after work are the best times to handle the Reiki.

Know why you are Into Reiki

You need to understand why you took up Reiki in the first place. Was it for relaxation, was it for healing? Was it to recover? Well, all in all, you need to understand the benefits that you stand to gain before you start doing Reiki. Remember what you felt in the first session before you get into it. Mae sure you relate to the past successes so that you can use them for the present motivations. Imagine what you wish to achieve, then see what Reiki has done for you so far, then use this motivation to see how you will feel later on if you do the same routine. Make sure you connect to your benefits at all times so that you have a goal in mind at all times.

Understand the Limitations

When you try to create the perfect self-practice, you might have to remind yourself why you decided to go for Reiki in the first instance. Remind yourself of the various consequences that might happen when you fail to do Reiki. For instance, your worry might grow. Try to know the reasons why you took up Reiki in the first place and what you will lose if you give it up.

Use a Guide

You need to have a guided meditation so that you don't get distracted at all. Many times our minds are too busy to focus on the meditation practice, but with guided meditation, you will be able to keep your mind on many things. You can also set a timer so that it goes off in a few minutes so that you can move to the next position. You can also use mantras so that you can focus your mind on a single object.

Lower Expectations

What are your expectations when you get into a session? Are you out to improve the existing session or you just want to get something out of it? Either way, you need to come up with goals and make sure you follow them to the latter. Many people think that they have their goals well set out only to discover later that they don't have anything.

Reiki on the Go

You don't have to be in a single position to enjoy Reiki. What you need to know is that you can perform Reiki whenever and wherever you can. People have gone to the extent of performing healing sessions on a plane, or deep in the mountains. Either way, they get the same feeling that they get when they are in a setup position. The aim of self-healing is not to show anything rather to be at peace with ourselves.

Believe You Can

Anyone can learn the basics of Reiki and use them to make their life easier. Regardless of age, personality, and history, you can still make sense of Reiki. However, many people think that they can't do it, and this is why they never even try to.

Chapter 30: Advanced Reiki meditation session

Emotional Healing Reiki Healing Meditation

Find a comfortable and safe place in your home to perform the self-treatment. It can be your bedroom, or living room, wherever you seem comfortable. Whichever space you pick, you will have to use it continuously if possible. These treatments can be performed on a bed, the floor, and the sofa while lying down or sitting in a chair if you'd like. Lock your doors, turn your phone on silent, and ask to be not disturbed during this time. It is recommended that you are alone during these self-treatments unless someone that you require to have someone in the room to make you feel safe and secure then you are welcome to bring them along. Just ask them to not speak or disturb you in any way.

When making your environment quiet and comforting, you can choose to play some music, not the kind that has lyrics; otherwise, you will find yourself singing along and distracted. Pick any instrumental music or meditational music which is known to be quite relaxing. Sounds have a specific effect on our brain. They have the power to stimulate relaxation chemicals or brainpower chemicals, all depending on what you hear.

When you feel as if you are ready to start your Reiki self-treatment, change into some comfortable loose clothes, go to your desired space where you will be performing the treatment, turn on your music for further relaxation, and take off your shoes and socks. Many practitioners and receivers can't relax with shoes and socks on. If you decide to lay down, place one pillow underneath your head while placing another pillow, rolled-up preferably, under your knees. If you'd like, you can also place a blanket on top of you for comfort and warmth throughout the treatment.

When balancing a specific element, you must first look at what particular space they are associated with. Since in this practice, we are focusing on water, this element is associated with ponds, rivers, oceans, and waterfalls. It will be easier for you to go to any of those destinations to achieve a balance within the water element. But you can also choose to stay at home. There is water within you; in fact, seventy percent of the body is made out of water. You should also consider taking a bowl or cup of water and placing it beside you if you are lying down or in front of you if you are sitting up. You should also consider doing this treatment after you've gone for a swim or taken a shower when your hair is wet, it will bring better results.

Start by drinking some water before filling up the cup or bowl with water, preferably river or ocean water, but tap will do fine. Get yourself comfortable, either sitting up or lying down. Begin to close your eyes slowly, as if you are falling asleep. Take a deep breath in, hold it for a second or two before exhaling it slowly, pulling it for a second or two. Continue to breathe deeply for a couple of minutes, try to relax your body the best that you can. Get into the habit of deep breathing. Make a mental reminder through this treatment that Reiki is being used for the greater and higher good. If your mind and thoughts slip away during the breathing exercise, simply draw the attention back to the way your chest rises and falls or the way you breathe in and out.

Somewhere in the middle of your breathing exercise, say your Reiki prayer in your head or out loud if you wish. Ask to channel the Reiki energy, ask for guidance throughout the treatment, ask for the Reiki energy to resurface within your body, and set your intentions to heal the water element within your body and your mind. Call out to the element of water, ask it to help guide you through this session.

You can use the Power symbol and then the Mental/Emotional symbol by calling out their names three times and visualizing their symbol in your head. Repeat the words Choku Rei (Cho-Koo-Ray), the Power symbol, call out the name three times. Take some time to visualize the symbol in your head or draw it in the air in front of you. Set the right intention for the Power symbol, such as asking to enhance the energy and power of this treatment. Then repeat the words Sei He Ki (Say-Hay-Key), the Mental/Emotional symbol, call out the name three times. Take some time to visualize the symbol in your head or draw it in the air in front of you, besides the Power symbol. Set the right intention for the Mental/Emotional symbol such as asking to heal and balance the water element which represents your mind.

Go back to breathing deeply; make sure your mind is clear while you focus on breathing. After a couple of minutes of the breathing exercise, begin to visualize a lake, the ocean, or the pond. Take in the many details of your scenery. If you are physically present at that destination, then listen to the water but still make sure to visualize it in your head making you feel as if your eyes are open. The Heart and the Sacral chakras are mainly related to this treatment, but you can choose to give Reiki to all the other chakras since the water element is spread through your body within your veins.

If the lake or whatever place you are visualizing, imagine it as the core of the water element. Think of this water element and this big and round pond. Imagine yourself walking towards it, and carefully going in until the water is up to your waist. Visualize your body falling back, floating on the water, and feeling as light as a feather. Think of all your emotions coming in tune with the water. This water is balanced while your emotions and the water within you is not, so let the balanced water surround your body as you take a deep breath in. Feel tingling sensations throughout your body as both the energy radiating from you and the balanced water come in touch. Visualize the positive energy filling your entire body; you are swimming in a pond of positivity and emotional balance. It's so overwhelming that it influences the imbalance within your mind.

Imagine your anxiety fading into the water; let the water suck out all of your negative emotions, fears, and doubts. Let this water cleanse your whole being. All the negative feelings are replacing with the flow of Reiki energy, now that the negativity is gone, you can feel the flow of Reiki more precisely as more of the negative emotions leave your body. The water is encouraging the pure energy flow and guides it to your most tense area, which is the mind. Visualize all the negativity leaving your body, replacing it with emotional balance and the feelings of love, gratitude, self-care, and everything good and positive.

Encourage the flow of Reiki throughout your entire body and concentrate on the areas of the Heart chakra, which is located in your heart, and the Sacral chakra, which is located in your lower abdomen, a couple of inches below your belly button. Imagine the feelings of happiness, joy, pleasure, satisfaction, self-respect, love, and abundance fill you up until you become part of the pure water and this pure energy. Feel the Reiki healing your Heart and Sacral chakras, expanding the love capacity and the feelings of safety. The water within you has turned into pure and light energy, intertwining with the water around you.

When you feel as if you have visualized enough and that your mind is healed and any anxiety or negative emotions are all in the past, then you can begin by closing the treatment. Thank the universe or the Higher beings for their guidance. Thank the symbols for helping you balance your emotions and give more power to the treatment. Thank the element of water for being present, helping you through this process, and providing you with a lot of water to drink and use. Thank the Reiki healing energy for being able to give you the power to heal your emotional imbalance.

Finally, open your eyes and breathe normally. Take a minute or two to reflect on the treatment and notice any sensations throughout your body. Compare how you felt at the beginning of the session and the end of the session. Drink the water that you have left in front of or beside you.

Full Physical Body Reiki Healing Meditation

Make sure to get rid of any distractions beforehand. Start off sitting upon the sacred place of your choosing. Your arms should lay right by your sides with the palms on your knees and facing upwards.

Take a deep breath in a while setting an intention for your body to relax. Slowly and gently, close your eyes and start breathing deeply. Inhale and hold the breath for a second and exhale, pulling the breath for another second. This breathing exercise ensures that your body will relax and it also provides you a focus point on something other than your thoughts. Think of nothing, meaning let your mind clear and empty itself as it brings focus on the way your chest rises and falls with each breath you take. If you find your mind drifting away and thinking about something, bring your attention back to the breathing by either paying attention to every time you inhale or exhale or simply to the way the chest rises and falls.

Activate the Power symbol, Choku Rei, by visualizing it hovering right in front of you. Hold the image for a minute while breathing deeply. Since this meditation will be focusing on giving healing to your whole body, you will also need to envision the Master symbol, Dai Ko Myo. Visualize the image of the symbol and hold it in your vision.

In your head, call out to the Universe or the Higher being and ask for guidance. Ask to channel the Reiki energy to be able to heal yourself effectively. Make an intention to help and heal the body and restore it to its natural flow of energy. If you'd like, you can form the Gassho hand position while asking the Universe for guidance.

Allow for the Reiki healing energy to resurface your body, glowing a bright white bulb of light as it takes a form all around your body. Imagine your Reiki resurfacing throughout your body, channeling its energy. Let the Reiki energy be harnessed before setting an intention to center it on the palms of your hand. Imagine and focus on all of the Reiki energy being absorbed by the palms, forming a bright bulb of light.

Take a deep breath and begin by hovering your hands in front of your head. You will feel a strong pull towards the areas that will require your healing once you access the Reiki healing energy. Allow for your auric field to guide you and pull your hands to where you need healing the most as you complete a quick body scan, that involves you hovering both of your hands from the head and making your way to the bottom to your feet, scanning the body in all areas. You will feel some tension, tingling, or a pull towards certain areas within the body.

Follow your intuition when doing a body scan, take a mental note of any areas that you can feel the tension in. Once you reach the end of the body where the feet are, make your way back up towards the head, double-checking if you missed any tension spots. Begin at the top where the head is, hover your hands in the air and imagine the Reiki light reemerging from within your hands and healing that area. Hover the hands in front of your head, do not make any skin-to-skin contact. Let the energy sink in as you slowly move your hands around the area, covering and hovering over each part of the head. From the very crown of the head to the sides and the temples. Make sure to cover all the ground. Allow for your hands to hover for at least thirty seconds before moving on, making its way down to the cheeks, the third eye region, the chin, and the rest of the face.

When you come across the area that possesses tension or something that pulls you in or away from it, then make physical contact with that part of the body. Place your hands on top of that tension, imagine the Reiki healing energy entering deeper and healing that area, releasing any tension, and encouraging the proper flow of Ki. Keep your hands on that area for about two to three minutes to ensure that it is healing before moving on.

Take your time as you move from place to place, once you pass the head, allow for your hands to hover around the throat region, making their way down to the shoulders. When it comes to your arms, use the opposite hand that is getting healed while hovering it over each of the arms. Allow for your hands to hover over your chest, stomach, lower abdomen, making their way to your legs, knees, and finally to your feet. You should spend at least thirty seconds hovering over each area, slowly moving around and making their way down to the bottom of the body.

Once you reach the feet, allow for the process to repeat, but this time, let your hands travel from the feet up to the crown of the chakra, covering and hovering over the tensed areas that you discovered during your quick body scan. Allow your hands to rest on those areas, making skin-to-skin contact for at least two to three minutes before moving on. Imagine cleansing the mind, healing from physical or mental trauma, lifting any tensions, purifying negative feelings, and healing the body.

Once your hands reach the crown, allow them to turn to the back of the body, which might be challenging to cover. Hold your hands over the back of the head, making their way to the back of the neck, the upper back, the lower back, the lower abdomen, and to your feet. Rest your hands at the bottom before repeating the process and moving back to the top of the head while breathing in deeply.

Once you've finished with cleansing the mind, lift your hands and form a Gassho position. Focus on the Completion symbol, Raku, and visualize the symbol in your head to activate it. Set an intention to seal the Reiki healing energy within your body. Thank the Universe or the Higher being for guidance and thank the Reiki energy for being able to give you the power to heal the receiver. Return the Reiki energy and spread it evenly around your body by visualizing your body glowing white before letting that white energy sunk inside.

Take a minute to casually rest and meditate normally, giving some time for the energy to sink in and for your body to heal. Once you are ready, gently open your eyes and lay down. Simply look up while taking another brief minute to reflect on your healing, take in on what you have experienced while the Reiki energy heals your body. Throughout the day, do not push yourself but rather take a break and give some time for your body to heal.

Chapter 31: How to practice Reiki on others

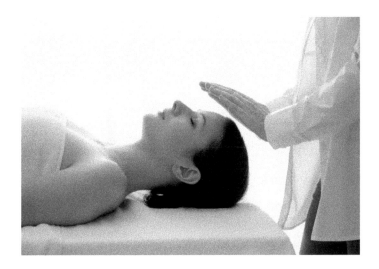

Developing your Reiki Practice

Once you experience the benefits of practicing Reiki on yourself, you'll want to share this practice and the same positive outcome with others.

This can take time to develop and find people who are interested in experiencing the benefits of Reiki, though, with patience and perseverance, you'll find many people are willing to try the benefits of Reiki at least once.

If the experience is positive, they may return for another session.

There are some key factors to keep in mind once you reach a level of Reiki practitioner, and want to share your healing energy with others:

- Gently introduce your new practice to friends, acquaintances, and co-workers.

Keep it light and brief and be open to a variety of questions and feedback. Some people will show skepticism right away, while others will respond with enthusiasm, and others with some interest.

- Receive Reiki treatments from a practitioner to gain a different perspective.

Without analyzing too much, consider the areas of the session that seemed to be most powerful and use this as a guide for your practice.

Keep in mind that what works for you may vary on other people. Relay your experiences to other people and let them know how Reiki made an impact on you.

This anecdotal piece may be what motivates someone to try a session with you!

- Don't think of Reiki as a business but more of a type of service to your community.

While the practice of Reiki is a popular business that can be successful for many practitioners, it is done by building strong connections within your community and avoiding too much business.

Offer one free session for beginners to Reiki and get used to a variety of different responses and opinions on the practice itself.

If there are local Reiki schools or health clinics that may be interested in having someone perform Reiki as a supportive service to patients, this can be an excellent way to become a stronger part of the community.

- Be realistic with expectations.

Some people may expect to be completely healed of an ailment or illness because of Reiki or consider replacing their medicine and doctor's treatment with Reiki.

It's important to advise them, under all circumstances, that they should not substitute their regular treatment for Reiki, as Reiki is meant to complement or support their health, not take the place of medication and other forms of therapy that are medically necessary.

Once people understand the purpose of Reiki and the realistic outcome to expect, this will work in everyone's favor, as they will have a good reason to place their trust in you, for being honest, and know what they can expect as a result.

- If you are looking to practice Reiki as a source of income only, and not for any other reason, it will show in time, and people will discover the lack of insincerity.

Reiki should be practiced by practitioners who have a passion for the treatment, and this will become apparent in how they share their enthusiasm and positivity about the practice.

Reiki is not a technical process and shouldn't be treated as just a novelty item or just a business-making opportunity.

While Reiki can be successful for many people who practice and teach, it must be done with selflessness to be truly valuable and effective.

- If you have a family open and interested in experiencing Reiki treatment, as well as pets, you may want to try different techniques on them and determine which areas of your practice you would like to work on more.

Some people may already have experience with receiving Reiki and can provide some feedback on what works (or has worked) best for them in previous treatment sessions.

This is a good opportunity to become accustomed to practicing Reiki and observing the benefits it provides to others.

Creating a Powerful Reiki Healing Process for Others

When you begin your practice of Reiki on others, you'll want to give each person the best possible experience and benefit they can have during each session.

Setting realistic expectations, is a good foundation for building a trusting relationship.

Even with a high level of energy, you may find that some people don't feel the same sensation, or their experience may differ from what they expect (or you expect).

How can you harness a powerful effect of energy through Reiki for others?

There are some simple, mindful ways to keep your energy levels strong while maintaining good, healthy habits to support your Reiki practice.

Always keep in mind that people will take note of your lifestyle and habits and validate them with the principles of Reiki.

For example, if you smoke or eat unhealthy foods, someone may not be as included to accept an offer for Reiki treatment from you.

While everyone needs to make decisions on how they live, a Reiki practitioner may be viewed in a special light, as they channel the energy that is used for healing, and if they present themselves in a positive way (healthy lifestyle, for example), this will make a great first impression and a good appearance overall.

There are some practical, easy suggestions for creating and maintaining strong energy for healing others:

- Practice self-care, not only by treating yourself to Reiki (by yourself or another practitioner) but also by checking in with your feelings and state of well-being.

This coincides with eating well, getting plenty of movement, exercise, and living a life that supports the principles of Reiki.

- Where you practice Reiki is important: the ambiance of the room and temperature, and the level of comfort.

There should be some options available to choose between sitting or lying down, depending on the comfort level.

The atmosphere should feel calm and soothing, not too clinical or sterile. Choose a temperature that is moderate, not too hot or cool.

A moderate temperature can be adjusted according to preference, which can also create a more positive environment for the practice.

- Some Reiki practitioners use smudging to cleanse and purify the room before practice.

There are various methods for smudging, which is done using a variety of specific herbs.

Some people choose sage, as this is used in certain aboriginal ceremonies, there are variations in the types of herbs and practices, depending on the region and culture.

- Avoid clutter and/or numerous objects in a room where Reiki is practiced.

A room should be as clear and simple as possible, to allow for maximum energy flow and activity.

Too much clutter can be a distraction, even if unintended.

To enhance the function of the space in coordination with Reiki, Feng Shui guidelines on the placement of furniture and items in the room can improve the quality of the energy level.

- Before you practice on someone, prepare with meditation just before their arrival.

This can also be practiced when treating someone remotely, by sending energy to them and allowing them to relax and calm.

In some practices, this is done for Reiki clients on their way to a session, so that they feel at ease just before their treatment begins.

Meditating before they arrive allows the practitioner to harness stronger energy, which can be done with one or more symbols, drawing the energy or power into the room, in preparation for the session.

- The energy transferred by the placement of hands doesn't need any specific wording to work, as long as the energy is harnessed and present during the treatment.

For example, you could carry on a conversation with the client during a session that is completely unrelated to Reiki, and the energy would continue to flow.

To increase or maximize the energy, it's best to avoid distractions, and this includes regular conversation during the treatment.

Make the most of the energy channeling by meditating on it as you guide it with your hands.

In doing this, the recipient of the treatment will appreciate your intent to focus on the energy and making sure it works as best as possible for their benefit.

- Some practitioners choose to pray aloud or internally.

This can be a welcome addition to a Reiki session, and depending on the client, the prayer may incorporate their beliefs or faith, or simply a way to ask for a blessing for the Reiki treatment.

For some people, prayer is something they may want to include, and for others, a silent calm or mantra may be the preference.

- Some practitioners use guides with Reiki, such as crystals, mantras, and/or background music or sound.

This can help create a calm, steady environment, which makes it easier to practice, and allow the client to relax, and benefit fully from the treatment.

Chapter 32: How to practice reiki on animals

Powerful Reiki Healing for Animals and the Benefits

If you have a pet or spend a lot of time with animals, you'll notice how well they thrive from the power of positive energy and happiness.

Animals benefit from Reiki treatments, and this can be powerful in helping pets who have been injured or otherwise can feel peace and less tension from a treatment session.

If you have a cat or dog as a pet, they can receive Reiki treatments for a variety of reasons and outcomes.

Other pets that may benefit from Reiki include birds, and small animals (rabbits, hamsters, Guinea pigs).

They can receive energy during a Reiki session, which can promote their sense of peace and security.

Some of the benefits of Reiki with animals include the following:

• Reiki can strengthen an animal's immune system before they undergo surgery or medical treatment. Some pets are receptive to Reiki in that they heal quickly afterward, and regain their strength within a relatively short time frame.

• Animals with behavioral issues may also improvements with several Reiki treatments. They may become approachable and gentler after just one or two sessions.

- Reiki can animals with and can no longer  help comfort terminal diseases conditions that be treated or improved. Providing them with positive energy through hand placement is a powerful experience and gives them a sense of peace and reduced pain during the process.

- Animals who are feral or otherwise challenging when trying to help them can improve with Reiki treatments.

A frightened squirrel or stray dog may quickly become less worried and scared, and more receptive to people who want to help them

- Large animals, such as horses and elephants, may benefit from the positive effects of Reiki.

Depending on their location and the circumstances, they may be a bit hesitant at first, though with an experienced handler or trainer working with a Reiki practitioner, the animal will calm enough to enjoy the benefits of Reiki and become more likely to enjoy it next time

Relieving pain and discomfort are two major benefits of Reiki practice on animals.

As they become more comfortable and trusting in you, they will become even more receptive to treatment, knowing from before, how pain relief and feeling better will result from every time.

When treating pets with a terminal condition, by giving them positive energy to manage their pain and discomfort, there is also the opportunity to treat their owners in the same way, by helping them cope in advance with the eventual passing if their pet.

Strengthening the bond between pets their owners is a powerful way to help them both develop a sense of trust and connection.

For many people, the idea of bonding well with their pets can take time, depending on the circumstances.

For example, a stray cat or dog may be hesitant to accepting kindness from a stranger, even if they are later adopted and well cared for.

There still may exist a distrust if they experienced mistreatment or neglect from a previous owner or situation.

A Reiki session, whether in person or done remotely, is a way to relieve the tension and fear, and help soothe the animal, so they are more willing to receive love and be able to eat and relax.

This has a profound effect on their physical well-being and allows them to achieve a sense of peace.

If a pet owner is anticipating the loss of a pet, they may benefit from sessions that include both their pet and them together.

This combined treatment can also be done remotely if there are no Reiki practitioners available in your immediate area.

People will feel a sense of relief and calmness, along with their pets, and realize the connections we all have to the universe.

This knowledge will provide a sense of comfort, knowing that once our loved pet passes, their energy is still present as a part of the universe, which is within us as well.

Reiki is becoming more commonly used in veterinarian offices to support animals during stressful and difficult treatments.

Some people have felt comfort and connection with their pets when they've become lost, even temporarily, giving them a sense of peace during a challenging time.

Many animals rescued from difficult situations or mistreatment may experience PTSD (post-traumatic stress disorder) and find it difficult to trust anyone, whether it is another animal or a human.

Reiki can provide a soothing experience for them during this time and may work in animal shelters or support rescue groups that locate animals in need of help.

Performing Reiki on your pet follows the same principles as and guidelines.

You may choose to meditate and prepare the space with energy and symbols.

If you are in a position to practice Reiki remotely, either for your pet (if they are with someone else) or someone else' pet, it is helpful to have a personal belonging of theirs and/or details on the animal (including photos and characteristics about them) to begin the practice for a meaningful and powerful experience.

It is important to realize that animals are very receptive to Reiki, even if they are initially unapproachable because they can also channel energy and receive it.

The treatment is also non-invasive for pets, especially animals that do not wish to be held or touched, which is why Reiki is so effective for them.

Chapter 33: Additional Therapies to Use with Reiki

Often, Reiki is not used as a standalone therapy. While it can produce results on its own, especially when it is performed by someone that has earned the title of Reiki Master, there are additional therapies that can be used to increase the results of Reiki healing. This chapter will go over some of them so that you can get the most of your Reiki healing sessions.

Crystal Therapy

Crystals are made up of elements of the earth. They carry a unique vibrational energy depending on what they are made out of. This vibrational energy allows them to attune to your body, producing certain effects. It is not uncommon for people to wear certain stones or carry them around. They can also be used during Reiki and other practices, as a way to enhance the results.

To add crystals to your Reiki session, you can put your hands into position over the chakras as you focus your intention and your healing energy. Hold the appropriate crystal in your hand and channel the energy into yourself or the person you are healing. The crystal that you use depends on which chakra you are trying to heal, excite, or calm. You can choose whichever crystal has the strongest pull or seems to call to you, or you can choose one that goes with the specific chakra you are trying to heal. Here are some of the crystals that should be used for each of the chakras:

• Crown Chakra- Clear Quartz, Diamond, Ametrine, Clear Calcite, Amethyst/Violet

• Third Eye Chakra- Lazuli, Lapis/Indigo, Quartz, Sodalite

• Throat Chakra- Turquoise/Blue, Celestite, Blue Lace Agate, Aquamarine

• Heart Chakra- Pink Calcite, Emerald/Green, Rose Quartz, Tourmaline

• Solar Plexus Chakra- Amber/Yellow, Malachite, Aragonite, Moonstone, Topaz

• Sacral Chakra- Carnelian, Orange Stones, Smoky Quartz, Red Jasper

• Root Chakra- Lodestone/Red, Bloodstone, Tiger's Eye, Ruby, Garnet, Hematite

Something to keep in mind is that crystals can take on negative energy as people would. Some people choose to release negative energy on their crystal by performing a Reiki session to clean the crystal's aura before their own. There are several other options, including burning sage to cleanse the crystal or soaking it in saltwater. Some people also bury their crystals in salt, especially if they are soft and will be harmed by a saltwater bath. To amplify the power of a crystal, you can stick it on a windowsill or in direct moonlight. This works best when the moon is highly visible.

Yoga

Yoga originally comes from India, however, it has recently become popular around the world. It is used for physical activity but also encourages the development of a more spiritual mindset. The type of yoga that you participate in has a lot to do with the effects, as the positions and breathing patterns can invoke certain results.

As you do yoga, you should always use the breathing practice called 'Pranayama.' This type of breathing is necessary for people who are trying to bring results to their yoga session. It allows you to connect with the Universe, while improving your physical and mental strength, increasing your memory power, and even extending your lifespan. You can take a class for yoga. Alternatively, lookup positions or videos online. You'd be surprised how much information is available once you know where to look!

Pray

Many people stay away from the prayer option because they believe they must claim a religion or choose a specific God if they are to pray. However, prayer does not have to be directed at anyone or anything specific. If you are not comfortable praying, you could also meditate.

This is a time when you should focus on your intentions. Get in the habit of focusing on the positives of what you want. Instead of saying that you do not want pain, say that you want to heal. Even when you say something negatively, by reflecting on it as you meditate, you are giving it your focus and energy. This can draw that thing into your life or cancel out what you are trying to achieve with the prayer.

You should always look at meditation and prayer as an opportunity to reflect and look inward. Even if you are speaking outward, whether to your God, the Universe, or whatever you believe in, it is important to look inward. Speaking out loud can help trigger insights that you may not have realized otherwise.

It does not matter how long you pray or when you pray. Simply set aside time each day, whether a few minutes or longer. Make it a habit. If you can, speak out loud as you pray and focus on the things that you need to be happy in your life.

Serve Others

We may do the things that our family, friends, and co-workers ask us regularly. However, fewer people take time out of their busy weeks to help those who truly need it. The reality is that every person is fighting a battle that nobody else understands. For example, someone who is homeless is not necessarily lazy—they are the result of a collection of life circumstances that could just as easily happen to you or me.

As you start to explore the world and help the people that truly need it, you will find yourself better prepared to help others. You will find a newfound sense of satisfaction in yourself and the responsibilities of life, as you realize that you can be responsible for more than just your normal day-to-day routine. As a person that connects to the Universe, you have the knowledge and wisdom to help those around you. Additionally, helping those who are less fortunate allows you to gain your maturity, strength, and knowledge when it comes to fighting battles in your life.

Nourish Your Soul

Nourishing the soul is all about learning those things that make you happy and bring you peace—and then making an effort to do them. When you work long hours or have a hectic family life, it is hard to find time for yourself. It is important to remember that you owe yourself this nourishment. You must take care of yourself if you want to connect to the Universal consciousness and connect with others.

In addition to nourishing yourself by committing time to yourself, you must take care of your physical body and mind. Be sure that you get enough sleep each night. Practice relaxation techniques if you need to. You should also choose nutrient-dense foods, rather than those that are filled with empty calories. By nourishing your body and mind, you will find yourself in the best possible state to encourage mental, emotional, and spiritual healing and wellness too.

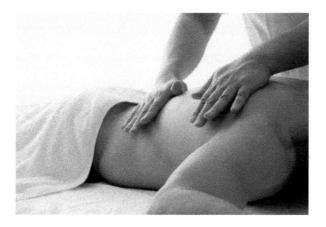

Be Mindful in Your Experience

People lead busy lives. As you rush from task to task, when do you make time to slow down? Think back to the last time that you had a meal. Were you rushing to get back to whatever task you were doing before or even checking your emails while you ate? What about your last trip to the store or work? Did you look around you as you went and observe the sights, or were you on autopilot mode as you just tried to get from A to B?

It is easy to become so immersed with the physical experience that we forget to slow down and experience the world in all its beauty. Instead of going on autopilot, make an effort to notice the things you are doing. When you are washing dishes or sweeping the floor, pay attention to the way the muscles move in your arms, shoulders, and back. As you eat, pay attention to the different flavors and textures you are getting from the food. Immerse yourself in the experience of eating and chew slowly enough that you can take it all in. Whenever you are driving or walking, notice your surroundings. Instead of staring at the carpet when you are rushing to your office in the morning, make an effort to smile at your coworkers. It doesn't take any extra time to move the muscles in your face. By immersing yourself in your human experience, you will find yourself more connected to your spiritual one as well.

Conclusion

Congratulations on your journey through the chakras and learning all you need to know about how to begin healing your energy! This book is a welcoming resource for you to start practicing the healing process and with all of your new knowledge about chakras, you can begin to explore in a more in-depth way on your own. Your intuition is all you need now, to help you achieve the level of balance and vibrational flow required to feel that wholeness and enlightenment that comes from an unblocked and healthy chakra system.

This book has shown you the beautiful history and discovery of the chakras as well as an understanding of how we can use modern science to explore and explain what is happening on the energetic level with our bodies. The connection between the chakras and the physical/emotional self is strong and I hope that you can now see how dynamic our total being truly is within that mind-body-spirit balance.

You have taken a unique road trip through the chakra system and learned about how each of them has distinct qualities and characteristics that set them apart from each other, and how all together, they create a uniform wholeness that leads to the transcendent self and connection to the truth and purpose of your life.

All of the information in this book is here to show you what kinds of ailments, issues and challenges can present themselves when your chakras are unhealthy, blocked and imbalanced. As you move forward, you can begin to identify these causes and side-effects in your own life and begin to energetically treat yourself through the healing process.

You have all of the techniques outlined for you to get started and any number of them will shift and transform your energy the more you practice them. Remember that daily or weekly energy clearing, using any of these methods, will keep you in a better balance overall.

The goal of this book is to show you how to work with your chakra energy for a fuller, happier, healthier life and how-to bring positivity into your vibration and frequency more regularly. The power of living in balance will bring into you in harmony with the life you have always wanted to live. Moving forward, keep your energy open and flowing using these chakra healing techniques and the knowledge you have gained about your own, unique energy system. Everything that you do in your life, and every person you encounter, will influence your energy and your chakras. We carry this energy around with us, sometimes for our whole lives and if you are wanting to heal the wounds of the past, traumatic circumstances, chronic health problems, emotional challenges and upheaval, to create a more balanced and energetically vibrant life, then all you have to do is listen to your energy and "read" your chakras.

Reiki healing, instead, allows you to connect with the energies of the Universe and use it in a way that encourages the body to heal itself. It can be used to treat aches and pains, overcome allergies and headaches, and even heal chronic or painful diseases. The results depend heavily on your abilities and your mindset, as it is important to be receptive to the Reiki energies for them to result.

Often, the emotional and physical health problems that we struggle with stem from blocked energy channels in the body. Energy channels can be blocked after certain life circumstances or from being neglected. As you learn to encourage the flow of Universal energy through your body, you can promote overall health and wellness. You can stop at learning to heal yourself or you can continue our practice to strengthen your abilities and possibly heal others.

Hopefully, this book has been able to hep provide the foundation for Reiki knowledge that you can build upon later. Forl the time being, however, you should know what you need to put your Reiki skills to work. The only thing left to do is practice! Your abilities will strengthen with time and as you become more aware of the way that the energies of the universe and your body affect you.

Best of luck!

Book 2

THIRD EYE AWAKENING:

A GUIDED MEDITATION TO OPEN YOUR THIRD EYE CHAKRA, ACHIEVE HIGHER CONSCIOUSNESS, ENHANCE YOUR PSYCHIC ABILITIES DEVELOPMENT, MIND POWER AND SPIRITUAL INTUITION

By Ellen Cure

Introduction

What is the Third Eye?

If you study various societies and religions, you will learn that the third eye is something that exists as a commonality among them. Though the message and the name change from group to group, each of them relates to the third eye, located above the brows, as being a sense of empowerment or enlightenment. Some describe it as a heightened all-knowingness, while others experience it as a sight into the future. Some people simply describe it as an unwavering intuition that guides them through life.

However, it feels, the third eye opens doors into a type of knowingness. Even though not all people will experience what could be considered 'powers' like telepathy or clairvoyance, everyone has the potential to unlock the third eye.

Unified Field Theory: The Science Behind the Third Eye

Up until he laid on his deathbed, Albert Einstein sought out a unified field theory that could explain the relativity of matter within a single field. It is even said that he asked for his latest notes just three days before his passing.

This was just one part of the bigger picture—James Clerk Maxwell had proposed the first field theory regarding electromagnetism in the mid-1800s, and Einstein proposed the second, the general theory of relativity, at the beginning of the 20th century. Einstein was obsessed with the idea that there must be a 'unified field theory.' His evidence as that electromagnetism and gravity manifested in different ways—but still functioned in the same field.

This led to the greater idea of quantum theory, which is gaining more acceptance in the scientific community. The theory of relativity and gravity both look at things on a macroscopic level, which describes things that are visible through the naked eye—your natural sight. The third eye relates heavily to the information on quantum theory because it includes the nature and behaviors of things on an atomic and subatomic (microscopic) level.

One theory is that the third eye offers a deeper insight into the past, present, and even future in some cases because it helps uncover things on the microscopic level. This gives a greater and more in-depth understanding of the world around you and explains why some people experience certain 'powers' after unveiling their third eye. They develop their ability to see things on the subatomic level, and then the mind uses this newfound information to alter their perception.

The Third Eye Across Various Cultures and Religions

The third eye is not some mystical discovery that has happened in the past few decades. If you look into the history and practices of various cultures and religions around the world, there is mention of the third eye. Under the Taoist way of living, for example, there is an emphasis on connecting with oneself spiritually by opening the third eye. The Christian Bible also mentions the third eye—but it recommends and even condemns trying to open it. While the intentions and 'goodness' of the third eye are disputed, this makes it clear at the very least that it is a real, studied thing.

The third eye that is spoken of in religions, cultures, and meditative practices is the pineal gland. Symbolically, the third eye is a single eye that exists on the forehead. It is positioned between the two eyebrows. It is said that by creating the connection between the third eye and the mind, we connect with our inner selves and the outside world.

The Third Eye and the Bible

One of the earliest references to the third eye in the Bible is in Matthew 6:22, where it is said, 'If thine eye is single, the whole body shall be full of light.' Though this comes across as positive, the text further goes on to discuss the connection to the third eye as having the potential to be one of light or darkness, depending on if the intentions of the eye-opener are good or evil.

However, later in the Bible, passages in Leviticus, Chronicles, Romans, John, and Ephesians go against this idea that the third eye may be good or evil. It is even said that those who practice acts of the third eye like fortune-telling and the like should be punished by death, as well as those who have chosen to associate with them. Eventually, the earlier support for the third eye is explained—the third eye or sixth sense that is spoken of is a connection to the Holy Spirit, and it is this spirit that should be used for guidance. This taking in of the Holy Spirit should be so much that it fills, which keeps out the evil spirits because there is no room for them.

The Third Eye Chakra

It is common to hear the third eye referred to as a chakra, with it being one of seven that are found at various points in the body. These chakras align with the unified field theory and ideas presented in quantum physics—that humans are not single entities but instead made up of atoms and molecules that have aggregated together.

Each 'human' entity is just a physical body that has been assigned to contain the seven chakras. The chakras explain different energy centers found in the body, each of them with its location and 'color.' Many cultures believe that the flow of energy is important to health—that is why treatments which align 'qi' or energy like Reiki and acupuncture are used to treat some conditions, according to traditional medicine practices. It has been used for high blood pressure, pain in the joints, back, or anywhere else, migraines, and more.

If the third eye is considered as a chakra, it speaks to the importance of having the right environment and mindset before attempting to open the third eye. Total, there are seven chakras in the body. Most cultures that focus on opening the third eye require you to access a free flow of energy through all the other chakras before you reach this heightened state of enlightenment, where the third eye is open and perceptive to the world around you.

• The seven chakras start with the root chakra, which is related to feelings of grounding and stability. The root chakra is located at the base of the spine.

• From here, the lower abdomen is home to the sacral chakra, which is related to feelings of pleasure and emotionalism.

• Above this is the solar plexus, which is above the navel. This area is related to self-worth and confidence.

• Sitting on the solar plexus is the heart chakra, which is related to all things involving love.

• Next is the throat chakra, which is related to all types of communication.

• Finally, you reach the third eye chakra or Anja chakra. Traditionally, this is related to a sense of empowerment and perception, which describes the heightened sense of enlightenment when the third eye is open. It is related to intuition, heightened perception, intuition, and imaginative prowess.

• The last chakra sits above the third eye chakra; the crown chakra. It is at the top of the head and is home to spiritual energy.

Skull Caps

Another commonality regarding the third eye is the principle of a skull cap. Over time, the idea of a skull cap has been watered down so that it is related to customs and tradition. In the earlier days, however, the skull cap was positioned in that way to represent closeness to the third eye, the eye that allows access to the Divine. The Jews wear the skull cap as a 'yarmulke,' and the Pope wears it as a 'zucchetto.' The skull cap can also be found in the Muslim religion, where it is called a 'Taliyah.' Regardless of what it is called, it has been worn as a way of sanctifying the crown of the head, where the third eye is said to be located.

Other Mentions of the Third Eye

In the Quran, these energy fields are called the seven heavens. In 2: 164, it says, "Then He directed Himself to the heaven and made them seven heavens, and He knows of all things."

The third eye is also called the 'bridge to the Divine' for this reason. Once the third eye is activated, it allows the experience known as 'God-consciousness' or 'Samadhi.'

Numerous other names refer to the third eye. Metaphysicians call it the 'All-Seeing Eye of Consciousness," while Hindus refer to it as 'Anja.' The Ancient Egyptians call it the 'Eye of Horus," and the Muslims call it 'Khafi.' According to Descartes, who is a great philosopher, the third eye is the 'seat of the soul.'

One common symbol in Ancient Egyptian hierarchy is the upright cobra that the Pharaoh wears on their headdress. This is called the 'uraeus' and represents wisdom and royalty, as well as the awareness of the third eye.

In the Vedas, which are the ancient Hindu texts that the opening of the third eye connects one with their godliness. Only when the eyes of sight and the third eye are open can their spirit connect with the Gods and Goddesses. It is said that no master of the Hindu religion ignores this connection—they are constantly working toward opening the third eye.

Chapter 1   : Third Eye

What is the Third Eye?

Across different religions and practices in the world, the third eye has many meanings. In general, it is considered a concept that has a certain mystical quality to it. It is used to describe a perception that exists beyond seeing with just your eyes. Some people refer to the third eye as a type of 'meta' organ. It uses the mind, as well as the information collected from all the senses, to seek out patterns and new perceptions of the world. In this way, you gain insight that you didn't have before and a deeper understanding of the next steps that you need to take in your life.

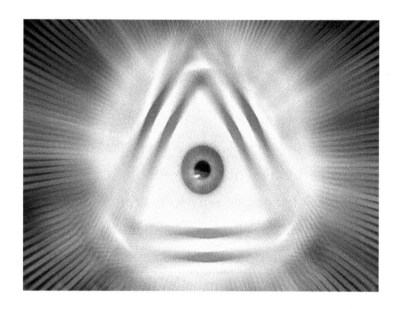

The third eye has been a mystical concept for centuries. Very few people have known this power and they kept it a secret for very long. It has widely been a misrepresented and misinterpreted concept. Opening the third eye is no magic. It will not happen through some gadgets or accessories. It is a journey within. You will have to undertake it alone. You can open your third eye with devotion, willpower, and meditation. It is possible and thousands of people are doing it. The best thing about this process is not only the result but the journey in itself is also very beautiful.

The third eye is the most eloquent source of intuitive wisdom. A power only possessed by the yogis, psychics and fortune tellers in the past. If you meditate and open your third eye then you can get insights, prior warnings of danger and high level of intelligence at the time. The keyword to achieve this objective is meditation.

The Ajna chakra or the third eye is located in the pineal gland. For centuries, the occultists and the spiritual masters have called it the 'seat of the soul'. Once you are able to open your third eye, the difference between the truth and reality becomes crystal clear. You are able to connect yourself with the higher energy field and feel what is impossible to feel in any other way. Getting very high intuitive power is another aspect of it. You become highly aware and establish a connection with your surroundings. Your gut feeling gets stronger. Your sixth sense starts working predominantly.

The third eye awakens your inner self. You easily establish a connection with your surroundings. The reason for most of the sorrows in our lives is our discontent. The new awakening introduces you to a world of new realization. Your perception of good and bad will change. You can see things deeply and not from the superficial level. You react differently and in a much matured way. This is a completely new feeling. It is like an intellectual looking at the immature quarrels of the kids.

Seeing the Third Eye

To know the eye functions, let us look at the way that it is likely to utilize the Third Eye and translate energy. It is expected to view Motion (for instance, a car moving), Action (you driving the car), and Exchange of Energy (burning off the gasoline). Insert in our capability of projecting & sensing potential (being able to forecast where the car goes dependent on the streets and understanding the motorist), Quite only regarding where energy, movement, and actions will flow into overtime. Add all this together into an inner visual map, and then you've just enlarged the best way to view Energy playing (the outcomes of working with the car/gasoline/intention to push you up the mountain). By viewing energy, it turns into a property of lifestyle, which we may discover how to interact and feel inside a manner.

The Powers of an Open Third Eye

Freedom from Anxiety, Stress, and Worries

With every meditation session, your consciousness level increases. You will start achieving higher states of consciousness. The light inside you illuminates you. It takes away your insecurities and fears. Our worries are a product of our worldly burdens. With every step we take in our lives, the Karma has its effect. It keeps on piling up. We fail to recognize the impact of Karma and keep fretting over the results. Meditation gives us the power to ponder upon our actions and the resultant Karma. It all starts making sense and you can make amends. Clear thoughts give birth to reasoning. We also start giving weight to cause and not just the results. This helps in balancing the effect of Karma.

The illumination also makes you realize the importance of various things in life. You can prioritize things better. We do many things without setting up clear priorities. This creates a lot of backlash in the form of pending mortgage, student loan, or unpaid credit card bills. These keep haunting our thoughts. Once you can see clearly inside yourself, you start understanding that most of the actions were unnecessary. You can also get out of them once you reason and align them properly. This is the best way to come clear from this vicious cycle of debts and liabilities.

Victory over Emotions

One of the biggest reasons for our distress is our emotions. Love, hatred, dislike, and affection are some of the free-flowing emotions. We attach undue importance to things. The negative energies and emotions accumulate and make us sad. Most of these emotions and energies are avoidable. When you look deep inside yourself, you find that most of your outbursts were unreasonable and uncalled for. You could have avoided the negative energies by suppressing them. These eventually lead to sadness. Your inner light will give you the wisdom to introspect. This time is entirely yours. At this moment, you are unchallenged. There is no victory or loss. You are in complete control. There is no ego or tussle. You make rational decisions. This leads to the birth of positive decisions. You are able to shun negative energies. It is relieving and light. You become happy from within. You get mature and become affable in real terms. You can take proactive steps towards improving your health and relationships. You can make prudent decisions towards strengthening your career and financial situation. The intuitive power of the third eye will help you in assessing your future course of action.

You Start Changing from Within

Now, we know that meditation helps you in self-introspection. You understand the impact of Karma. You also understand the impact that even the small steps would have on your life. You can predict the consequences of those actions. This knowledge helps in shaping up a new you. You become a better and improved human being. Your thought process starts changing from the root. Your worries and insecurities vanish slowly and gradually. This makes you more confident and stronger. As your Third eye opens up your physical, emotional and mental wellbeing improves. This starts reflecting in your overall personality. You mellow down. You become calm yet confident.

Your path to success becomes clear. Your goals become clear and the path leading up to them also gets crystal clear. There is no confusion. The mind makes its way through the darkness. It is no more just an entangled structure of nerve cells. It gets illuminated.

You start realizing the power of your mind. It is a powerhouse. It gets illuminated and you know the things in place. Once the light comes the path gets clear. The challenge lies in bringing the light. The pineal gland or the Ajna chakra needs to be illuminated and activated. This requires focus, dedication, and discipline. You will have to work your way till here with meditation. You will have to open your Third eye inwards. This will need patience and determination. It is a doable task. You will just have to dedicate yourself to it. The path is not tough. It only requires you to keep walking on it. The journey is calming and rewarding. You only need to take the first step towards it. It will lead you from there.

What is the Pineal Gland?

The pineal gland has remained an enigma and been the subject of controversy for ages. In ancient times, it was regarded as "a mystery gland," and theories abounded about its mystical powers. For this reason, it was sometimes called "the pineal eye."

The pineal gland is a small reddish-gray gland shaped like a pine cone, from which its name is derived. It was first depicted as the symbol of a pine cone by the Sumerians. This pine cone symbol can be seen in the art of many ancient cultures, suggesting that it held great importance.

The pineal gland is about one-third of an inch long and belongs to the endocrine system (the system of hormone-producing glands necessary for various bodily functions). It is located in the midbrain; it is embedded within the crevice between the left and right hemispheres.

For a long time, the pineal gland was regarded as an unimportant vestigial organ that was unworthy of in-depth investigation. Even today, science has not fully discovered all of its functions—but what is known so far signifies its vital importance in the regulation of several bodily functions.

The Function of the Pineal Gland

• Its main function is the production of the hormone melatonin. Melatonin regulates the body's circadian rhythm (sleep-wake cycle).

• Melatonin promotes sexual development in both sexes.

• It induces sleep.

• It connects the nervous system with the endocrine system by converting neural signals into hormone secretion.

• It helps regulate immune system functions.

• Melatonin regulates the mood and helps us adapt to change. It plays an important role in our happiness and contentment.

• It interacts with many other organs, as well as the blood.

• Studies indicate that the melatonin secreted by the pineal gland may affect cardiovascular health and blood pressure, but more research is needed.

• Other studies indicate that the pineal gland may play a role in regulating female hormones and could be linked to irregular menstrual cycles and fertility. Again, more research is needed to confirm this.

The Pineal Gland and the Third Eye

The pineal gland was sometimes considered the third eye itself, perhaps because of its location deep in the center of the brain.

French Philosopher René Descartes was so fascinated with the enigmatic pineal gland that he wrote extensively on it, calling it "the seat of the soul" and the area where all thoughts are shaped. The gland was also known to the ancient Greeks, who shared Descartes' view that is was the center of thought.

Although these opinions have been thoroughly dismissed by science, amazingly, recent research may confirm that Descartes and the Greeks were right! A revolutionary study has reported a connection between the pineal gland and a compound called dimethyltryptamine (DMT). This substance is found naturally in many types of plants and has psychedelic properties. It is known to cause psychic visions and profoundly heightened and vivid perceptions.

Clinical psychiatrist Dr. Rick Strassman has done extensive research on DMT, after being commissioned by the U.S. government to research psychedelic drugs.

During his extensive studies on natural psychedelic substances, including DMT, Dr. Strassman made the astonishing discovery that the pineal gland also secretes the substance in certain situations.

In his book *DMT: The Spirit Molecule,* he details all of his truly groundbreaking findings. His theory is that DMT secreted by the pineal gland allows for the life force to transition into this life from another realm (during birth). It also enables the transition of life force from this life into the next dimension (at death). Strassman asserts that DMT is released in the pineal gland during extremely stressful and traumatic situations, such as birth and death.

Strassman describes the pineal gland as "the intermediary between the physical and the spiritual." In other words, the pineal gland has a purpose very similar to the third eye chakra.

Needless to say, Dr Strassman's study has caused immense excitement and debate. Many studies are now underway to uncover the full story of the tiny, enigmatic pineal gland.

The long-ignored pineal gland, like the third eye chakra, may well be the doorway to psychic experiences and other realms. Descartes and the Greeks were not so far off base after all. The pineal gland and its associated third eye chakra may indeed be the seat of the soul!

In the meantime, there is still very little known about the pineal gland and its full spectrum of functions, other than its secretion of melatonin. Let's wait and see what more research tells us in the future.

Ten Fascinating Facts about the Pineal Gland

The pineal gland is thought to be the third eye by many spiritual schools. Here are some facts that may confirm this:

1. The pineal gland stops growing somewhere between one and two years of age. From puberty onwards, it begins to increase slightly in weight.

2. It contains pigment similar to that found in the eyes.

3. It gets its name from the Latin "pinea" which translates as "pine cone."

4. When it is cut open, it appears very similar to an eye.

5. It contains light receptors that are thought to be responsible for inner sight or insight.

6. Unlike other parts of the brain, it is not isolated by the blood-brain barrier and receives a direct and abundant blood flow. The only other body organ which has the same function is the kidney.

7. It appears to be related to near-death experiences, visions, and when overstimulated, to hallucinations.

8. Many scientists consider it to be some form of an eye.

9. In 1886, anatomists discovered that the pineal gland contains retina cells, pigment cells and a direct response to light, just like a physical eye.

10. Ancient texts and drawings from almost all cultures of the world regarded it as a third eye.

Calcification of the Pineal Gland

Calcium, fluoride, and phosphorus can build up in the pineal gland over time. These deposits cause what is known as "calcification." A calcified pineal gland can be easily diagnosed with normal x-rays.

Calcification of the pineal gland is more likely to occur when the third eye is dormant—meaning that the majority of people today have some degree of calcification in the pineal gland. An awakened and active third eye chakra keeps the pineal gland healthy, and is the best way to prevent calcification from occurring.

Calcification is basically where a hard, solid ridge builds up around the pineal gland, effectively blocking the door to other realms. It can also cause other physical problems, if ignored. Studies have shown that a calcified pineal gland can cause the following symptoms and disorders:

• Slow production of melatonin, which can wreak havoc on the body's sleep cycle and circadian rhythm.

• A slow or lethargic thyroid, which has its own set of physical problems.

• Low melatonin production may lead to mood swings and even mental disorders.

• Poor blood circulation.

• Weight gain and sometimes obesity.

- Kidney disorders.

- Digestive disorders.

- Confusion.

- Depression.

- Fatigue.

- Poor sense of direction.

- Spiritual disconnection.

Chapter 2 : Opening the Third Eye

What is Third Eye Activation

Third Eye is referred to as the pineal gland within one's brain. The pineal gland produces and regulates melatonin, which is the hormone responsible for our sleep/wake cycles and how we handle external stressors. Philosopher Descartes has described the pineal gland as "the principal seat of the soul". The pituitary gland is also important to the Third Eye awakening and the sixth chakra in general, as it is responsible for multiple other hormone glands in the body. The pituitary gland, in biology, is often referred to as the "master gland".

When the Third Eye chakra is fully balanced or has been activated, both of your brain's hemispheres are able to function with complete synchrony. The Third Eye is sometimes referred to as our body's spiritual center, and works diligently to break down thoughts that have been brought on by illusion, strength, and fear; to open the mind to promote spiritual healing. The Third Eye differentiates what we believe to be true with what we know to be factual (or what is true). This chakra houses your psychological skills as well as mental abilities and determines how we evaluate certain situations, attitudes, and beliefs.

The Third Eye is about not only the idea of seeing but more deeply than that the idea of truly understanding what is. This chakra is the source of our sense of ethics, morality, and justice (the Third Eye has also been said to be the part of us that receives messages from spiritual guides). Psychological functions associated with the Third Eye (or the pineal gland) are those of intuition and imagination.

There are numerous benefits to awakening your sixth chakra, or Third Eye, and below we have listed four ways for you to open your Third Eye followed by five signs that your Third Eye is opening.

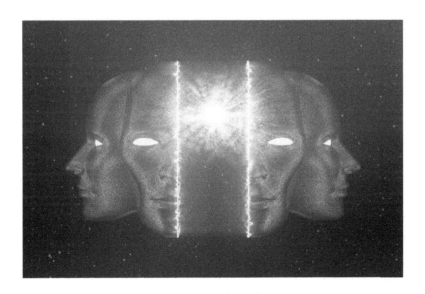

How to Open the Third Eye:

1. Touch- Using your index finger, gently touch the area of your forehead located directly between your eyebrows. Rub this small spot in slow circles as you breathe deeply (inhaling and exhaling slowly), and imagine the chakra opening.

2. Essential Oils: Using essential oils is a great way to relax while working to awaken your Third Eye. Essential oils can be used to promote general wellness while you are sleeping or meditating to balance your chakras. Using an oil diffuser, diffuse several drops of sandalwood, chamomile, or myrrh to promote the awakening of your Third Eye.

3. Breathe: This technique can be used continuously throughout the day to promote the opening of your Third Eye. Many people practice the bad habit of shallow breathing without even realizing it. To effectively awaken your sixth chakra, it is important that you focus on and regularly practice deep breathing. When inhaling, be sure that you are breathing deep enough that your abdomen expands with each breathe.

4   <u>Clairvoyance Meditation:</u> To practice this technique, find a comfortable spot to sit and relax your body completely. Once relaxed in a sitting position, practice the deep breathing mentioned above for several minutes. Next, visualize the number 1 in the center of your head between your eyebrows (while still utilizing the deep breathing exercises). Once you have clearly visualized the number 1, move up to the number 2, and repeat this exercise up to the number 10. This meditation exercise will help practice not only relaxation and breathing techniques but also can help to practice visualizing different shapes and symbols.

Five Signs that Assert the Third Eye is Open:

Once you begin regularly exercising your mental strength to attempt to open the Third Eye, you may notice certain changes in the way you see or perceive things. Below are five signs or symptoms that you may notice and often act as a sign that you are becoming successful in awakening your Third Eye:

1   You may feel a gentle pressure or spread of warmth between your eyebrows when encouraging your Third Eye to open.

2   You may notice an increased feeling of intuition, or a stronger "feeling" about what is right to do when you are faced with making a decision.

3   As you encourage your Third Eye to awaken, you may begin to notice a slight sensitivity to bright light.

4   You may feel a continuous feeling of change within yourself (body and mind).

5   As your Third Eye begins to open or awaken, you may experience mild headaches, though these typically occur less and less frequently as you continue exercising opening your Third Eye.

Symptoms and Side-Effects

After opening your third eye, you are going to experience some different things that will tell you whether or not your opening meditation was successful. Now, since everyone is different, we may not experience the same things or to the same extend. Some will have very subtle symptoms, while others will have some very overwhelming results. However, no matter how intensely you experience these symptoms, there seem to be some symptoms most people experience.

Short Term Symptoms and Side Effects

Here are some of the symptoms you can expect right after opening your third eye, and which will go away after a couple of days or weeks.

Pressure on Forehead: A pressure on the forehead is for many the very first symptom they get and is something most people experience during, or right after completing the third eye opening meditation. The pressure can become quite intense when you meditate or think about your third eye, as it is much more sensitive now. This is a sign that your third eye opening has been successful and that you are now ready to start activating your third eye with third eye meditation.

Tingling Sensation: A tingling sensation on the forehead or crown chakra is also one of the very first symptoms you can expect when you open your third eye. It will be a constant itchy or buzzing feeling on your forehead that does not go away when you scratch it.

Headache: In addition to the feeling of pressure on your head, you may also experience headaches. So, take some time to rest and allow the headache to go away.

Crackling or Popping Sound: Some people say they hear a crackling or loud popping sound inside their head after opening the third eye. This is the activation of the pineal gland, which is located in the middle of the brain, which is also where the sound tends to originate from.

Seeing Lights While Meditating: Many people see lights when meditating after they have opened the third eye. This is often in forms of string or spiral-shaped lights in green, purple or white (though can be any color).

Seeing Images While Meditation: Many people experience seeing images, oftentimes an eye-shaped object, while meditating. This is quite common and is a sign that your mental sight is improving.

Emotional Imbalance: Opening the third eye can have some strange effects on people's emotions and some experience mood swings and episodes of sadness where they feel like crying for no good reason.

Nightmares: An open third eye can give nightmares more frequently in the beginning, which should go away after a couple of days or weeks. You may also notice that your dreams become much more vivid and that you remember more of your dreams.

Long Term Symptoms and Benefits

Improved Visual Awareness: An open third eye can improve your awareness and eyesight, and make you more sensitive to impressions around you.

Improved Focus: Your focus can also increase greatly and you become much more concentrated and clear-minded.

Improved Memory: You may experience that your concentration improves and you have a much easier time remembering details.

Sensitive to Energies: As part of the spiritual awareness, you become much more sensitive to energies around you. This can help you in your development of psychic abilities.

Improved Intuition: opening the third eye can also greatly improve your intuition and you have an easier time making decisions based on your intuitive senses and not on your logical and physical senses alone.

Otherworldly Impressions: One symptom that can frighten many people is the fact that you may get impressions from beings not of this physical world such as spirits or entities.

Ability to Sense the Truth: Many people experience the feeling of knowing the truth in different situations and be able to see things more clearly.

Psychic Abilities: Opening the third eye can greatly benefit you in your process of developing psychic abilities and is something many people advise when it comes to psychic practice, as you will connect with your spirituality and universal energies.

Third Eye Awakening Checklist

Check the boxes below to document the different symptoms you have from your third eye awakening practice.

After 1 week   *After 1 month or more*

Tingling sensation on forehead		Improved Visual awareness	
Tingling sensation on Crown Chakra		Improved Intuition	
Pressure on Forehead		Improved concentration	
Crackling or popping sound		Sensing the truth in situations	
Seeing lights while meditating		Otherworldly Impressions	
Nightmares or vivid dreams		Sensitive to energies	
Emotional Imbalance		Improved Focus	

Seeing images while meditating		Clairvoyant impressions	

Chapter 3   : Clairvoyance Power

Clairvoyance Meaning

This is the ability to clearly see with the mind's eye, as is described by the name itself, which means "clear seeing". Although clairvoyance is a single term, there are numerous forms of clairvoyance, each unique in its way. For example, some people can see events in other people's lives by tapping into their clairvoyant ability. This is where the image of a fortune teller using a crystal ball comes into play. While few clairvoyants use a crystal ball to harness their visions, the image itself is what is important. Such a person can see an image as clear as day in their mind, one that involves another person or group of people. These images can be warnings of impending danger or good omens pointing to job promotions, meeting a future spouse, or even the birth of a child. In the end, it is a bit like daydreaming about someone else's life—the only difference being that, in this case, the dream comes true.

Most people have experienced clairvoyance at least once in their life, whether or not they realize it. This is where the second form of clairvoyance comes into play, namely that of seeing a person in your mind that you will cross paths with in real life in the immediate future. Countless stories exist where a person sees an image of a friend or loved one, sometimes someone whom they haven't seen in a long time, only to get a phone call or surprise visit from that person during the day. A good example of this is a story where a store manager for a retail store always knew when the district manager would make a surprise visit because he would see his district manager's face either in a dream the previous night or in his mind's eye during the morning as he got ready for work. Needless to say, this gave him a huge advantage as he was always prepared before the "surprise" visit, making him look good in his boss' eyes.

Another form of clairvoyance is the ability to see a place or an event that you will come in contact with before the fact. Numerous accounts exist of people "seeing" their next house before deciding to look for another place to live. At first glance, this might not seem like an important ability; however, it can have very profound implications. While the mere fact that a person sees a house even before looking for it is amazing, the message beneath the phenomenon will, more often than not, be one of validation. In other words, knowing what your future house will look like can help you to make the right decision, turning down the other options until you find the one your intuition has prepared you for. The very same thing can happen in terms of choosing a new job, car, or even significant other. Any time you see the outcome, you no longer have to guess at what decision to make. This ensures that you make the right decision every time.

Even so, while almost everyone has had a clairvoyant experience at one time or another, it doesn't mean that clairvoyance is everyone's psychic ability. The question, therefore, is how do you know if it is your personal ability? The simple answer comes down to two things: frequency and intensity. If you have had numerous experiences of seeing a person or event before it happens, even making it ordinary and mundane in your mind, then you have the knack of clairvoyance. Additionally, if your dreams are vivid, or you can imagine things in your mind with great clarity and detail, then clairvoyance is probably your gift. Once you make that determination, the next step is to develop your ability to the highest level possible.

The very first step to achieving this goal is to practice meditation regularly. You don't have to do anything elaborate; simply engage in a practice that enables you to clear your mind at the beginning and end of each day. Clearing your mind in the morning will help you to tap into your clairvoyance during the waking day, enabling you to see things before they unfold. Performing the practice at the end of the day will help you to dream better at night, giving you a clear mind that will be more open to vivid images from the spirit realm. Another proven technique for developing your clairvoyance is to keep a clairvoyant journal. In this journal, you will record all of your dreams, along with the images you receive during the regular day. Next to each vision, you will record the corresponding event that unfolds, reflecting the accuracy of your vision. The purpose of this exercise is twofold. First, it will create a sense of confidence in your ability, thereby causing you to pay more attention to the phenomenon as well as accepting the messages you are receiving. Second, it will increase your connection to your mind's eye. The more time you spend focusing on your experiences, the stronger and more frequent they will become. In the end, by ensuring that your mind is clear and by recording your visions as they occur, you will soon develop your clairvoyance to the point where you will see any event or outcome by simply tuning into your inner vision, thereby giving you an untold advantage when it comes to making the right choices and decisions every single time.

Steps to Improve Your Clairvoyant Abilities

Step 1: Unblock as well as Release Your Clairvoyant Fears

You may experience clairvoyance manifestation in one way or the other in your life. In some time, you may block it, and you may not recognize what exactly it is. What you need to do as the first step is to unblock as well as release the fears that are build up in you regarding the excellent gift you have. You need to find a cool place and focus on your breath as a way of trying to identify the primary source of your fear. Do not be afraid that you may go off the deep or you may experience the psychic episodes. Know that there is a difference between the psychotic and psychic episodes. Do not worry about what the other people will say or think when they realize you got this precious gift in you. You may think to turn that off as a way to respond, but that should not be the case. You need to find a way to release the fear that is in you and find an affirmation to repeat from time to time. Repeat that statement as many times as you can, and your concern will no more be there.

Step 2: Keep Your Focus on the Third Eye

When you get through with the first step, it is time to put in practice the second step; which is focusing on your third eye. The third eye chancre is just above the eyebrows. It is responsible for the visual abilities that are seeing visions, symbols as well as flashes. What you need to do is close your eyes and pay attention to the area between the eyebrows. You have to imagine that is has a horizontal-oval shape which is between you're your eyes. Notice whether the eyelid of the third eye is opening or closing. If it is closed, you need to ask it to open and repeat that until it obeys. When the third eye opens, you will feel some love as well as a warm rush in your body. It will be so since you are having an encounter with the part of you that had blocked. It may be reasonable if you are not able to visualize your third eye on the first attempt. You need to keep on doing that, and with the time you will get it. You need to rub the third eye, and in that way, you will stimulate as well as awaken it. As the power of your abilities increase, your other senses will increase their power as well.

Step 3: Boost Your Visual Imagination

The moment your third eye agrees to open, you will start to see glittering lights, dots, pictures as well as floating shadows. The images can come in different forms or colors. It can either in black and white or either full colors. They can be in movement or not moving, and it can have life or looks like a cartoon. The first image you are likely to see may not be very clear and somehow fizzy. That is the reason you need to increase the visual imagination before you start making use of the clairvoyant ability that. You will use that ability to answer some specific questions. You need to increase the visual creativity, and you can request the image to be a bit clear brighter as well as grow in size and strength. You have to make sure that you use all the power as well as intention within you to request that. All you need to do is visualize yourself while standing in a garden or a field with flowers. While standing, imagine that you are holding several balloons and not of the same color. Continue believing that you release one of them as you watch it floating up the sky. Once the balloon has entirely disappeared, go to the next one and have a similar imagination. You have to repeat that until the moment you will see clearly when each balloon is no longer visible.

Step 4: You Need to Answer Some Specific Questions Using Clairvoyance

When you feel you are ready to answer specific questions using your abilities, you have to practice with questions. The questions should have a focus and be on particular matters. You have to stick to questions that are not broad since broad questions will consume your energy and without any positive yields. You always have to ask questions that are precise and formulated. Be very specific on the thing that you want instead of asking general questions.

Step 5: Interpret Clairvoyant Images

You will see the mental pictures from time to time. Once you can see them, you also need to be in a position to understand as well as interpret them so that you can make use of your visions. If you think that the images are not sensible, you can decide to ask silently or loudly for clarity from the higher spirits. The answers that the higher senses will give you will come as a feeling, sound, or thought. In the beginning, you may see them as vague or random, but you need not worry. It is normal, and you need to trust yourself as well as the higher spirits, and you may opt to repeat the question. The higher spirits will make sure that they send you the answer until you are satisfied, and it is clear to you.

Step 6: You Need to Believe as Well as Work with Faith

It is an important step that will improve the clairvoyant abilities that you have. You have to believe as well as have confidence in the things that you will see or hear. You need to discredit your skills, and you think it is a daydream or the mind is just wondering. A Wishful thinking, as well as the imagination, will help you to achieve a lot of things, and you will be in a position to exercise your potential fully. By doing that, you will use your clairvoyance power, and you will appreciate life more and see things from a better perspective.

Step 7: Write down About the Psychic Experiences

When you are done with doing all that is in step number six, you are ready to move to step number seven. You have to create a journal concerning the psychic experiences that you have had at a particular time. That will be an excellent way to help you develop further as well as understand the psychic abilities that you pose. When you can recognize such skills, you will appreciate the person you are becoming, and you will get an opportunity to grow in terms of power. It does not matter whether you are developing claircognizance, clairaudience, clairvoyance as well as clairsentience you need to put that in writing. When you write that down, you will keep a habit of getting back to the journal and reading what is in it. You will access to how valuable, real as well as reliable the clairvoyance ability that you have can be. You will have more insight into the most reliable psychic and the intrusive skills that are in you. In that way, you will get more power and have more strength to exercise control in you. You will appreciate the kind of life you are living and the precious gift that is in you.

Step 8: Find a Clairvoyant Person

Each person has a way of how they look into things. Having a different perspective of the entire thing from a person who as similar powers will help you to appreciate yourself. You will know that you are not the only person out there who has such skills and the fear in you will be over. Find a person you can open up to about the clairvoyance experiences you have had, and it will be of much help to you. You will have time to learn from one another and share things from everyone's point of the angle. That way, you will be in a position to support one another and grow together. The journey will be more comfortable, knowing that there is someone you can talk to when you feel overwhelmed.

Step 9: Meditate

If you want to grow as well as develop the psychic ability that you pose, you need to have sessions of meditation from time to time. When in the meditation process, you will connect with your higher person as well as be more receptive to intuitive messages. Meditation will be essential in helping you open up the third eye and improving the mind's eye to visualize more. Meditate with a specific intention, and that is to strengthen the clairvoyant ability. You will be in a position to open and strengthen the third eye. You can either choose to go on a guided meditation or do the meditation on your own. It can be either a short one or the one that you decide to go, but you have to put in mind it should be regular. When you get a guided meditation, you will be in a position to trust the visions that you are having. You will believe that whatever images you are experiencing is a big part of developing clairvoyant abilities.

As you work out to increase the power of clairvoyance, you need not forget that it is an experience that is close to daydreaming. You need patience when you are going through this process so that it will be successful. It will take quite some time, and you have practiced all this to the end if you fail along the way that will mean that you have just been wasting your time and energy. Your time and energy are so precious, and so you need to take care of how you use them. Spending them will not be such a good idea, after all. There are no shortcuts when it comes to boosting your clairvoyance power.

The psychic energy will come in a more natural way to one person compared to the other one. People are not similar, and so you should not worry if the gift is not stronger in you than it is in the other person. The psychic power in you is not in any way connected to curses or the dark side. It is a way to connect you better to your creator, and you will go to greater heights spiritually. You need to let the message in despite the busy schedule that you have. Give your mind some time to calm and audit every experience that you have come through. You have to let you go and let God. Do away with any negativity that you have before you start the journey of taking your spiritual connection to the next level. Make sure that you have a positive energy that is surrounding you, and you will be clear the negativity that is in you. That will serve as a protection, and there will be no blockages along the way. As you go on with the journey, you may realize that it is getting more enjoyable. It will be evident to you that if you get closer to God as well as your spirituality, the clearer all things will become.

Chapter 4 : Achieving Higher Consciousness

Mankind has always tried to find ways to fight stress, anxieties, and worries in spirituality and devotion. When questions become too confusing and your mind has no answers, you turn to the powers of the unseen. Science couldn't understand it and hence rejected it. The same was the fate of the concept of the third eye. Our ancestors across all cultures of the east and the west have believed in the concept of the third eye. They believed that it had the answers to the most complex problems. Modern medicine leaves many people to understand that they should only consider what can be seen, heard, or touched. Stress, anxiety, and worry remained problems that could only be treated through pills. Such treatments only treat symptoms and are never lasting.

Until recently, the third eye was considered a concept suited for the occult or an idea favored by spirituality. Scientists were not ready to believe that such amazing things could be done with simple techniques like meditation. They thought the higher sense of perception or consciousness was not possible in general. This has been answered now. New research carried out by neurologists and psychotherapists have changed the way science looks at the pineal gland now.

Serotonin and melatonin are two important hormones stimulated by the pineal. It is known now that these hormones play a very important role in regulating your mood and cycles of sleep and wakefulness. These two things have a profound impact on the way we function in life. Our knowledge and experience of the world as we know it is governed by these things. In a mental state of unpleasantness, you will not be able to enjoy even the most beautiful things in the world. If you are sad, stressed, or unhappy, even the tastiest food would not look appealing to you. In opposition, when you feel pleasant, even your least favorite foods might taste slightly better to you. The pineal gland regulates both these hormones. If your pineal gland is functioning smoothly, you can keep stress and anxiety at bay.

Meditation has been considered as one of the most effective ways to activate the pineal gland and improve its abilities. Science has proven that meditation can bring real physiological changes in the brain that help in the evolution and growth of the pineal gland. This makes the concept of higher consciousness a possibility.

Meditation also helps in reducing the release of the stress hormone called cortisol. This hormone can start several negative processes. It has a strong physiological impact on your body. From obesity to adverse inflammatory responses, cortisol is a big offender. Meditation can help you in suppressing the release of this hormone.

It has also been proven that an active pineal gland can help you in bringing down your sense of fear. If your sense of fear goes down, you won't show frequent 'fight or flight' responses at the drop of a hat. Your reactions to situations will become subtler.

Sages, seers, monks, and people indulged in devotion are known to show reduced signs of fear. Spiritual consciousness brings down such responses. We now know that spirituality has a deep connection with the pineal gland

and the third eye. The third eye opens the gate for spiritual consciousness. Your sixth chakra helps you in raising your consciousness and opening up the seventh chakra of the spiritual dimension.

So, if your pineal gland is healthy and your third eye is active, you will have fewer worries. Your anxiety levels would go down. Your reactions to situations in life become stable, and you react in a calm and composed manner.

Our reactions to situations are as per our worldly experience and the way our brain processes that information. Between your eye and the pineal gland lies the very important orbitofrontal cortex. It gathers information as you view and experience things in the outside world and distributes it to the other parts of the brain for use. This is the primary point where all information comes and goes. The output of this part would dictate your behavior, emotional, and physiological responses.

A healthy pineal gland working with the orbitofrontal cortex helps in forming a sync between the information that's coming and going. An increased sense of consciousness led by the pineal gland can help in bringing stable reactions. Your level of tolerance to situations can rise phenomenally. The pineal gland can help in moderating reactions to a great extent. People who meditate for longer periods and have a healthy pineal and an activated third eye will have very controlled heart rate, blood flow, pain threshold, etc.

The hippocampus in our brain is one specific area that has a deep impact on your memory and consciousness. You can proactively work to expand your hippocampus through third eye meditation. It is humanly possible to do this knowingly. Stress, on the other hand, can lead to shrinkage in the size of the hippocampus. The more stressful you remain, the lower would be your levels of consciousness.

Therefore, it is possible to get over the feelings of stress, anxiety, and worry. These are responses to the way our brain processes the information received from the world. We can actively improve the mechanism that processes this information correctly.

Stress, worry, and anxiety kick in the survival mechanism. These feelings keep us confined to the roots. We always remain busy with thoughts of self-preservation and never look beyond although we want to do so.

A quest for knowledge and a sense of greater purpose has always intrigued humankind. Survival hasn't been the sole focus of our race, and this makes us different from other species. The third eye helps us in this pursuit.

We have always aspired to look beyond the limits of the things that can be seen. We want to know things that are beyond comprehension. We all want to know what is in store for us in the future. However, all this isn't possible through the available physical means. The physical eyes have limitations. This is the point from which the all-seeing third eye gains prominence.

The third eye can help us in having a greater vision. It brings with itself the power of wisdom and foresight. It opens the portals to cosmic vision. It is believed that the awakened third eye can dilute the barriers of time and space. It works beyond the known four dimensions.

The physical location of the mystical third eye is the pineal gland. Once activated, this gland can help you in gaining greater consciousness and also psychic abilities. The ethereal energy in your body becomes intense.

Activating the third eye will help you in rising above these restrictions. It will expand the depth of your thought and consciousness. You will experience the world in a new light.

Chapter 5 : Mindfulness Meditation - Higher levels of consciousness

The higher the released energy flows, the greater the spiritual uplift the meditator feels. Fire sparks emanating from the mouth of the kundalini snake reach the hemispheres of the brain, stimulating them more and more to vigorous activity. The meditator begins to experience the deepest ecstasy, joy, and peace. It seems that the whole body is plunged into an ocean of happiness and bliss.

With the stimulation of the right hemisphere, hidden possibilities of extrasensory perception, such as clairvoyance, clairaudience, telepathy, providence, and so on, come to the surface. Consciousness begins to expand and go beyond its borders, opening up new dimensions of cosmic unity. The sense of self-identity begins to make quantum leaps into the ever-increasing orbits of the cosmic mind. This stage of comprehension of time and space is a reward to the adept for all his efforts.

Here are a few meditations that help rise to higher levels of consciousness and control internal energy.

Meditation on the Clouds of Light

Find a comfortable place to relax. Let your thoughts flow freely, come, and go; you are only an observer. Take a deep breath, hold your breath. Check for tension in the body. If you find such areas, free them - and on the exhale to get rid of everything that prevents you from completely relaxing. Take a deep breath again. As you exhale, release all energy and all your thoughts from the body. Take a deep breath. Feel new energy entering the body; you breathe in new possibilities and allow the body to become light. Relax more and more - until you stop feeling the body.

When fully relaxed, imagine a colorful mist vibrating around you. You, being light, smoothly pass into this fog, just your being has a slightly higher density. Clouds of energy slowly float around you. Relax on one of them, feel safe. This cloud lifts you up and takes you to an infinite world. The boundaries between time and space are erased. You are immersed in a world of infinite beauty and endless possibilities. You are floating in the cloud, feeling how light you have become. Suddenly you see a giant rock below; the cloud softly and easily lands, you descend on a rock.

Feel the strength of the stone, feel the power emanating from the rock. You look back, and you see a big river. You cannot make out where it begins and where it ends. You are fascinated by the water stream. It is an endless river of energy, a river of life. You come closer to the water and try to examine its color, to feel it with your whole being. What sounds do you hear? You are the light, so you can safely enter the water, cross it, rush along with the stream, and when you want, stop.

Relax and try to realize what you need most at the moment. What is your main intention? What emotions will accompany you on the way to the chosen goal? Feel the energy of these emotions, feel how it moves through your light body, burns, pulsates. Inhale energy with your whole being. Try to see the paintings, images, symbols associated with it: they will appear in front of the inner eye themselves; you can only focus on them.

When you are completely filled with this energy, enter the river, dissolve for a moment in it, purify the energy, and then release it into the water. See how the energy cloud comes out of you, touches the water, and gradually disappears in the stream. Take a deep breath. Your desire merges with the source of life. Enjoy the river of life for some more time. Take a deep breath again and exit the river. Notice that the colored fog surrounds you again, and you rise up with it. You descend to the cloud and return. With each deep breath, you return to the outside world and feel peace and satisfaction.

Sacred Space Meditation

Relax, sit in a comfortable position. Close your eyes, calm your mind. Breathe slowly and deeply; breathing comes from the diaphragm. For a while, just breathe and pay attention to the spine. It is a pillar connecting earth and heaven.

Feel the energy being concentrated at both ends of this pillar. Let the flow of earthly energy move upward, exit the crown of the head, and disperse into the Universe. Together with the energy flow, all negative emotions, pain, anxiety, tension are carried away.

Your whole being is filled with peace. Let the mind be like the ocean, and thoughts - bubbles appearing on the surface of the water. You may remember your thoughts better, but for now, remain a simple observer. Breathe deeper, gradually slow down your breathing. With each breath, relax your body and mind more and more.

Feel the cool red fog enveloping you. It is not hot, not cold: you can only feel it with your skin.

Feel yourself on a cloud firm enough to hold you on yourself, but very cozy and comfortable. Each part of your body rests on a cloud: legs, arms, back, neck, head - all organs feel calm. The cloud begins to plunge slowly into the red fog, and you plunge with it. Immersion is very slow; you go deeper and deeper and relax even more. The fog begins to change its color: from brilliant red to red-orange.

Gradually, the orange color changes to yellow-lemon. Your body is also painted in lemon color. You are floating on a cloud that carries you to the green summer lawn. You can even hear the wind shaking the grass, feel the flowing blue light from heaven.

Blue light turns into purple; moonless night comes, dark, peaceful, and quiet. The cloud you were floating on gently lands.

The fog disappears. You lie on your back on the green grass. You feel light blows of the wind; you can hear the faint chatter of night insects.

Wherever you are, there is always something that pulls you toward you. It may be someplace, person, impression. What you are thinking about may appear right next to you because you are in a sacred place of fulfillment of desires. Everything can change here, but any changes will occur only at your request. You built this place, inhabited it. Rise, explore the sacred space in which you are. May you meet with something (or about whom) have long dreamed of.

After a while, you will realize that the time has come to leave the sacred place. Say goodbye to what you saw, leave without regret, because you can always come back here whenever you want.

Lie on your back and again feel the fog enveloping you. This time it is dark, like a moonless sky. Feel the cloud again under your feet, arms, back, neck, and head. It supports you - and begins to rise very slowly.

Breathe deeply, watch the gradual change of colors: the dark color of the sky turns into blue, cyan, green, yellow. All this time, you continue to rise slowly; yellow turns to summer orange, then red. Let your mind still float, and your body will slowly return to the tangible world. You begin to feel the floor with your back, to realize the room in which you are. You are coming back.

Understanding the Benefits of a Strong Meditation Practice

The mindfulness movement is rapidly gaining popularity in the Western world. If before meditation was practiced only by people who are fond of various kinds of spiritual practices, now it is considered the most common thing. Now in Europe and here in the USA, the phrase "I practice meditation" no longer causes a wary-detached attitude, as before. So, what's the point? What are some of the benefits of meditation or mindfulness? Why are more and more people doing it? I will try to answer these questions in this chapter. But let's take it in order.

What Meditation Is

In 2007, a study was published that experimentally confirmed the previously existing hypothesis that a person has two different forms of self-consciousness, and different parts of the brain are responsible for them. These two forms of self-awareness are called the narrative mode (story mode, narrative mode of self-reference), and the experience mode (empirical mode, experiential mode of self-reference).

The narrative mode is a mechanism by which we can think about the past, present, and future. Its essence is that our attention is partially or completely captured by thoughts that give meaning to what is happening. The story mode is responsible for our understanding of who we are, what is happening around us, what we are striving for, what connects us with others, and so on. The story mode connects the past, present, and future for us into one semantic picture.

The empirical mode is the ability to perceive our direct experience, what is happening to us at this second. Our direct experience consists of several parts. This is, firstly, the sensations realized with the help of the senses (hearing, sight, touch, smell, taste, balance). Secondly, these are internal sensations - thoughts, imagination, emotions, and internal states.

Meditation is the training of attention. When we meditate, we train to keep our focus on exactly what we are experiencing at the moment. That is, we train to be in the mode of experience.

Why Do We Need Each of These Forms of Self-Awareness?

Both forms of self-awareness are necessary. Narrative mode serves to perform any action. To do something, you need to make a decision. To make a decision, you need to somehow explain to yourself what is happening. Medicine knows cases of damage to the part of the brain that is responsible for the narrative regimen. In cases where this department completely loses its working capacity, a person turns into a vegetable. He does nothing more and does not say anything.

Once I read about one case when such a person fell into the pool and drowned. He could not have a motive to perform any actions for his salvation. For a motive to appear, one must first give the event some meaning. If the narrative mode does not work, what is happening seems pointless.

The empirical regime allows us to be in the present moment and feel what is happening to us. In addition to the fact that we get complete satisfaction from any pleasant sensations (for example, the pleasure of eating, music, sex, etc.), we are better aware of what is happening around us. That is, we can give the event meaning more accurately. The empirical mode allows us to adjust how we explain what is happening, taking into account what is happening here and now.

If the empirical regime is poorly trained, then our thoughts are more based on our ideas about ourselves and the world and to a lesser extent, on what is happening here and now.

Let's look at an example:

Victor works in sales. He is new to this business. He attended several trainings where he was told the theory. But he is not good at applying this theory in practice. When he speaks with the client, usually at some point, the client begins to close, and the contact disappears. Victor began to practice meditation. Now he notices that the contact disappears when he begins to feel excitement amid a desire to close the deal as soon as possible. Gradually, he began to recognize this sensation at an early stage and learned to behave more calmly, despite the excitement. Over time, he noticed that he began to feel more relaxed.

In this example, the practice of meditation helps Victor to pay attention to his feelings during a conversation with a client. This led to the fact that he understood the reason for the disappearance of contact with the client. As a result, over time, he first managed to adjust his behavior, and then his emotional reactions became adequate.

Awareness is a kind of feedback mechanism that allows you to adjust behavior. Without realizing what we feel, we usually act on autopilot.

Yet another example:

Andrew is a conflict person in terms of his personality. When he was angry, he could not stop. The conflict simply unwound according to a previously known scenario. But Andrew never thought about it. Each time he drew conclusions for himself and lived on. Conclusions usually came down to the fact that the other side is to blame.

When Andrew began to practice meditation, first of all, it helped him realize that he was behaving aggressively. Then he noticed that often in a conflict, he doesn't react to the essence of the issue, but to the form in which the other side answers him. This allowed him to react less emotionally. Andrew realized that from time to time, he spoke stingy, offensive phrases, the purpose of which was to offend another person. He began to learn to stop in time. The practice of mindfulness helps Andrew more often and faster turn off the autopilot in a conflict and do something for a peaceful resolution of the situation.

What Other Benefits Does Meditation Provide?

The fact is that the mechanisms of attention are the most low-level mechanisms of our consciousness. Therefore, the practice of meditation affects absolutely all aspects of our lives. Known and research-confirmed effects include:

- Increased attention span. Reducing the number of random distractions.

- Improving self-control ability.

- Increasing the pain threshold.

- Improving learning and memorization.

- Reduces irritability and stress.

Meditation to Attain Your Divine Self

As you have seen in the mediation guides, the most common meditation technique is observing breathing. Even though it is very good for training concentration, in terms of awareness of your divine self, you need to take it up a notch. For this, I recommend trying a technique called marking or mental noting.

Marking is a technique from the attention category without a choice. In other words, we are not trying to concentrate on something specific, but simply try to notice what is happening to us, whatever that is. And when we notice, we call it one word. Perhaps we feel some sensations in the body. Perhaps we are thinking about something. Maybe we want something. Maybe we imagine something. Anything. In a word.

There are various marking options without a choice. You can start with anyone. The easiest option is to use only three words: see, hear, and feel. Moreover, each word can refer to both external sensation and internal. For example, the word "hear" can denote perception by the hearing organs and the thought that "sounds" in the head.

As for the time for meditation, 10-15 minutes a day is enough to start. It is advisable to find the time when no one will bother you.

While meditating, you can sit, lie, stand, or walk. Eyes may be open or closed. You can sit on a chair or the floor. All this is not so important at first. It is important to remember that the practice of meditation is a long game. And therefore, at the first stage, it is advisable not to overdo it.

The practice of meditation is usually associated with people with Buddhist monasteries, where people come to live to someday achieve enlightenment. At the same time, enlightenment itself is usually not taken seriously but is used to denote a certain unattainable ideal that one will have to strive for a lifetime.

Probably, touching upon this topic, I may seem strange to some but still, take a chance. Enlightenment is an absolutely real and quite strong change in the work of the human psyche that can occur as a result of the practice of meditation. I know because it happened to me. It happens suddenly, at one point. In Buddhist texts, one can find descriptions of several stages of enlightenment. Each of these steps leads to a radical increase in the basic level of awareness.

Achieving enlightenment is no easy task. But it is not impossible. According to Daniel Ingram, whose book gave me an understanding of the technical side of meditation, it is no more difficult than graduating from a university.

And for this, it is not necessary to go to live in a monastery. If you meditate an hour a day and receive personal recommendations from an experienced teacher, I think it can take from several months to several years without interruption from your usual life. If you are interested, try to find such a teacher.

Meditation has a hugely positive effect on my life. I believe that the further you go, the more you will understand what I mean. Good luck!

Chapter 6 : Pineal Gland Activation and Chakras

Activation of the Pineal Gland Through Guided Meditation (10-15 Minutes)

The pineal gland is the physical location of the Ajna chakra.

This small pine shaped gland is placed in the middle of the brain.

It controls your sleep cycle, sexual maturation, and many other vital hormones. It produces the DMT, the brain's natural psychedelic drug. It helps us in connecting with our spirituality.

Stimulating this small gland will help you in awakening you spiritually. It will help you in interacting with your divine energies. It will help you in seeing through life.

Start with the breathing exercise.

Inhale slowly, take the fresh air deep into your gut. Gather your worries, tensions, and thoughts. Now exhale slowly. Release all your worries and tension with the air.

Clear your mind. Racing thoughts are a distraction. You need peace and calm. Soothe your senses. Clear your mind.

Once again, inhale slowly, take the fresh air deep into your gut. Gather your worries, tensions, and thoughts. Now exhale slowly. Release all your worries and tension with the air.

Clear the waste from your mind. Nothing is important at this very moment. You are the prime source of energy. You are embarking on a journey to enlightenment. Start with peace of mind. Tranquility must prevail everywhere.

One more time, inhale slowly, take the fresh air deep into your gut. Gather your worries, tensions, and thoughts. Now exhale slowly. Release all your worries and tension with the air.

Close your eyes and focus.

Focus on the center of your brain. The pineal gland is located here. Establish contact with it. Let it know that you want to connect.

It is very powerful. It is the source of immense power. It is the seat of the soul. The place of the Ajna chakra.

It has spiritual powers. It will help in your unification with the universe. You will become a part of the great network. You do not need an external source. You are the source.

Breathe into the pineal gland. Fill it with divine power. Energize it. You can charge and activate it.

You will feel some throbbing sensation. It is the pineal gland activating.

Focus on it. Let it know that you want to connect with it. You want to become one with your greater self. The eternal light inside you.

Breathe deeply. You want to amalgamate with this divine light. You want to become one with it. Leave all the negative energies behind. Move towards the source of pure and pious energy. The unblemished aura.

It will fill you. It will enlighten you. It will awaken you. Seek and you will find.

Expunge the pollution out of your system. You will not carry anything this point forward. There is no place for worldly feelings. Love, hate, and animosities become meaningless. They create Karma. You are a forgiving soul.

Move ahead. As one with the power. Focus deep. Breathe Deeper.

It is a long journey. Keep moving.

You will feel immense calm. Light all around you. It isn't hot. It is soothing. This is the light of the soul. Your soul is emanating radiance. Absorb it. It is all for you. Relish it.

Enjoy the moment. It is blissful. It is the moment. You have always desired it.

Now, take a deep breath. Inhale slowly, take the fresh air deep into your gut. Wait for a few moments. Now exhale slowly.

Again, take a deep breath. Inhale slowly, take the fresh air deep into your gut. Wait for a few moments. Exhale.

Rub your palms vigorously. Make them warm. Cover your eyes with them. Keep them covered for a moment.

Now open your eyes very slowly. Do not rush. Loosen your body. Do not get up immediately.

Ponder over your achievements in the process.

Chakras Meaning

Another aspect of spiritual awakening is recognizing and working with the chakra system. Chakras are centers where energy collects throughout the body. They are generally centered around major organ systems, and manipulating the energy and clearing blockages of energy in these areas can help bring more balance to your life and alleviate symptoms associated with a specific chakra.

The chakra system was originally developed in India, centuries ago, and it still plays a major role in Eastern medicine today. Chakras are all about energy balance. Just like your spine, the alignment of your chakras must be just right, or there will be a pain. Learning to pinpoint when a chakra point is out of alignment is the key to fixing it. The body and mind are in a constant state of finding balance. Energy flows and changes, and it is necessary to take stock of your needs, both physical and emotional, as it relates to your chakras, on the regular.

Types of Chakras

There are seven major chakras in total, all aligned along the centerline of the body. They are as follows:

Root Chakra: This energy point is located at the base of the spine, at the tailbone. It is called the root chakra because it is meant to be the energy that grounds you. As you sit on the floor, this chakra is directly in line with the energy of the earth, literally grounding you to it. On a spiritual level, this energy is what keeps you humble and centered in everyday life. It is what gives you purpose, and continually reminds you of your purpose.

A misaligned root chakra can have you feeling as if you are not grounded, unstable. It can manifest itself as having money issues, insecurity finding housing, or a place to call your own. Energy imbalance in this area may lead to trouble securing food or feeling as if you are satisfied. It is associated with the color red.

An imbalance may manifest itself as stiffness in the legs, knee issues, sciatica, a weak immune system, and eating disorders.

Sacral Chakra: This chakra gives us the ability to interact and accept others. It is the energy that drives exploration and new experiences. It is located just above the root chakra, about two inches below the navel. Energy from this chakra drives passion and sexual desire, pleasure, and abundance.

A disrupted flow of energy in this chakra can cause a decrease in sex drive, little ability to connect with others on an emotional level and show interest or desire in anything. This chakra is commonly associated with the symptoms of malaise and disinterest during depression. Lack of energy here makes it difficult to show compassion for others and find common ground. It also makes you less able to accept inevitable change in life.

Lack of energy here can manifest itself physically as urinary or sexual issues, kidney problems, and lower back pain.

Solar Plexus Chakra: This concentration of energy is centered in the upper abdomen, near the stomach. It is the driving force for our self-confidence and self-esteem. Without this energy, we do not dare to follow through with our goals and aspirations. Without it, we are meek and have no confidence in our capability of success.

Like our pineal gland, the solar plexus helps guide and drive life forward. You may recognize its power as that itch to do something new, to try new things and become more successful. This power waxes and wanes as the chakra moves in and out of alignment. It is associated with the color yellow.

Energy drops may manifest with general fatigue, digestive issues, and gallbladder or pancreas issues, including diabetes.

Heart Chakra: It's no surprise that this mass of energy is located on the spine right next to the heart. It is responsible for joy, love and peace. Our heart organ often gets the credit for love, but it is a beaming ray of energy from our heart chakra that fills our chest cavity with feelings of excitement and warmth.

Strengthening this chakra increases our ability and capacity to love, and at what magnitude. It defines the relationships we have and keep. It is associated with the color green, not red, as you might expect!

Issues with respiratory infections, asthma, heart disease and circulatory issues can be a physical manifestation of low energy in the heart chakra.

Throat Chakra: This little gem is centered right in the center of our throat. It is responsible for our ability for good communication. When in good alignment, this chakra gives us the energy to articulate our ideas and needs in a way that others can easily understand.

When out of alignment, it may be difficult to work with others and get your point across. We all have moments when it seems like no matter how well you explain something, people don't understand you. Not enough energy is available to formulate your words and emotions in such a way that makes an impact on others.

Issues with the thyroid, laryngitis, ear infections, and shoulder or neck pain are a good indicator that your throat chakra is out of alignment.

Third Eye Chakra: Yes, it has its own chakra! It is no wonder that a great mass of energy is centered right where the third eye is located, just above the eyes in the center of your forehead. This chakra is responsible for your intuition and decision-making skills.

You may have felt a decrease in this chakra's energy before, manifested as an inability to make a decision. Generally, wishy-washy people lack energy in this chakra, as their inner self is unable to guide their decisions, leaving them hanging, wondering what to do. Realigning this chakra invites wisdom and confidence that you are making educated decisions.

Chronic headaches, blurry vision, and hormonal imbalance, can all be signs of a third eye energy deficiency. We also cannot forget about depression and anxiety as possible symptoms.

Crown Chakra: Last, but not least, the crown chakra represents our ability to be connected spiritually. It is located at the very top of the skull. It represents our ability to see the beauty in the world and have joy within us. As you sit in a seated position, you are rooted in your root chakra, and your spine stands lengthened with your crown chakra pointed straight up to the heavens.

In meditation, this chakra will attract and accept energy in through your head and radiate it throughout your body. Lacking energy in this area means you will find little joy in your surroundings and the rest of your chakras will suffer from lack of energy as well.

Sensitivity to light and sound, as well as depression and the inability to concentrate or learn, are good indications of a problem with your crown chakra.

Knowing the spiritual functions of each chakra makes it easier to pinpoint when anyone is out of alignment. Our bodies and spirits are in a constant state of fluctuation, so at any given time, any chakra may not be functioning properly, even on a day to day basis. It is important to recognize these subtle changes so that adjustments can be made to realign the energy balance.

If one chakra is out of alignment for a long time, it begins to show. For example, if your root chakra is out of whack, you may notice that you lose your ability to control spending, pay bills and keep a secure home. There just isn't enough energy to focus on these things. Over time, the problems mount, creating stress. Aligning this chakra at subtle hints of a problem can help avoid things like financial ruin, loss of relationships or declines in health.

The imbalance of one chakra also causes the overcompensation of others, to try and balance themselves. This can manifest in several ways, depending on which is acting up. You may be doing very well in one aspect of life, but completely failing in another, something many of us recognize. The goal is to balance all energies, so we are strong and successful in all areas of life.

Sixth Sense – Developing Psychic Awareness

Have you ever had a feeling about something and you just know what others might not feel, or see? Have you ever heard the thoughts of another, but second-guessed that you did? Have you had a dream before that come true days later? Do you ever feel the presence of things that are not of the earthly realm? This is just scratching the surface of some of the things that begin to happen when you awaken your psychic awareness.

As part of Kundalini rising and the process of clearing and releasing blockages and negativity from your subtle body, you shift your perception of reality to the extent that you are able to crack open your latent abilities to receive input from other dimensions. This ability isn't reserved for a select few or passed down genetically through generations, although that has been known to happen. This power to feel beyond the physical realm exists in us all and can be nurtured and grown into everyday use and understanding.

Many people have fear about this level of input because it can feel uncomfortable or vulnerable to tap into the unknown, into things that on the Earth plane we call magic, witchcraft, or superstition. Really, it's truly available to anyone to use this ability. When we are locked in our sleeping state (pre-kundalini rising), we cannot fathom the possibilities of such an existence, but as we allow our awakening to progress fully and reach the state of higher consciousness, we can open the brow and crown chakras to receive and accept our abilities as psychics.

These abilities can manifest in a variety of ways and have been reported as some of the side effects of the awakening process.

Chapter 7   : Mindfulness

What is Mindfulness?

Mindfulness is a standard for each human being. It's not you only need to understand how to get it.

It may be cultivated through while mindfulness is inherent Proven methods, mainly walking, seated, standing, and moving meditation (it is also potential lying down but frequently results in sleep); brief bursts we fit into regular life; and joining meditation exercise along with different activities, like sports or yoga.

When we meditate, it will not help to fixate the advantages, but instead to do the clinic, and there is no one or benefits. After we're conscious, we reduce anxiety, improve functionality through celebrating our mind, gain ness, and boost our focus on other people's well-being.

Meditation provides us a moment in our lives when we can suspend judgment and unleash curiosity about the workings of their mind, coming to our expertise to other people and ourselves -- with kindness and warmth.

According to the American Psychological Association (APA.org, 2012), mindfulness is:

"...a moment-to-moment sense of one's encounter without Judgment. Mindfulness is a condition rather than a trait. When it may be encouraged by specific activities or practices, such as meditation, it isn't equal to or interchangeable with them."

Mindfulness is as we could see through training. It isn't static, nor are several people born more cognizant compared to many others. About that which we profit from this consciousness, it involves comprehension and impartiality. In an era of networking, in which comments, likes, and opinions are coming, it's simple to learn how reflection may be a welcome change.

Another definition comes from Jon Kabat-Zinn, that enjoys Significant worldwide renowned for his job on mindfulness-based stress reduction (MBSR):

This is the definition in practitioner and academic more descriptive, and even literature. In addition to consciousness, Kabat-Zinn informs us to concentrate focus that is conscious about the 'right here, right.' It is a theory that many that practice meditation will be acquainted with, and it is why the two go together.

Mindful Meditation

One important type of meditation is mindfulness meditation. Mindfulness is the practice of bringing your attention to what is happening at the present moment, in which you develop this ability through practice and meditation.

In Buddhist traditions, it is believed that mindfulness will bring you to spiritual enlightenment and end your suffering.

Many studies have been done about mindfulness, and they have found that it will help you to live a better, happier life. When you spend your life worrying, and ruminating over things that you either can't change, or are yet to come, you are living your life in negative, and this can lead to anxiety, depression, and other mental illnesses.

When you first start practicing mindfulness meditation, start with ten minutes a day for your first few sessions. Once you have become used to the practice, increase the amount of time by five or ten increments, whichever you think you can do successfully. The goal is to get to 30 minutes a day. You can practice for longer if you want, but it isn't necessary.

The goal of mindfulness if teach you how to live in the moment. While you may think you already do, stop and think about where your mind is when you're living. When you eat your breakfast, do you taste your food appreciate what it is doing for your body? Probably not. With mindfulness, you will learn how to have your mind and body doing the same thing.

The best place to learn about mindfulness is within the Buddhist tradition. We get the term "mindfulness" from the Pali word "sati" and the Sanskrit word "smriti". Smriti means "to bear in mind," "to remember," or "to recollect." Sati's meaning is also "to remember."

Now that you understand what mindfulness is let's move onto a few meditations to help you get started living mindfully.

Three Minute Body and Sound

Start by taking notice of your posture at this moment. You could be lying down, standing, or sitting. Notice how your body feels as it is at this moment. Now see if you can notice the sensations that are currently present in your body at this moment in time.

You may notice a lightness or heaviness, weight or pressure. You may even notice coolness, warmth, movement, pulsating, or vibration. You can notice these sensations anywhere throughout your body. The only thing you have to do is notice them.

Notice these things with interest and curiosity. Take a deep breath in. As you breathe in, allow your body to relax. Don't do anything other than be present and aware of your body.

Now allow all of those sensations to release. Now turn your focus to the sounds around. These can be inside or outside of your room. There could be many different types of sounds. Quiet sounds, or loud sounds. You should also take notice of the silence that happens between the sounds. Notice how the sound come and go.

The mind tends to want to concentrate on those sounds. It starts to come up with a story for the sound. Or you think you have to react to it: I don't like that, I like that.

Instead, see if you can only listen. Take notice of it with interest and curiosity. The sounds are just coming and going.

Now turn your focus again to your body; presently standing, lying, or seated. Take note of obvious body sensations. Take another deep breath. Allow your body to soften. Once you are ready, slowly open your eyes.

Nine Minute Loving Meditation

To start this meditation, allow yourself to feel relaxed and comfortable where you are seated. In this practice, you will cultivate positive emotions, particularly, loving-kindness. Which means your desire someone to be happy, or for yourself to feel happy.

This isn't dependent on anything, and it's not conditional. This is only allowing your heart to open to yourself or someone else. Take this moment to check in with yourself to see how you feel right now. Allow whatever is here, to be here.

Allow your mind to think of something. This should include someone, as soon as you think of them, you feel happy. See if you can bring someone to mind. This could be a friend or a relative. It's best if it's somebody that you have a non-complicated relationship with. It should just be a general sense, which once they come to mind you feel happy. You can even choose a child.

If you are having a hard time of thinking of a person, you can also choose a pet. Any creature that is easy to feel love for. Allow them to come to mind.

Feel as if they are standing in front of you. You can see, feel, and sense them. As you picture this, take note of how you feel inside. You could feel the warmth, or your face may feel warm. You could also start smiling or have a sense of expansiveness. This is loving-kindness.

This feeling is natural, and everybody can access it at any given moment. Now that you have this loved one in front of you, start wishing them well. I wish them to be protected from danger, and to be safe. I wish them to be peaceful, and happy. I wish them to be strong and healthy. I wish them to have well-being, and ease. You can wish them exactly what I said, or you can use your words.

Notice the sense of allowing this loving-kindness come from you, and how you are being touched by your loved one.

During this, you may have images come to mind, notice light or color, or you could have a feeling. The words you say to your loved one can bring more of these feelings. Say whatever is most meaningful to yours. I wish them to be free of anxiety, stress, and fear.

While you are sending them these words and feelings of loving-kindness, check with yourself to see how you feel. Picture your loved one has turned around and has started to send these feelings back to you. See if you can receive this loving-kindness from them and take it in.

They're wishing you well, to be happy. This means you. I wish you to be at ease and peace. I wish you to be protected and safe from all danger. I wish you to have wellbeing and joy.

Allow yourself to take this in. If you have not started to feel this loving-kindness, or you never have in other meditations, it's not a big deal. This practice is to plant seeds. If you start feeling something other than this loving-kindness, check into that feeling. What is it that you're feeling? You may need to learn from this feeling.

If you are ready, and this isn't always going to be easy, but try to send yourself some loving-kindness. You can picture this as a light flowing down your body from the heart. All you need is a sense of it. Say to yourself; I wish to be protected and safe from danger. I wish to be strong and healthy. I wish to be peaceful and happy. I wish to accept myself for who I am.

Then, when you ask yourself, "what will make me happy?" notice what comes up, and offer yourself that. I wish to have meaningful work, close family, and friends, a joyful life.

Now check in again and notice how you are feeling. Now think of one person, or group of people, that you want to send loving-kindness to; picture them sitting or standing in front of you. Sense and feel them.

I wish them to be peaceful and happy. I wish them to be free of all fear, anxiety, and stress. Worry, grief. I wish them to have happiness and joy. Wellbeing.

Allow this loving-kindness to expand outward. Allow it to spread and touch everybody that you want this feeling to touch at this moment; in every direction. This can be people you do or don't know. People you have problems with. People who you love unconditionally. Imagine this feeling touching and expanding, and every animal or person it touches is filled with loving-kindness. Every person is changed.

You can picture that everybody, everywhere is peaceful and happy and at ease. Once you're ready, take a deep breath in, and open your eyes.

Chapter 8 : Meditation

What is Meditation?

Meditation is the way to open this third eye. It helps you in awakening your energy power wheels, the chakras. It takes you on the path of consciousness, knowledge, and calm. It helps you in self-realization and understanding this world better.

It is your guide on the journey to the light inside your mind. It helps you in activating the pineal gland, which is the originating source of this light. This small but crucial gland performs many actions for you. It regulates your sleep, desires and other such functions. It gets calcified with impurities over time and the search for the third eye gets difficult. This guide will help you in activating and decalcifying the pineal gland through guided meditation.

You will take on an amazing journey of self-consciousness and awakening. You will learn the ways to open your third eye. You will learn the ways to decalcify your pineal gland, the source of power. You will also learn various meditation techniques to awaken and activate your chakras and balance them. It will show you the path to awaken your psychic abilities and improve your power of intuition. The third eye is the source of these powers.

Know the healing powers inside you. This book is a journey to yourself. It will take you a bit closer to understanding and consciousness. You need no tools. You are the tool. You are the machinery. You are the operator. In this amazing world, you will learn that only you are the consumer. Everything is just centered around you. You are the focal point in the spiritual domain. This is an exploration. You will learn a lot more.

How Meditation Can Help You Activating Your Third Eye

Meditation 1: Trataka Meditation

This is an ancient meditation derived from the Tantra and Hatha yoga practices. In Sanskrit, Trataka means "to gaze" or "to look."

• This meditation requires you to sit perfectly still on the floor with legs crossed in the lotus position. If this is not comfortable, sit in a straight-backed chair where you can keep your spine straight.

- Close your eyes and breathe deeply from your belly for two-to-three minutes until your body is completely relaxed.

- Focus deeply on the area of your third eye chakra. Continue to focus on the area for a few moments.

- With both of your eyes still closed, draw them upwards towards the inner eye chakra as if you are looking at it. You may feel a strain in your eyes as you try and hold them in that position. You will know that it is the correct position when you feel your eyes "lock" slightly above the bridge of your nose, and the position does not feel too strained.

- Keep your closed eyes in that position and slowly start counting backward from 100 (with about two seconds between each count).

- Keep your closed eyes focused on the third eye chakra until you have finished counting backward to zero.

- Draw your eyes back to their normal position and breathe deeply three times to ground yourself. Allow your eyes to return to their normal movement.

- Feel yourself become grounded and open your eyes. The meditation should last between ten-to-fifteen minutes.

Some people report that when doing this meditation, they can see their thoughts as if seeing a dream. You may feel warmth in the area of the inner eye, which indicates that it is attracting energy. Also, not only is this a very powerful meditation for awakening the third eye, but it is also a great workout that keeps the eyes healthy.

Note: This meditation should be practiced in moderation to prevent the over-activation of the third eye chakra. Once a week will be enough to keep everything in balance.

Meditation 2: Body Scan Meditation for Third Eye Intuition

This meditation is specifically oriented toward increasing your intuition through the third eye chakra.

• Sit in a comfortable position with your back straight.

• Close your eyes and do the mindful breathing exercise to ground yourself. This should take two-to-three minutes, or until all the tension is released from your body and you feel completely relaxed.

• Start the body scan from the very top of your head or the crown chakra. Focus on this area until you begin to notice the sensations there. This could be tingling, pressure, a slight warmth, burning, or buzzing. Don't worry if you don't feel anything the first couple of times you practice this meditation. Your mind will become trained to pick up on these sensations over time.

• When you are ready, move down to the whole forehead area from the front to the back of your head. Focus on this area—again, noticing any sensations there.

• When you are ready, move down to the eyes, then the nose, the area above the mouth then the mouth itself. Spend a few minutes on each area and notice the sensations.

• Continue the body scan by moving downwards and exploring every part of your body; chin, neck, shoulders, arms, torso, top of the stomach, lower belly, upper thighs, legs, and finally end with the feet.

• Do not react to or judge any negative sensations that you may feel. Simply acknowledge them and move on.

• If you want, you can repeat the body scan starting once again from the top of your head.

The meditation heightens the intuition by making you more aware of the subtle sensations in your body. You may receive certain insights or "aha!" moments as you are meditating—or even days after the meditation.

Meditation 3: Golden Ball of Light

• Sit in the lotus position or a comfortable chair with your back straight.

• Breathe deeply and feel the tension leave your muscles with every breath.

• Visualize a warm stream of energy flowing through your body from the top of your head down to your toes. Continue to visualize and feel this energy slowly circulating around your body.

• Next, direct your focus to the third eye chakra and the warm energy filling the space between your brows.

• Visualize the energy coming together to form a rotating ball of golden light in the center of your third eye chakra.

- Focus on the rotating ball and the beautiful golden light that emanates from it.

- When you feel ready, allow the light to expand until it fills all of your third eye chakra. Visualize it expanding slowly until it finally emerges out of your forehead in a bright ray of incandescent golden light.

- Gaze at the beautiful ray of light with your inner eye and notice any colors or pictures that appear within it.

- Simply acknowledge what you see without judgment.

- Now, still gazing into the light with your third eye, ask your third eye if it has a message for you. Take as much time as you need.

- When you are ready, bring yourself back to reality with deep breathing and slowly open your eyes.

Again, don't worry if you don't see anything the first few times you practice this meditation. The more you advance, the stronger the ray of light will become as well as the images and messages from your third eye.

Meditation 4: Third Eye Awakening and Decalcifying the Pineal Gland

- Sit in a comfortable position and allow your body a few moments to settle and relax.

- Close your eyes, take a deep breath, and hold it for as long as you can, feeling the fullness in your lungs. Exhale slowly through your mouth.

• Bring your full focus to the third eye chakra. If it helps, you can visualize it as a small ball of light.

• Allow your senses to become vividly and intensely aware of everything around you; any sounds in the background like voices or the hum of electrical appliances, the seat beneath you, the feel of your clothes against your skin, and any smells that may come to you.

• Allow your senses to fully experience all of these things while dismissing any thoughts about them.

• Visualize your third eye absorbing and processing all of these sounds, smells, and sensations.

• When you are ready, end the meditation by taking a few deep breaths.

This meditation can be practiced daily. It energizes both the third eye chakra and the pineal gland and heightens awareness and the senses.

Meditation 5: Mindfulness Breathing Cues

This is a great meditation to keep you grounded throughout your day and regularly mindful of your third eye.

• Choose a certain cue from your daily life, such as whenever you look in the mirror or brush your teeth; when your phone rings or you have ended the call. It could be every time you look out of the window or hear a dog bark or a car horn. Just choose a cue that occurs regularly in your daily life—ideally, more than one.

- Each time they come up, breathe mindfully for a few minutes while focusing on your third eye chakra.

- Repeat the exercise whenever the cue occurs.

- This exercise allows you to relax and ground your overactive mind while also checking in with your third eye.

Tips to Get the Most out of Meditation

Here are a few suggestions to help you meditate better. These are not mandatory rules but just useful tips to consider.

Place. The ideal place to meditate should be relaxing and welcoming, with as little noise or disturbance as possible. It does not necessarily have to be indoors. Meditating in nature to the sounds of birds singing or waves sweeping onto the shore is a wonderful experience. The choice is up to you: just a calming environment that resonates with you.

Time. It is best if you are able to meditate at the same time each day; having a consistent meditation schedule really helps to ground your mind and creates a regular pattern of time-out for the body and mind. Many people find that having a regular meditation schedule gives them something to look forward to during a hectic day. Their meditation time is a quiet, energizing haven from the havoc of daily life.

Position. Whether you choose to sit on the floor or in a chair, the important thing is that you are totally comfortable. The ideal position is one where you can nod off if you want you. Always give your body time to settle down and relax before you start, as fidgeting during the meditation will break your focus.

• Try to clear your mind. Connecting with the third eye chakra and receiving information from the higher plane requires extreme clarity and calmness of the mind. This is easier said than done, especially if you are new to meditation. The best way to maintain clarity is to remain focused on the third eye for as long as possible during each meditation.

• Coming out of a meditative state is just as important as entering it. Never just open your eyes and jump up. Always bring your focus back to the physical world slowly and ground yourself with a few deep breaths until you are fully aware of your surroundings.

• Take your time. Each meditation should last for at least 30 minutes.

• Wear loose, comfortable clothing, and no shoes.

• Don't be alarmed when you suddenly receive a poignant message or thought, from your third eye. This may disrupt your concentration.

• Learn how to sit in the proper lotus position as it allows the best alignment of the body.

• Turn off cell phones, TVs, and other sources of distraction.

• Feel free to explore other forms of meditation such as guided meditation and meditating to nature sounds or music, or meditation that incorporates physical movement.

• Enjoy the experience.

How to Meditate (Guided Meditation)

These meditation sessions, when utilized correctly, can be extremely beneficial in numerous ways: from relieving stress to balancing and aligning the seven chakras. To best utilize this chapter, which offers numerous guided meditation sessions, read each of the provided meditation sessions out loud to a recording device. Make sure to use a calm, soothing, comfortable voice as you read these exercises for recording. Also, it is important to stop for an adequate amount of time between each step in the guided meditation exercises so that you do not feel rushed when you play the audio file back and are performing the meditation practices. To help you relax for these guided meditation sessions, you can also try some warm-up yoga routines or drink herbal teas (both yoga and tea have been shown to help the body relax and greatly reduce tension from the body's muscles). It is important to remember that meditation does not require you to sit alone in an empty, quiet room for twenty minutes. Many of the following meditation exercises provided are only two to ten minutes long, so they should be fairly easy to incorporate into your day. Also, you can meditate anyway. Meditation is simply the act of breathing, clearing your mind, and adjusting your focus to positive areas of thought (this you can do anywhere, which will be a very helpful tool in relieving stress and handling the various stressful situations which you no doubt encounter every day). For some soft, soothing music to listen to practice these guided meditation sessions, check Amazon or your local bookstore for a CD dedicated to sounds and musical compilations dedicated to helping you relax and free your mind from stress or negative energies.

Two-Minute Calming Meditation

1. To begin this meditation session, first find a place where you can sit or lay and be completely relaxed. Try to find a place to be alone with minimal external noise or distractions. Lightly close your eyes (they don't have to be forced shut tight) and breathe slowly, deeply. Inhale and exhale, focusing your energy only on breathing deeply.

2. Now, imagine yourself in a completely calm state. Feel your body relax completely, notice any remaining tension in your limbs and try to relieve that stress through deep breathing. Picture yourself as being completely relaxed and peaceful as you continue to inhale/exhale deeply.

3. As you continue the deep breathing, imagine what environment would allow you to be calm and peaceful. What sights make you feel calm? What smells or sounds bring you peace? Try to hold these images or other senses in your mind to improve your calm demeanor.

4. As your mind obtains these calming images, sounds, or smells; focus on the calm state that you have allowed yourself to experience. Continue your deep breathing, and recognize the relaxation that your body is currently experiencing.

5. Consider how it would be possible for you to incorporate this sense of calm and peace into your daily life. How nice it would be for you to experience this every day. Is there a way you can achieve this? Could you set

aside two minutes each day to allow yourself to relax and feel at peace with your thoughts?

6. As you continue your deep breathing, slowly allow your focus to return to the room in which you are in. Listen to the external sounds from your environment, and slowly open your eyes. Don't come back all at once, slowly incorporate your environment back into your thoughts and senses.

7. Stay in your calm and relaxed state, continue your deep breathing for a moment longer after your eyes have opened. Remember, don't try to come back all at once. Once your thoughts and senses have returned to your environment, allow yourself to continue the meditative breathing exercises for another minute before standing and moving on with your day.

Five-Minute Meditation Session- Tension Relief

1. Either sit on the floor or lay flat on your back, take a moment to pause, and then gently place your feet flat on the floor. You do not have to put weight on your feet, but make sure they are FLAT on the floor.

2. Feel your connection to the floor through your feet. Close your eyes lightly, and begin deep breathing while concentrating all your energy on the connection between your feet and the floor beneath you.

3. Beginning with your toes, tense and then relax each area of your body. Curl your toes, then after a moment relax your toes as you deeply exhale and push any tension out from that area. Next, flex your ankles and exhale deeply as you relax your ankle joints, releasing tension from your ankles. Do the same with your calves, your knees, your thighs. Next, relax your buttocks

and pelvis, feel your hips and lower back relax completely as you continue the deep breathing.

4. Continue these steps up to your head. Tense and relax your shoulders, your arms, your wrists, your fingers, and your neck. After you have allowed your whole body to feel complete and total relaxation, take 4 more deep breathes in, completely exhaling each before beginning the next breath.

5. As you continue your deep breathing, slowly allow your focus to return to the room in which you are in. Listen to the external sounds from your environment, and slowly open your eyes. Don't come back all at once, slowly incorporate your environment back into your thoughts and senses.

6. Stay in your calm and relaxed state, continue your deep breathing for a moment longer after your eyes have opened. Remember, don't try to come back all at once. Once your thoughts and senses have returned to your environment, allow yourself to continue the meditative breathing exercises for another minute before standing and moving on with your day.

Chapter 9 : Common Experiences during Third Eye Awakening

In this part, we will further discuss the most common experiences, and feelings you may encounter while using the various third eye-opening techniques in this book.

Tingling in various body parts

Vibrations and tingling sensations indicate that something in your ethereal body is activated, which means the vitality layer or prana. When meditating if such feelings occur in your hands, arms, legs, or any part of your body, it just indicates that some of your energy is rearranging. For example, some blocked channels may begin to flow again, or a specific cycle is suddenly stimulated

These minor symptoms are not meaningful in themselves. They come and go. It is best not to pay too much attention to them.

Let things come and go

If you deal with energy the general principle is that different kinds of little emotions and experiences are going to be felt now and then. These may include spasms, little pain, seeing colors, hearing inner sounds, and so on. They appear and then disappear. As long as they don't remain permanently, they don't mean anything at all. Consider them as little releases or energy rearrangements. Don't just stay on them, just follow your process.

It is only if any of these were to return regularly that you should take them into the evaluation and try to know what they mean.

Can meditation be too intense? That's very controversial! In high-intensity cases, it is always best to remain very calm and watch what happens without responding.

If you start feeling uncomfortable for some reason and want to stop the experience, all you need to do is open your eyes and stop. Just by opening your eyes, the burden of life will immediately decrease, and you will be taken back to your normal state of consciousness.

Feeling sensation higher up than between the eyebrows A potential feeling is to feel pressure and light on the top of the forehead, around one inch above the region between the eyebrows, around the boundary between the forehead and the scalp. Pressure and light may be continuous, even outside meditation, and even if you are not trying to keep your eye vigilant. Such pressure means the energy is being pumped into your eye. It's like cutting off your unconscious organs of clairvoyance, powered by non-physical helpers.

Another potential experience is the "saw" of light in the middle of the head (in the upper part). The sensation of vibration and light is experienced that seems to be trying to divide the two hemispheres of the brain.

All these symptoms are good signs, showing that you are making progress. However, these are not obligatory. You can complete the whole cycle of opening without experiencing any of them.

If they occur, just observe them. They can last a certain time and then fade away when this phase of the building process is finished.

Feeling Heat

It may be that heat is released during your practice. There's nothing bad about that. It is a common occurrence during certain phases of awakening, and it normally does not last very long.

There's nothing special to change if you don't drink any alcohol. It is recommendable, however, to abstain from eating meat during the heat release period, to have as pure a diet as possible, and to eliminate spices. You can also take very long showers and release heat into the flow of running water, as in the process of washing your hands. Having a bath in the rivers and the ocean is also very appropriate.

In Kundalini-yoga, a form of meditation practice in which strong heatwaves can be released, ingesting yogurt is sometimes recommended to counterbalance the body's warming. Consumption of alcohol including any type of alcoholic beverage. It is very risky during third eye awakening procedures. This opens the door to several negative forces and can lead to problems. Practically no kind of protection will work effectively for someone who consumes alcohol

At some stage in your meditation, breathing stops.

It's quite common to feel that the breath stops. Some people tend to get a little nervous about this. They think: what if I do not start breathing again? Meanwhile, you need not worry about it, because no one has ever died of a normal suspension of breath. The body knows exactly what it's doing! You just have to wait for a few seconds, and regular breathing will resume.

Indeed, the time when the breath stops is important. All comes to an end inside, as in a celestial standstill. It's an opportunity to dive deeper into space and get in contact with the extended dimensions of your Self.

Pressure in the eye becomes painful. In some situations, pressure in the eye may become uncomfortable, bordering on headaches.

What's going to happen? It is possible to envisage a mixture of different variables.

You're catching up.

It's never been suggested that you focus on the third eye, but just keep your mind off it. But when you fight to stay in the eye, it's very easy to start grasping the eye instead of just being aware of it. Unnecessary tension is generated, which can turn into a kind of headache. So, whenever this occurs, the first thing you need to do is make sure you keep a good conscience and don't push anything.

The energy is trying to pull you up and you are unconsciously resisting.

From time to time, as you practice being in the eye, your consciousness will be lifted from the eyebrow to the top of your head. This is quite natural and is due to the close connection between the third eye and the center of the crown at the top of the head. When this occurs, just let yourself be pulled up and enjoy being above your head for a while. Then come back to the eye once the experience is over.

It often happens at the beginning that you don't know the "pull" and that you resist instinctively, actively holding yourself between the eyebrows. Your resolve to stay fixed in the eye, a true ambition, unconsciously makes you resist the normal flow of energy. The outcome is simple: a headache.

What's going to be done? The answer is clear: shift your emphasis for a while. Shift the mind from the eyebrows to the top of your head. The excess energy accumulated in your head will be released upwards.

Here's a strategy to help you achieve this result.

Controlling headaches

Close your eyes and notice about 10 to 15 cm above your head. This area has an energy center, the chakra. Some teachers call it "the center of the hissing snake" because when people come into contact with the chakra, hissing is heard.

So, tune to the 3 to 5-inch area above your head and spend 1 minute consciously and listening. Remember, there is no imagination. Staying conscious is much better than composing a sound.

Then keep your consciousness at the same height, about 15 cm above the head, while making a continuous hissing sound: "sssssssss ..." for a minute or two (a physical sound, not just a psychological sound). One). Not only repeat "ssss," but also make a proper hissing sound as if you were a big snake. Keep yourself focused while keeping your head clear. Then stay above your head and repeat the sound silently within yourself for 2 to 3 minutes. At this level, in a lot of cases, you will be surprised to find that the headache has vanished. The more proficient you are at this technique, the more you will be able to release the bad energy above your head.

Tips

- Tiger balm on the forehead is often effective in treating energy-related headaches, especially during attacks.

- If you have difficulty moving energy up through the top of your head, try going through the back of the skull's head instead of the middle. This area is located around the acupuncture point Baihui and is an easier way out.

- Another way to encourage energy to move up is to raise your eyebrows and tighten them as much as possible from the beginning to the end of the exercise.

- This technique is a way to release extra head pressure due to "over-training." But in reality, once you master the trick, you can use it to eliminate almost all headaches, even if it is caused by a completely different cause. As long as patients are prepared to learn to process energy, the technology can be used to control migraines of various origins.

Other possible causes of headache

Let us study other possible causes of headaches in the context of internal alchemy (hence not mentioning all headaches related to medical illness).

- If you meditate, sleep or work on harmful earth lines, you may have various negative symptoms, including headaches. Turning on your perception may reveal these symptoms and make them look worse. The truth is that you are not getting worse, but you are becoming more aware of energy disorders. By correcting this situation (moving bed or whatever), you can avoid a lot of trouble in the long run.

- Meditating or sleeping near refrigerators, televisions, electric heaters, cables, electric blankets, electronic devices, synthetic carpets, or any metal structure that stores static electricity can also cause headaches. Eliminating the cause will eliminate headaches.

All in all, in addition to the above reasons, it is usually not easy to have headaches due to eye work. If you have a headache and you have checked that none of the above is the cause, then the problem is likely to come from a completely different source than mental practice. In this situation, the best thing is to discuss with your doctor or pharmacist

Dizziness

After some exercises that will take you into space, you will feel a little dizzy. There is nothing wrong with that. In some states of increased awareness, you will feel extremely relaxed and happy, as if you were drinking a glass or two of champagne. However, it is not always you that are clear-headed, but others are "heavy-headed"! Life in Putonghua's thinking produces suffocating thoughts and emotions.

As you move forward, the modest lightness of the exercise will become "normal" and integrated into your usual way of working. You won't even notice it. Even if it feels a little "different" at first, you will soon find it easier and more efficient to operate in this lightweight state.

If for some reason the frivolous feeling becomes uncomfortable, the following suggestions are likely to restore the situation:

Eat! Eating is perhaps the easiest way to create a short-term structure. If your friend is dissipated after meditation, and if there is an urgent reason to bring him back, then feed him. Strong food in an emergency: cookies, and even poultry. This is dramatically effective, but do not misuse it: proper grounding is supposed to come from your mastery of energy, not from a questionable diet.

Getting fed-up or emotional

What happens when you feel fed-up or emotional as a direct consequence of your meditation? Your mental blockages are being exposed by your practice of opening up. It's quite reasonable and it's important. When you try to simplify and purify your body, you get to learn all that's unknown inside, so you can unlock it and cure it. Such mental blockages are like smears on your astral body. It's often through clearing them that you're going to have major shifts in opening up your thinking.

If it is difficult to have access to any technique of emotional release, a lot of physical exercises will help. Gardening and working in the soil are also very pacifying. But you should not forget that even though physical exercise may make you feel better, it doesn't solve any of the problems. You have to go deeper to deal with conflicts of mind through effective techniques. Neglecting the task of emotional clearing is probably the main reason why some people practice a meditation technique or a cycle of spiritual development, sometimes for as long as thirty years, without any real breakthrough.

Hearing Sounds

The hearing of non-physical noises is a very normal experience on the road. It often begins with a buzzing type of sound inside your head, and slowly, slowly, the harmony of the spheres is refined. If you have sounds in your head, just listen to them. They're a good focus to preserve your mind. The best zone to position your awareness to tune into non-physical sounds is behind the area between the eyebrows, in the center of the head.

When there's no energy, it's somewhere else!

Some days the energy connection is intense, and the experiences flow naturally and easily. Other days, there doesn't seem to be any energy at all, and it's much harder to get into the experience.

It's the nature of the energy that can vary. For example, the vibration around the Full Moon is very strong, while sometimes it is barely noticeable just around the New Moon. On the other hand, space, the purple space of the third eye, is often easier to reach by the New Moon. Many other energy variations can be observed, some predictable, some not. Perhaps one day a reliable "energy meteorology" will be discovered. This is supposed to be the purpose of true astrology.

For your practice to be successful, you need to learn how to feel these variations and work in harmony with them. For example, if you're having one of those days when you're automatically projected into purple space as soon as you close your eyes, there's no need to waste your time battling for clear channel releases, because the vibration can hardly be felt anyway. Rather, concentrate on meditation, seeking to get as deeply into space as possible. Very often, when nothing seems to happen in your work, it doesn't mean there's no energy, but you're looking for energy in the wrong place. Tune in and seek to get in contact with a higher layer, and you might be shocked at what you're going to find.

Upon Sattva, Tamas. The Battle with the Tamas: Rajas.

In the Indian philosophy, all the evolutions of the creation are interpreted throughout terms of the three modes of existence, called tamas, rajas, and sattva. Tamas has to do with fatigue, obscurity, and cloudiness, dullness, lack of initiative, a sense of laziness, etc.

Rajas is an action, a movement, a wish. Once Rajas is triggered inside of you, you start running around, pursuing the things you want, interested in the pursuits of the universe. Too many rajas contribute to frustration and restlessness.

Sattva produces pure and clear states of consciousness, transparency of mind and vision, receptivity to light, higher awareness. Spiritual growth can be interpreted as a gradual unfolding of sattva within yourself to allow it to reflect on your Higher Self.

One of the basic laws of interaction between the three gunas is that after a large dose of sattva (clarity), tamas (inertia) is enabled. In basic terminology, this means that after an unusually clear experience of consciousness, it is quite normal to feel tired for a while. Under these tamasic circumstances, it will not be easy t to re-enter the inner space of the sattva directly. It's going to be easier to have a rajas change first and then look for your sattva again. Practically, this means that if you feel inert and unreceptive the day after a brilliant awakening, it is good not to try to meditate for long periods. It's better to keep moving for a while: go out, walk in the countryside, do some physical work–and try to stay as conscious as possible. Then you can start looking for clarity again.

Chapter 10: Activate Sixth Chakra to Awaken Spiritual Intuition

The sixth chakra is one of the most important of all of the seven ones. It is found in between the two eyes. It is therefore commonly known as the third eye. It is concerned with knowledge, intuition and even sight. Some people say that it deals with human conscience. It mostly affects the aspects of the brain such as memory and even great things such as the human imagination. This chakra tries to bring our conscious mind to always be present and alive. It also shows the energy flow going up to the brain. This sixth chakra is very nice, but it should not be too much. This is to avoid someone having psychological issues or even physical and mental problems. An overactive mind can lead to constant thoughts that are not good for someone's health. So, the third eye chakra has to be very clear. The most effective of all ways to clear this chakra is to meditate. Other ways include aromatherapy or even sound therapy. Knowing ways to clear a blockage of this chakra is important but what are some of these blockages? The most common blockages are anxiety, depression and also paranoia.

The first way to activate or clear your third eye chakra is to meditate. Meditation involves clearing one's mind from all the things the world may bring in. This helps to bring the third eye chakra to restoration. As people will clear their head, their mind will function much better as their worries and fears have been taken far. As one meditates, then, is able to focus one something then he or she will have an open mind to the things that come his or her way. Meditation ensures the body's energy flow is going in the right manner. So, what are the steps one takes as they meditate?

- The first thing is to find a quiet place where you will not get any disturbances. Make sure you are comfortable enough from the clothes to the place you have chosen.

- The next step is to breathe and to relax your whole body. Ensure that you let the air you have taken in to go through you and for you to let yourself feel it.

- Then bring your focus to your eyebrows, this is to bring yourself close to the third eye so that you can be fully aware of it.

- Once you become aware of it you can let all your worries and fears of. This is mostly done by you breathing out through your mouth. This helps your mind to calm down.

- Allow the light to come in and out of your third eye chakra. This brings a new sense to one's mind. Here too you should allow your soul and mind to become one.

- Take a minute of your time and see if you have a message from your third eye chakra.

- The next step is to tell yourself that you are fully aware of it.

- Finally, breathe and stretch your body out.

The other way to activate your third eye chakra is to start doing yoga. This is an Indian tradition that has become popular over the years. It has been there to ensure the harmony of body, mind, and soul. Yoga ensures that the working of all the three is in tip-top shape. It helps to keep the energy of the body circling through as it should. Yoga has meditation processes in it but with exercises in them too. So, what are the most common yoga poses one can take on?

- The first is the downward-facing dog. Its name says how it looks. This is where someone stands then he or she bends forward. This mostly helps with the body muscles. It is a very common pose

- The other pose is known as the big toe. This consists of one taking a deep bend on the front side.

- This next one is very associated with the sixth chakra; it is the child pose. It allows one to rest and to open up their minds. It is also known as the respite pose.

- The final one is the shoulder stand. Here one stretches there should then put their neck in an inverted position. It mainly helps in the clearing of one's mind.

There many more poses that can be used in yoga these are just but a few.

The other thing that helps in activating the sixth chakra is some essential oils. They are usually applied on one's forehead on the specific place in which the third eye chakra is located. They are believed to have some healing power. One can use them to anoint or even bath with. Some include rosemary, the Roman chamomile, and some people use frankincense.

Gemstones or crystals also help to activate one's sixth chakra. One uses the chakra color that is similar to the third eye's chakra. This helps to balance the energy of the chakra and the crystal. These stones help to take away all the bad vibes and to put back in all good vibes that are needed by a particular person. These stones have to be placed where your sixth chakra is for it to work. There should also lay other stones on your body so that the energy can be circulated throughout the body. This helps to clear the mind, body and also soul. So, of the examples of the gems and crystals that are used for the sixth chakra are:

- The first deals with amplifying one's intuition. The amethyst does this. The sixth chakra is associated with intuition and if you need to work on yours then this is the right stone to use.

- The other stone is known as fluorite. This is supposed to work one someone's positivity. It looks to making every aspect of a person to be calm, cool, and stable too. It also helps someone to work on their emotions especially those that they have hidden away.

There many more ways to achieve an active sixth chakra. One is following a good diet and also being mindful.

Chapter 11 : Astral Travel

How to Astral Travel

The process of astral traveling has been simplified into small steps that an individual can be able to comprehend. There are three parts with their engraved steps, and they include:

Part 1: Preparation

Starting in the Morning

Some people prefer to practice the astral process in the evening. The practice is done by several people across the globe just before they break their day to sleep. However, the process can be effectively done in the morning when one is waking up. An individual is always drowsy during this moment of the day. It is more effective for an individual to get the optimum experience of astral travel during this moment. There is a heightened form of awareness from the body when it is dawning. However, this does not put restrictions over time barrier to astral travel since it can be done at any time of the day. One is advised to practice it in the morning, but the best results are also achieved when an individual feels empowered to do it.

Creation of the Right Atmosphere

Astral travel requires the presence of a deep state form of relaxation from an individual performing it. Therefore, an individual is required to be performed at home. The selected room in the house is supposed to be comfortable and place out of the noise. One can lie on his or her bed and make sure he or she relaxes his or her mind. An individual is supposed to be out of people present while performing astral travel. It is bound to be successful when a person has his or her privacy. It is also a way to reduce distractions that affect one's concentration on the exercise.

If an individual has a partner, he or she is advised to take a room that he or she can perform astral travel. If there is no way around getting another room, the process is supposed to be conducted at a time there are minimal interruptions. Any type of interruption has a detrimental effect on the process. One can be in a position of not being able to achieve a state of relaxation in the presence of any slight interference. Therefore, the curtains can also be drawn to minimize the presence of light distractions.

Lying Down and Relaxing

An individual is supposed to lie down in the room he or she has chosen. He or she is supposed to lie of the back facing the ceiling. The next step involves an individual closing his or her eyes. During this moment, one is supposed to be able to clear thoughts in his or her mind. One of the most focused thoughts that seem distractive is supposed to be the priority. One will now be able to focus on the state of his or her body and how it feels. It is because the goal of this step is to be able to achieve an absolute state of relaxation

Flex your muscles during this step and then loosen after a while. The process is supposed to be systematic and gradual. This means that an individual is supposed to start from the toes as he or she is working his or her way to the head. The process is successful when every muscle in an individual's body is relaxed. The second step entails an individual focusing on how he or she is breathing. A person is supposed to make sure he or she breaths deeply and exhales everything out. The shoulder muscles are not supposed to be held or be tense rather they are supposed to be relaxed.

Focusing on breathing can be tricky. However, one has to go a milestone and not get distracted by the thoughts of outside worry. It is not advised for one to start thinking of the soul getting out of the body at this stage. So, a person is supposed to let him or herself to sink at the moment. One can be able to increase his or her speed of getting the vibration intended by the usage of quartz crystals. The process of using the quartz crystal entails an individual holding the crystal on the third which is faintly above the center of an individual's eyebrows.

During this moment a person is supposed to have his or her eyes closed and breathing deeply. As the vibrations emanating from the crystal a person is supposed to consistently clear his or her mind. One goes to different notch to envision of any color in his or her head. An individual is then allowed to hold the crystal in his or her hand and place it on his chest or abdomen. The crystal functions are enormous since it produces high vibration, unlike negative energy which produces low vibrations.

Part 2: Moving of the Soul from the Body

Reaching of the Hypnotic Stage

The hypnotic state is the first stage of the second part of astral traveling. Several people commonly refer to the hypnagogic state as the hypnotic state. At this point, an individual is supposed to let his or her mind and body to approach sleep. However, an individual is not supposed to lose his or her consciousness. Several people tend to term this stage as the edge of sleep and wakefulness. It is an important stage for astral travel to be successful.

There are simple steps that an individual can use to achieve this state of astral travel. The first step involves an individual keeping his or her eyes closed and let his or her body to wander to the other parts of the body. The mind can be left to wander to parts of the body such as the toe, foot, or the hand. Focusing on the desired part when eyes closed is supposed to be done intensely until one can visualize the part perfectly.

The focus is supposed to clear any form of distractive thoughts in a person's brain. The brain of an individual is a powerful component. A person is required to use his or her mind to flex the visualized part. The movement is not supposed to be physical rather mental. An individual can imagine his or her toe-curling and uncurling or clenching and unclenching of the fingers. It has to be continuously done until one feels like it is happening. The last step in this part is the broadening of an individual focus on other parts of the body. The success is achieved when a person is able to move the whole body with the mind.

Entering into a State of Vibration

Several people have reported feeling vibration at this stage. These waves tend to come at different frequencies depending on an individual. It is always a stage that the soul is ready to leave the body. A person is not supposed to fear any of the happenings at this point. It is because fear has the potential of making an individual leave the state of meditation. Therefore, one is supposed to handle the vibrations as the soul leaves the body.

Using the Soul to Move One from the Body

One can imagine he or she is in a room he or she is lying. A person is supposed to be able to try to move his or her body to stand up using the mind. He or she can look around, walk, and look at him or herself lying on the bed or the coach. The state is successful when an individual can be able to gaze on his or her body.

Returning to One's Body

The soul is always connected to the body of an individual even if it leaves. The happening is commonly termed as the silver cord. An individual is supposed to let the forces guide him or her back to his or her body. The soul is back to the body in the event a person can move his or her toes physically. The consciousness of a person is retrieved later.

Part 3: Exploration of the Astral Space

Confirming You Are Projecting the Soul from the Body

Once one has mastered the art of self-projection, he or she is supposed to be able to confirm the two separate planes. Therefore, the following time an individual performs this act, here or she is supposed to go a notch higher and walk in the house. This will be a progressive feature from observing the body in the room. One can go ahead to observing other things in his or her room that he or she had noted earlier on. The referred to about items are supposed to be physical with a unique shape and color.

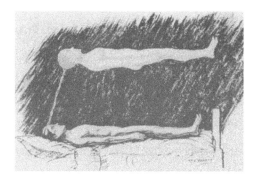

Astral Projection

Further Exploration

One can go to different locations that feel like they are less familiar to him or her. This is supposed to be done over subsequent astral travel sessions. One is supposed to note something new in each session he or she engages in. The new places an individual travels to are supposed to have different physical features from each other.

Chapter 12: Common Mistakes People Make Trying to Activate the Third Eye

If there is something worse than not doing something, then it is doing it in the wrong way. The same is true for third eye activation. If you are trying to awaken your third eye and doing it incorrectly, then you are up for some pretty bad experiences. Third eye awakening is a powerful practice that must be done carefully and with great dedication.

If you are looking for quick results or instant gratification, then you will be stepping in the wrong realm. Some people keep trying but never have any luck with their third eye activation. It isn't that the third eye is not present in them, it seems that they are improperly looking for something. Not understanding the signs or misinterpreting them can also lead to failure or desperation.

The following are some of the mistakes people make while trying to activate their third eye. You must avoid them.

Indulging in Misinformation

TV, media, and internet are great tools for spreading misinformation. They have a knack for making a mountain of a molehill. They can make you believe absurd things that may lead to desperation in the end. Before you begin your third eye activation, you must make yourself aware of the things you are going to encounter on your way. Do not expect too much or too little. Judging the gap always prevents falling in it. Do your homework properly before you embark on the journey of activating your third eye.

Lack of Trust

Trust is a very important factor when you go on any journey, especially the ones involving adventure. Third eye activation is an adventure trip like you have never taken. To experience it, you must have trust in yourself and your instincts. You must not distrust anything that you see or feel while you are trying to activate your third eye. You must also give proper importance to the changes you experience on the way. Remaining conscious of even the smallest of events is very important.

Lack of Purpose

People who lack a clear purpose for activating their third eye will face failures. Activating the third eye is not a walk in the park. You can't shake it off as you do with other things. It starts some irreversible processes. You must have a definite purpose for activating the third eye. Only then will you be able to judge the amount of success you have achieved in your pursuits. If you are not looking for something specific, you may not find anything at all.

Lack of Technique

Following a proper technique is very important for activating the third eye. Third eye activation may look like an undefined path. The journey inside doesn't have a definite route, but using the right technique is very important or you can start feeling lost. Pick a technique that suits you the best, and please follow it carefully. Do not keep changing your methods or you may not achieve anything at all. Remain regular in your practice and do it with great devotion. People who take this lightly end up wasting their time.

Trying too hard

Do not try too hard. Those who want quick success often start trying too hard in the beginning. It may lead to desperation or your mind will start cooking up false stories, and both will lead to failure. When trying to activate your third eye, focus on the technique and let things happen on their own. Do not try to force your mind to think in a particular way or imagine things. Overdependence on visualization will lead to the framing of false notions in your mind. You may start viewing things that you want to see without having achieved anything at all.

Stop Looking for the Wrong Signs

You must look for the right signs. Some so-called experts have attached some wrong notions with the third eye activation method. They have made people believe that third eye activation will only happen if they get specific signs. This is inaccurate. Look for the subtle changes taking place inside you. Trust your instincts and take a lead. Do not go by the wrong notions. Your experience with third eye awakening may be totally different than others. If you keep looking for the experiences of others you may never feel satisfied.

No Instant Results

Third eye activation is not similar to ordering anything on the internet. It doesn't happen instantaneously. Even after your third eye has awakened, you may not be able to see a significant change for a very long time. Honing your abilities takes much longer than that and requires a lot of practice. You must pay great attention to this aspect.

Not Enough Practice

This is a continuation of the previous point. You will need to practice your skills for quite some time to have measurable results. Even if your third eye is active, it will not give you significant results if you fail to practice it regularly. You have to train your mind to look in the right direction. Your mind must learn to recognize the signs. It must learn to look at things with better insight. All this will only happen when you practice regularly. Make meditation a part of your schedule. Do not miss it or give excuses to yourself. By doing so, you'll only be bringing failure to your pursuit.

Avoid Overpublicizing Your Efforts

The journey to awaken your third eye is a personal quest. It is a long journey, and the ride is never smooth. You must avoid talking about it to your friends. Such discussions spark negative criticism and envy. You may start getting labeled or ridiculed, and it may lead to doubts. Keep it to yourself, and keep practicing. It is one of the best ways to preserve your positive energies and get better results.

Chapter 13 : Dangers of Opening the Third Eye

Opening the third eye isn't a small change. It is a significant event. It leads to a total shift in your consciousness and that has its side effects. Understandably, several changes will start to take place in your mind. Some changes are at the level of your consciousness, and others are physiological. Our body is designed to resist change of any kind as it becomes alarmed. Therefore, before your third eye gets fully active, there will be some minute physiological side-effects like a headache, pressure on the forehead, tingling sensations, or even a migraine. You need to know how to deal with them.

Some changes also take place on the level of your consciousness. Seeing shapes, fear of the unknown, having vivid dreams, getting frightened, and feeling the presence of some entities are only a few of them. These things are a part of having an awakened third eye. You will have to learn to deal with these things and not be scared of them.

Potential Problems and How to Deal with Them

Headaches and pressure on the forehead

It is common for people to feel pressure on the forehead while they try to activate the third eye. It happens as you are putting a lot of focus on one point and trying to redirect your life energies to that point. Such headaches or pressure will not last long. However, for some people, the pressure can last for hours after they have finished their meditation. If you are also feeling something like that, then you shouldn't become alarmed. In the initial phases of third eye awakening, such things do happen. It is a clear sign that your third eye is getting stimulated.

Tingling sensation

You can also feel a tingling sensation on your forehead, as well as in other parts of your body during the process. This sensation can last for hours or even days after you are done with the process. However, this is also a temporary phase that ends very soon, and there is no reason to get alarmed.

Migraines

Migraine headaches can be a real problem. They can put you in some real pain. Such headaches last for a bit longer. If you are certain that the headache you are experiencing is due to your meditation and you haven't had it in the past, you must consult your physician. Not paying proper attention can aggravate the pain.

Seeing strange shapes

Many people start seeing strange shapes soon after their third eye activation meditation. There is no reason to get alarmed if you are also in that category. Meditation involves concentrating for long periods with your eyes closed while looking for light. This sometimes creates images in your mind. Most of the time, it is an image of an eye or light shapes.

Vivid dreams or nightmares

Vivid dreams and nightmares can be concerning for many people. When you activate your third eye, your mental vision gets strong; it can lead to such dreams. Although it has no other danger, still some people start feeling restless and have difficulty in sleeping. If you are experiencing this problem, try to calm your mind. When your thoughts are running too wild, such dreams become vivid and frequent. Meditation is the only cure for such dreams. Try to calm your mind and think only about positive thoughts. Such dreams are caused by an excessive accumulation of negative thoughts.

Third eye activation is a powerful tool to have better mind control and to help you avoid being controlled by it. It will empower you to use your mind as you desire. However, third eye awakening is not for everyone. If you have a weak mind and heart and have given to addictions, you should stay away from third eye activation.

You Shouldn't Try Third Eye Activation if:

You have a strong fear of the unknown

Fear is a natural phenomenon and we all have a fear of something. Ghosts, spirits, and other such entities can frighten anyone, and if you have a normal fear of such beings, then it can work for you. However, if you are too scared by such thoughts, then you should stay away from third eye activation until you have some reasonable control over your fears. Proceeding without caution will only increase your paranoia, and you will become restless.

You are already suffering from Schizophrenia

Schizophrenia is a serious mental condition where you keep switching between conceived realities. Practicing the third eye meditation can be dangerous with such a condition; you will end up adding more layers to an already complex situation. People with schizophrenia can start demonstrating strange symptoms. Such people shouldn't enter this dimension.

You have given to the addiction to drugs: psychosis and permanent hallucination

Any kind of addiction is bad when you are practicing third eye awakening. Addictions can complicate your mental state and cause problems putting your focus in one direction. Drugs and other such addictions can be very dangerous. If you are mixing third eye meditation with drugs, the result can be even worse. Psychosis and permanent hallucination can become a reality for you. The treatment of such conditions may be difficult, and you may never come out of the state. You should always avoid mixing addictions with third eye awakening.

You want to use the third eye for establishing a connection with spirits

Some people believe that they can use the powers of the third eye to talk to the spirits. Although it is a possibility, you must never do so. The full realm of the spirits and energies is unknown. We are only an insignificant part of this energy system. Meddling with energies that are beyond your knowledge spectrum can be dangerous. You have no way to gauge their power. Use the third eye awakening only for good and positive things. If you start interacting with ghosts and spirits, you may attract powerful negative energies and may never be able to get rid of them.

You have not researched well

Entering into anything without learning about it deeply can be dangerous. If you are thinking about third eye activation, you must do your research well. Do your homework and learn what the process involves. Ensure that it meets your goals. Only then should you enter this realm. Otherwise, you will end up wasting a lot of your time and energy on a futile quest.

Conclusion

Over the course of this book, the many benefits of opening and accessing the third eye should have become apparent. Activating the third eye chakra will open your connection to the world around you. It will deepen your intuition, boost your creativity, improve your relationships, and make you feel happier in all that you do. Your connection to the third eye can also increase your abilities in life, possibly allowing you to see into the future, make deep, insightful decisions, astral project, or discern information. Over time, you will find that your focus and attention on the third eye drastically changes your life.

Accessing the third eye is often something that cannot be achieved in a single session. It can take several attempts—spread across weeks, months, or even years to reach this heightened spiritual experience. Know as you continue forward that you are embarking on a journey that is going to change your life. Fortunately, you are now armed with the knowledge that is necessary to make these changes in a way that will improve all that you do.

Opening the third eye is not something you can do in your free time. You are going to live and experience life through the perception of the third way, especially as it interweaves with your conscious mind. There are many techniques that you can use to help you along the way, as you guide yourself into the purest version of yourself.

Best of luck as you welcome the influence of the third eye into your life!

CPSIA information can be obtained
at www.ICGtesting.com
Printed in the USA
LVHW021230140122
708525LV00005B/265